# Keep Pressing On, Brother

## Noel Braun

# ABOUT THE AUTHOR

Noel Braun commenced his working career as a country school teacher, then moved into a corporate career, which took him from Melbourne to Perth and Sydney. He has had a lifelong passion for writing and wrote the first words of his novels over forty years ago. After a busy career and raising a family of four, he has found the time in retirement to fulfill his long-held ambition to see his work in print.

Noel has published two novels: *Friend and Philosopher* and *Whistler Street*. He has published a memoir, *No Way to Behave at a Funeral* which describes his grief journey following the death by suicide of his wife Maris, and two explorations of the Camino de Santiago de Compostela *The Day was Made for Walking* and *I Guess I'll Just Keep on Walking*. *Keep Pressing On, Brother* is the third.

Noel is working on other manuscripts. He lives in the Snowy Mountains where he is involved in the community. He is a keen walker and enjoys getting out in the national parks surrounding his home.

---

Published in Australia by Sid Harta Publishers Pty Ltd,
ABN: 46 119 415 842
23 Stirling Crescent, Glen Waverley, Victoria
3150 Australia
Telephone: +61 3 9560 9920, Facsimile: +61 3 9545 1742
E-mail: author@sidharta.com.au
First published in Australia 2020
This edition published 2020
Copyright © Noel Braun 2020
Cover design, typesetting: WorkingType Studio
The right of Noel Braun to be identified as the Author of the Work has been asserted in accordance with the Copyright, Designs and Patents Act 1988.

All rights reserved. No part of this publication may be reproduced, stored in a retrieval system, or transmitted, in any form or by any means without the prior written permission of the publisher, nor be otherwise circulated in any form of binding or cover other than that in which it is published and without a similar condition being imposed on the subsequent purchaser.

Braun, Noel
*Keep Pressing on, Brother*
ISBN: 978-1-925707-26-7
pp326

*Dedicated to the memory of my cherished wife, Maris,
whose support, confidence and quiet encouragement
inspired me, and continues to do so*

*Dedicated to the memory of my dear friend*
*Fr. Peter McGrath cp*
*Mate, Beloved Larrikin, Spiritual Director*

## CONTENTS

| | | |
|---|---|---|
| Recap. | The story so far | 1 |
| 1 | Loves goes beyond the physical person of the beloved... | 3 |
| 2 | Keep Pressing On, Brother | 11 |
| | | |
| Act V | Voie de Vézelay | 17 |
| 3 | Time Out | 19 |
| 4 | One should walk gently and slowly | 29 |
| 5 | I'm slowing down the tune... | 47 |
| 6 | For age is opportunity, no less than youth itself... | 61 |
| 7 | Forgiving releases us. Until we forgive, we're imprisoned... | 79 |
| 8 | Hope is a feeling that life has a purpose and meaning... | 95 |
| 9 | Life without hope is an empty, boring and useless life... | 119 |
| 10 | Above all, do not lose your desire to walk... | 135 |
| | | |
| Act VI | Voie de Vézelay  Via Gebennensis | 161 |
| 11 | Many believe a pilgrimage is about going away, but it isn't... | 163 |
| 12 | Accept surprises that upset your plans... | 171 |
| 13 | Sometimes the bad things that happen to us... | 191 |
| 14 | Life is either a daring adventure, or nothing. | 201 |
| 15 | Difficulties are made to be broken down, not to break us down. | 213 |
| 16 | It is not enough to give the years to life | 231 |
| 17 | He who wishes to travel far spares his mount. | 241 |

| 18 | I am leaving not only on a journey, I will myself become a journey.. | 263 |
| 19 | Let us not forget hospitality. | 281 |
| 20 | Wasn't friendship its own miracle... | 287 |
| 21 | Brother, let me be your servant... | 297 |

Acknowledgements 317

Recap:
# The Story So Far

# 1.

*'Love goes very far beyond the physical person of the beloved. It finds its deepest meaning in his spiritual being, his inner self. Whether or not he is actually present, whether or not he is still alive at all ceases somehow to be of importance.'*
Viktor E. Frankl: *Man's Search for Meaning.*

I need to talk about, write about, my wife Maris. She died by suicide in 2004. She hid her depression; only a few knew of her constant battle with the demons of despair. Every day was a struggle. To the outside world, she had everything to live for; 42 years of a happy marriage, four children and, at that time, four grandchildren (four more since) and many loving friends. The family was looking forward to the wedding of my son Stephen. She could not hang around and died the week before.

It's still a mystery, trying to make sense of the catastrophe. One of a couple, I was alone. The role of loving husband was banished, assumptions and expectations overthrown. Life was uncertain, unpredictable, plans irrelevant. My world was shaken and in disarray. Nothing would ever be the same. I lost my identity. Identity is not something that we think about. It's how we regard ourselves, how we describe ourselves to others. I was no longer a husband and partner. What I had lost was so entwined with my identity that I was faced with the question of who I was. I looked in the mirror and saw a stranger.

How was I to cope with the pain and anguish, the immense guilt that I didn't do enough to save Maris from herself? I came to a decision. I had no control over her abrupt departure, but

I did have some control over how I coped. I could have gone off the rails, lost the plot completely, succumbed to anger, bitterness and despair, hit the grog, womanised, or turned in on myself. No way! This tragedy will not beat me. I will fight back. I saw no way around other than to meet my suffering head on. I was not going to be the strong silent type, but admit to my vulnerability. I'd show my emotions and tell the world how an insidious disease like depression could destroy a beautiful compassionate person. As a tribute to my Maris, I would endeavour to internalise her lovely qualities. I would ask myself what would she have done.

At first, it was difficult to see any hope in Maris's loss, but once the anguish subsided to a tolerable level, I saw opportunities for personal growth. I saw a different world and tried to evaluate what truly matters. I recognised my own vulnerability and limits more clearly.

So began my search for meaning. I did my 'grief work' and am grateful for the support from wise counsellors. I attended a Suicide Bereavement Support Group. At the same time, I attended to life's everyday tasks. I'd been a Lifeline counsellor for 5 years, working on the phones and in personal face-to-face counselling. Some telephone counsellors who experience a tragedy in their lives feel unable to continue. I was tempted, but that was a waste. I was good on the telephones and helped multiple callers. I resumed my shifts. My colleagues were most supportive. Indeed, one of them gave me a major breakthrough in dealing with my intrusive feelings of guilt that I had failed Maris and hadn't done enough. *'Think of the things you DID do,'* was her comment.

On my first shift back, I received a suicide-in-progress call. I dealt with it in a professional manner just as I'd been taught. I stayed with Lifeline for 10 years until I moved out of Sydney.

## 1.

In that time, I underwent training in Suicide Bereavement Support Group facilitation. I ran groups for people who had lost a loved one. In my role, I wore two hats: one as trained counsellor and the other as a fellow human being who was walking the same path. My own pain had made me vulnerable but more sensitive to the needs of people. Perhaps before Maris died, I reached out to people more with the head than the heart, but now in my brokenness, I felt I reached out in a modest and humble way with both my heart and my soul. Sometimes when you speak to a counsellor, friend or family member, you sense that they don't get you. They don't seem to understand why something has hurt so bad. Their eyes glaze over; you feel uncomfortable and misunderstood. I wonder whether I was like that. You never truly understand what a painful experience can do to another person, but when you have been through the mill yourself, you get a little closer.

I cannot stress enough the importance of my writing in my regeneration. In the month after Maris died, my first novel was published, based on my experience of teaching in one-teacher schools. In creating the setting of a remote community, I relied on my experience and on Maris's. She grew up in the bush and made many valuable contributions. She was an important sounding board. My books are dedicated to her memory. Her support and quiet encouragement inspired me, and continues to do so.

The novel filled the vacuum, allowed the storm to pass, and gave me purpose. Instead of succumbing or, to use Maris's term 'falling into a heap', I flogged the book with passion and intensity. I did grand tours in regional areas because I felt the nostalgia for an Australia long past would help it sell. I spoke of Maris's depression and suicide, the driving force restlessly pushing me. The first print sold out and a reprint as well.

I had a second novel ready for publishing about the friendship between two men set in both Perth and Sydney. One is unwittingly responsible for the death of the other's mother, the catalyst that drives the story. Nothing spectacular about the sales, just steady. I was halfway through another novel on the theme of unrequited love, but I detoured into writing about my grief experience. I had already spoken to many groups, and now was the time to put my story into print. It took two years to work my way through the raw intensity of my feelings before I was ready. I perused the grief books in book shops and libraries; they were mostly written by women. Men don't talk about their feelings, let alone write about them, particularly Aussie blokes. I found the grief books were sanitised; issues that I regarded as important were not discussed. The book that I wrote is described as 'brutally honest'. Writing it was therapy for me, but it has reached out to and helped many who were travelling along a similar path.

I was restless, running around like a headless chook trying to fill the vacuum. Travel was important. Maris and I had enjoyed our overseas trips, but in her last years, she could not bring herself around to spending the money because that was selfish; others could not even afford the basics. Three months after her death, I visited my daughter Jacinta in Idaho and son Stephen in Utah. Both were working in ski resorts, Stephen also on his honeymoon with his new wife Anthea. I travelled on to Washington, New York, London and Paris. Organising the trip distracted me from the pain of my grieving, but the demons were waiting for me when I returned. I was more prepared for travel a year later. I spent six months overseas mostly in France where I enrolled in a French language school. In their efforts to find themselves, some trek in Nepal, others sit on a remote beach, others sail around the world. I chose to

## 1.

learn French in Chambéry. Among the other students, I developed a close friendship with other lost souls. I believe I helped them cope with their journey. They certainly helped mine. I learned some French as well.

Each Sunday, I attended Mass in the cathedral. From time to time, groups of pilgrims were blessed and farewelled. They were walking to Santiago in north-west Spain along the Camino de Compostela or, in French, le Chemin de Saint Jacques de Compostelle. I had heard of the Camino, the ancient pilgrimage routes through Europe to Santiago, a few years earlier when one of my fellow parishioners in Sydney walked with his daughter. That's a good idea, I thought at the time. No way was Maris interested; she preferred comfortable modes of travel. Now, on my own, I decided I would be a pilgrim and walk the Camino. Four years later I took my first step.

Pilgrimage is a spiritual devotion that spans all major religions. It's an ancient concept. Embarking on a journey to seek spiritual aid at a particular shrine goes back thousands of years. The Jews went to Jerusalem, the Greeks to Delphi, Muslims to Mecca. Wherever a miraculous event occurred or a deity was located, people flocked. Pilgrimage seems to relate to a basic desire in the human heart to visit locations where heaven and earth met. It found its place in the Christian world. Christians visited those places where Jesus walked as well as the cities, tombs and churches of the saints. The Holy Land topped the list, but people were drawn to Rome and to Santiago in Spain, the place where the body of St James the Apostle was miraculously transported.

There is more to a pilgrimage than simply visiting the places. It's more than *'a get-fit course for the soul, a spiritual work-out for the spirit'* (*The Tablet*, 16 June 2007). It offers as much to the non-believer as to the believer. It offers a refuge from the din and clatter of the outside world, to take on an interior journey to confront your inner self. It involved travelling lightly. You leave most of your material goods behind, and in the peace of the track, you surrender your emotional baggage and shed your anxieties, fears and other demons. It focuses on the present, on what is happening right now without concern for the past or future. One step at a time, you place your feet on a well-trod path in the footprints of those who have walked before you. You acknowledge their essence just as others who follow will acknowledge yours. Your journey may be solitary, but you are bonded in a fellowship that encompasses the pilgrims of the past, the present and the future. In connecting with the earth, you commune with creation, with a greater power that the believer calls God.

> *A pilgrimage is a unique dimension to appreciate life's wonders and revel in its minutiae. It is the heady aroma drifting from fields of thyme, or the drone of bees in a sun-dappled forest. It is autumn frost blanketing a multi-hued trail, and the rough grain of your walking stick rubbing against your palm.*
> (Brandon Wilson: *Along the Templar Trail: Seven Million Steps for Peace*.)

Each pilgrim's journey along the Camino de Santiago is unique. It's from carrying everything on your back, sleeping in crowded dormitories and walking every metre of the way to engaging the services of the many companies who carry your luggage each day, put you up in five-star hotels with gourmet meals thrown in and provide a hop-on hop-off bus for the weary.

My first Camino pilgrimage began in 2010 on the porch of the Cathedral at Le Puy-en-Velay, France, and my first steps were down the long set of stairs leading into the town. I was searching for meaning. I dedicated my walk to Maris and was

## 1.

hoping the routine of the Camino would bring anchorage and structure into my life. I was on a spiritual quest of self-discovery. I finished at Saint-Jean-Pied-de-Port at the foot of the Pyrénées 39 days later and came home. Nine months later I continued on to Santiago. Although I was still walking for Maris, the Camino had taken on a life of its own and compelled me to return. That journey was the subject matter of my first book on the Camino.

One Camino is never enough. I had to keep on walking. It was like an addiction or a contagion, a viral infection. What drew me back? It could have been the scenery, or the challenge of endurance of walking hundreds of kilometres, or the call of many languages. Perhaps it was the call of the Spirit, luring me on into the unknown where I had to rely on a strength greater than my own to persevere. It was the camaraderie, the chance to meet many people of different languages and cultures and to form lifelong friendships.

Two years later in 2013 at the age of 80 I walked from Montpellier in France, crossed the Pyrénées at a different point (Col de Somport) and progressed to Puente la Reina in Spain. The compulsion did not diminish, and in 2015 I walked through Portugal from Lisbon to Santiago. My story was continued in my second Camino book.

Walking the Camino four times over six years presented profound opportunities for change. When I walk, I prefer to walk alone, although Maris is always with me. But in another sense, I am never alone because I meet many people. The most important person, of course, that I meet is myself. Although I endured hardships, anxieties and discomforts, I found joy and meaning. I was not finished.

## 2.
# Keep Pressing On, Brother

My pilgrimage began on Thursday 29 June 2017, the moment I walked out of my house in Jindabyne, a small town in the Snowy Mountains, into Act V of my Camino. I felt like the medieval pilgrims who left home, village or parish to walk to Santiago. I was like many modern pilgrims whom I met in earlier Caminos who had walked to Santiago from their homes, in little towns like mine, in Belgium or Holland or Germany.

I worked hard on preparing myself, walked many times in the lovely mountains surrounding my home and attended regularly the High-Country gym. I spent the last few days tidying up the loose ends. I was confused and anxious, worried that I hadn't got everything organised, that some little forgotten detail would trip me up. I should learn to trust in God. That was a lesson that needed constant repetition. You should plan what you can and then leave it to God. Somehow, things are always taken care of.

Before departing Australia, I stayed in Sydney with my daughter Angela and family. I made a nostalgic trip to Mass in St Anthony's in Terrey Hills. St Anthony's was our church for the 35 years when we lived in Sydney. Visiting St Anthony's is a pilgrimage in itself because it's one of my sacred places, a crucial influence in my life and that of my wife Maris.

That Sunday, I rediscovered St Anthony's. The morning was brilliant; the church grounds sparkled under the cloudless sky; the trees and shrubs had grown, and I had the impression of greenness and beauty. I felt a deep bonding with nature. I wandered around the garden and inspected the new plants. I could have abandoned my original intention of attending Mass and lost myself among this creation.

St Anthony's was so familiar. Over 36 years I had attended hundreds, even thousands of times, but, on this occasion, I saw it sharply, as if I was seeing it for the first time. Inside, people welcomed me. While Mass was under way, I looked around at all the familiar faces. Everyone was sitting in the same place. When I checked if certain people were present, I knew where to look. After Mass, I joined everyone for morning tea. The conversation continued as if I had never left.

I discovered St Anthony's-in-the-Fields about 1979.

At the first church we attended after moving to Sydney from Perth, it was hard to get to know people. They weren't friendly. Our joke was that if you tried to talk to someone after Mass, they'd call the police. One of the nuns at the school that Angela was attending told Maris that St Anthony's was far more open. One Sunday morning, we turned up. Fr. Peter McGrath, the parish priest, recognised us as new faces and grabbed other parishioners to say hello to us. The rest, as they say, is history. Maris said she would give Sydney three years, but it was St Anthony's that kept us. We bought a house in Frenchs Forest. We became fully involved in the life of the parish, joined a family group, and took on leadership roles. Our kids were confirmed and received First Communion. Our daughter, Angela, was married there, and sadly, Maris's funeral was held there. The support I received from my fellow parishioners was wonderful. St Anthony's became for me a Spirit-filled, sacred place where I had many encounters with God, that is, if God is love. I left part of me behind when I left Sydney for Jindabyne. St Anthony's will always be sacred.

It was charismatic Fr. Peter McGrath who created the special ambience of St Anthony's. He organised family groups as a means of creating community and getting parishioners to know each. From this small beginning the Passionist Family Group Movement spread to other parishes in Australia and eventually to other countries. Fr. Peter was elected Provincial of the Passionist Order, and we did not see him for a while. After his term, he returned to our region and eventually lived in a small house behind the Forestway Shopping Centre that was called Grace Cottage. Although now separate from the parish, he conducted meditation evenings, and many of the parishioners including Maris and I attended. Our lives are busy, and we rush from task to task, trying to fit everything in. To do more. To do a better job. But in meditation we pause and take breath. We become alive to the moment. Maris especially valued these sessions. Peter recorded some meditation tapes, and she listened to them every day up to her death.

One night I said to him, '*Peter, you God bless everyone but no one God blesses you. It's about time someone did.*' Every time we met, we did not part company without my blessing him. He used to look for it. If I made to leave, he'd demand, '*Where's my blessing?*' I'd place my hand on his head, say something about asking God to take care of this priest who was so human and gave his whole life to others. It was a joke at first, something between us, but I believe it was serious for Peter who saw his own failings too clearly. He described himself as a recovering alcoholic. He needed God's help desperately. For me, it was an opportunity to reach out to someone who relentlessly gave so much of himself to others.

After my visit to Taizé, France in 2013, I wanted to take home a souvenir of real significance. I found it in the bookshop. The Coptic Icon of Friendship dates from the sixth century, the original of which is in the Louvre. Jesus is shown with his arm around the shoulder of a friend named Menus. His eyes are not severe or judgemental but gentle. His face commands attention not in a triumphal way, but as a calm authority. I loved the icon because I identified with Menus. Jesus is my friend, my mate. He's not way up there, he's down here, always with us in the messiness of our lives. When I talk to him, he replies with an Aussie accent and calls me mate. But he's not just for me, Jesus is everyone's mate.

I bought three copies. I gave one to the parish Taizé group; that's a group which runs a monthly service in the Taizé style – chants, scripture readings, silence. (More about Taizé later.) The second was for me; I keep it by my bedside at home, and I gave the third to Fr. Peter. Fr. Peter treasured that icon. He kept it in a prominent place in Grace Cottage. Peter had a habit of giving gifts away, but not this one.

Peter's health deteriorated. He suffered from dementia and after spells in hospital, was in a nursing home in the care of War Veterans at Collaroy Plateau. After Mass, I visited Peter with old friends, Barbara and Bob Lunnon. It was confronting to see caring staff leading him into the room, his face covered with bruises and his walk a shuffle rather than the rapid stride that we used to know. He was restrained in his chair, which he didn't like and made him frustrated. We sat in a tight circle, placed the icon before him, lit a candle, joined our hands and prayed. He was hard to engage and kept slipping back into himself with flashes of anger at the restraint.

I put my arm around him just as Jesus placed his arm around his friend, Menus, and placed my hand on his head. I'd like to think Peter understood what was happening. He calmed down. I asked for God's blessing on Peter, and I thanked him for the tremendous contribution he had made to my life and that of my family. He married my children, buried my wife, baptised my grandchildren. I mentioned that innumerable people's lives had been touched by Peter. I was their spokesperson, and said to Peter that I was like Jesus in the icon putting my arm around him and blessing him. We are all like Christ whenever we put our arm around someone and support them.

Something profound stirred within me, like a yearning to have him back as he was. It was distressing leaving him to his suffering and bewilderment. Seeing Peter was confronting. I knew, however, that he was receiving loving care, not only from the staff at War Vets, but from the many friends who visited him regularly and those who helped him daily with his meals. Peter poured out so much love to others; now it was others' turn to show their love to him.

Barbara Lunnon and other Passionist priests continued with the meditation evenings. My Sydney visit on the way to Europe coincided with the monthly evening. I was invited to talk about 'Pilgrimage'. I mentioned I would be leaving soon for France. In an uncluttered moment I had an inspiration. I told them about my first pilgrimage in 2010 when I started at the cathedral in Le Puy. As part of the pilgrims' blessing, we were invited to take with us a petition, which someone had left to be conveyed to Santiago. Mine was a mother's prayer seeking help for her wayward son. I invited the people to give me a petition to carry. They responded enthusiastically as if I was releasing them of a burden. Some told the group the contents of their petition, and together we prayed. I wrote a petition myself asking for care for Fr. Peter. I exchanged each petition with a shell, the symbol of pilgrimage and Saint James. I felt a heavy sense of responsibility for the trust invested in me, as if I were a messenger to God. I felt inadequate for the task. I was not sure where I would leave these messages, but

I knew I would find a suitable sacred place. Perhaps by inviting the people to write and talk, I had already conveyed their prayers to God.

Before I left home, I straightened up my untidy office and came across a note from Fr. Peter, probably the last he wrote to me before dementia struck. He ended with this encouragement:

*Keep Pressing On, Brother.*

*The Icon of Friendship Jesus and his mate*

2017
**Act V**

Voie de Vézelay

# 3.
# Time Out

*If life is going at too fast a pace*
*When you feel it's one giant rat race,*
*Stop for a minute, feel a gentle breeze*
*Or listen to birds singing in the trees*
*Lay on the ground, watching clouds in the sky*
*And make out shapes as they roll on by.*
*Marvel at new plants, popping out of the ground;*
*Rejoice at the first buds on the orchard you've found*
*And in this crazy world of ours*
*Take some time to smell the flowers.*

Dorothy Francis
(Written on a seat in a front garden near Grace Cottage)

My son-in-law Guy drove me to Sydney Airport for the first leg of my flight to France via Korea. I like this flight with Korean Airlines. You leave early morning, fly all day in daylight and get to Seoul early evening where they put you up for the night. You then leave for Paris about midday and fly in daylight as the earth revolves all the way to Paris. You arrive early evening, which gives you time to find your hotel in daylight.

My mind drifted through all the arrangements, tying up loose ends and plans made before leaving Australia. I couldn't find anything to fret about, but I managed to worry about my credit cards, which were concealed in my back pack. What if they lose my pack? I had to remind myself: *'What I worry about never happens.'*

Since my last visit, Charles De Gaulle airport has been rebuilt. It's enormous and very different. I managed to track down the railway station (which was the same, as were their user-unfriendly ticket vending machines), catch the train into the city and the metro to Gare de Lyon. I was pleased I had survived the challenge of making my way to Hotel Corail and arrived after 9. It had been a long day and being too tired to go out to find a restaurant, I contented myself with a meal of a beer and packet of chips from the vending machine in the foyer.

I woke up about every two hours. A cold, which began in Sydney, was developing. Not a good start! I found the Gare de Paris Bercy, about 15 minutes by foot beyond the Gare de Lyon. Not as big or busy, the Gare de Bercy caters for travellers to Bourgogne and Pays d'Auvergne. I listened closely to the announcement that the train was in two sections and to get on the right one. I was still adjusting to French, and, of course, I had chosen the wrong carriage. A few questions got me back on the right path. A lesson I learned in earlier Caminos – ask!

I relaxed and watched the suburbs pass by and then the open country, fields of cereal interspersed with patches of woodlands. I was looking forward to walking in this beautiful country. I made a resolution. After hectic weeks racing around Australia, I was going to slow down and allow the region to absorb me.

The train finished at Avallon. The Voie de Vézelay began at Vézelay, another 18 kilometres. The railway station was on the edge of town. I walked to the centre and found my accommodation, the *Hôtel Le Saint-Vincent*, a picturesque building in the process of restoration. I explored the old town, charming with its windy cobblestone streets flanked by buildings in wood and stone. I stopped for a beer at the *Bar Tapis Le Seize* and fell into conversation with the young barman. I told him of my plans to walk from Vézelay to Saint-Jean-Pied-de-Port, about 900 kilometres, following the ancient pilgrimage route. He was respectful and intrigued. He concluded I was an old bloke (*'un vieux mec!'*), the French equivalent of long in the tooth. As I left, he and two patrons wished me *'Bon Courage!'* the first of many.

I could have taken a shuttle bus to Vézelay. My French guide book extolled the virtues of walking into Vézelay and, from afar, lifting the head and experiencing the joy of seeing the basilica on top of the hill, using it as your guide and enjoying the sight of its coming nearer and nearer. I was sold. The day began well. The walk out of the town was easy, and I had the choice of following the river Cousin. At first, the track was level, even, well-defined and passed by beautiful old stone bridges and buildings. I came to a warning:

> *Déconseillé aux personnes âgées et aux jeunes enfants non accompagnés. Passages délicats.(Warning to old people and unaccompanied children. Tricky route.)*

I should have acted my age and taken the road. But no! That's okay for other old folk, but I was fit and had already traversed hundreds of kilometres of difficult tracks. I wouldn't leap through like an antelope; my slow and steady pace would get me through.

Foolish Noël! The level, even and well-defined route gave way to a ramble along the river among large oak trees spreading their twisted roots in all directions. It became imperative to pick one's way carefully up and down the river bank amid obstacles intent on tripping me up, sometimes having to walk in the shallow water. The passage was slow, and I lost track of time. The good news: the weather was fine; I had many hours of daylight and no leeches. Thank God it wasn't raining. I made it through without breaking a leg, but though it was not yet midday, I was feeling exhausted.

Despite the discomfort, I had to admire the beauty surrounding me. The natural river environment, the interlacing patterns of the roots as they intertwined one with the other along its banks, the sounds of running water and bird song soothed my spirit. The canopy filtered the August sunshine down to a cool glow, with shafts of light picking out branches and roots. I paused many times for a breather and to absorb my surrounds and to allow my surrounds to absorb me. I put into action the resolution I'd made in the train — slow down and become part of Creation.

In this natural beauty, the people of Bourgogne had succeeded in preserving their heritage (*patrimoine*). I came across the remnants of an old mill, partly removed to allow the free movement of fish. A number of logs across a creek formed a bridge. The notice announced that it had been built by a local group on the weekend of 11.04.15, two years previously. I negotiated it successfully, but it would have been treacherous in wet weather.

After my slow start, I moved away from the river into open fields and forests, past small chapels and refuges. This was walking country. I passed through quaint medieval villages such as Vault-de-Lugny and Domecy-sur-le-Vault. I moved slowly and admired everything. I had to face the hills. Although none were of the killer variety, they were solid enough for my weary body. I had no lunch. I came across no facilities until, well into the afternoon, I arrived at Asquins just short of Vézelay. At the bar *L'Hirondelle* I enjoyed a much needed beer and sandwich. The Basilica Sainte Madelaine came into sight, just as my guidebook said, perched on the top of a distant hill. It got no closer the more I placed one aching leg after the other. The ground became steeper, and after leaving open country and passing through forest, I came on level ground and found myself at the rear of the basilica. What the guide book described as a 4 hours 30 minutes was an 11 hours slog. At least I didn't get lost as I did on my first day of walking from Le Puy-en-Velay in 2010. I hoped I had learned something in the intervening seven years. One piece of advice, which the old lag Camino addicts give to the novice, I had not heeded – go easy on your first day; do not exhaust yourself.

Vézelay's hilltop location has made it an obvious site for a town since ancient times. As I walked down the hill to the town, I was more intent on looking for my accommodation than on admiring the many fine heritage building. The *Relais du Morvan*, hotel, bar and restaurant, was old but charming for its makeshift appearance. I was pleased to have a private room, for the day's effort had freshened my cold, and it needed nursing. All my coughing and nose blowing would have made me a noisy roommate.

In the morning, I woke with an aching left hip. I was tired and battling with the dreaded lurgy. Feeling pretty average, I needed a spell before starting the Voie de Vézelay. Besides, the town looked as if it had a lot to offer, so I booked in for another night.

Now that I was here, I cranked myself up. I was pleased that I had approached Vézelay by foot. I could see how the basilica dominates both town and surrounding country. It began as a Benedictine monastery in the 9th century and was rebuilt as a basilica in the 12th century. As it claimed to guard the relics of St Mary Magdalene, Vézelay was a major medieval pilgrimage destination. It is well-known for its majestic sculpture of Christ over the main portal and for its capitals. It was among the many medieval buildings that the 19th century French architect Eugène Viollet-le-Duc restored following the neglect and damage of the French Revolution. Many historical figures are associated with the basilica. King Richard the Lionheart passed through on his way to the third crusade. The basilica saw the launch of the Second and Third Crusades. More peaceful were the pilgrims who, down the centuries, departed from here for Santiago (the French call it Compostelle) and the shrine of the apostle St James. The hillside is known as *'la colline éternelle'*, the land of faith where today pilgrims assemble for their blessing, the shell of St James on their backpacks, before departing on their way to Compostelle. I was about to join them.

I lit a candle for Maris, which I hoped would be the first of many. I paused to reflect. As with my previous Caminos, I dedicated my pilgrimage to her memory. I thought of the times we laughed, the times we cried, the times we were angry with each other, the silly things we did and the caring, love and joy we gave each other. May her light ever shine!

In a side chapel was a large wooden cross. I read the attached notice. My rough translation follows:

*The Cross of the German Prisoners*
*1946: Europe had emerged from a world war which had torn it apart. Christians felt the need to get together in prayer to vanquish the forces of hate which had racked the world, at the same time celebrating the 800th anniversary of the preaching on the crusade at Vézelay by St. Bernard in 1146.*

*This pilgrimage was an event of pardon and engagement with peace. Fourteen wooden crosses, carried on foot from England, Luxembourg, Belgium, Switzerland, and various parts of France converged on the basilica.*

*German prisoners, interned in a nearby camp, asked to join the procession. A fifteenth cross was made in haste. It became a powerful symbol of reconciliation for the world. 30,000 people gathered at Vézelay.*
*As an extension of this event, Vézelay became a place of prayer for reconciliation and for peace in Europe.*

I lit another candle and said a prayer for peace in this chapel. I was leaving behind a troubled world in which the leaders of the USA and North Korea were rattling swords at each other. The rest of the world was deafened by the fearful din of escalation. Sadly, we humans are such slow learners. The destruction and terrible aftermath caused by one war does not deter nations from plunging into another.

The crypt has reliquaries holding a few small relics of St Mary Magdalene. These are not the original relics that brought thousands of medieval pilgrims to Vézelay. They were burned by French Calvinists during the 16th century Wars of Religion. A basket invited visitors to leave petitions. I would not be visiting Santiago, and this crypt looked to me to be as sacred a place as any to leave the petitions that the people at Grace Avenue gave me before departing Australia, a fitting place because Mary Magdalene had faults and failings, just like us. She was both sinner and saint.

This basilica, the starting point of my pilgrimage, offered time for reflection. On this pilgrimage I should slow down, focus on each day and, as a concession to my age (in my 85th year), not be averse to taking the bus now and then.

Once upon a time, I walked with my full backpack every step of the way. I was critical, I'm afraid, of pilgrims who used the services of transport companies who carried their packs, which were left at the places they stayed at each evening. I was critical of those tour groups who were accompanied by a bus, provided a picnic lunch, gourmet meals at night; or groups of friends, one of whom drove a vehicle which carried the others' belongings. I realise, these days, that everyone embarks on the Camino in their own style and for any number of reasons. For some it's a test of stamina and perseverance. Others appreciate a little comfort. Some go on their own; others go with family or friends; some find new friends along the way, and some, such as myself, go in memory of a loved one whose pilgrimage is over. For everyone, however personally testing they may find the Camino, it has the promise to remain a source of inspiration.

The days of being a hardcore pilgrim, walking every step of the way, were over. Don't be so tough on yourself, Noël, I muttered to myself, still fragile from the cold and jet lag. Don't rush. I had given myself plenty of time, 49 days to reach Saint-Jean-Pied-de-Port.

*Abbaye de Sainte Madelaine de Vézelay*

*Voie de Vézelay* or *Via Lemovicensis*

# 4.

*Il faut marcher doucement et lentement*
*(One should walk gently and slowly)*

On Wednesday the 11th of August my pilgrimage along the Voie de Vézelay began. This route and this country were completely new to me. Just beyond the *Hôtel-Restaurant Le Relais du Morvan*, I had the choice of taking the northern route via Bourges or the southern route via Nevers. The routes join in the village of Gargilesse in the Berry region. The Bourges route is about 40 kilometres shorter, but the Nevers route, according to my guide book, offers more possibilities for refuge in the first days. I asked at the Pilgrim Centre if there were a preferred route, but they had nothing to offer. There was no indication one way was better than the other. A toss-up! What should the smart pilgrim do? Flip a coin? I didn't, but I leaned towards the longer walk with the better accommodation. Nevers, here I come! What challenges do you have in store? Nothing matters now but this adventure. With pack on my back, shell on my pack, walking poles in my hands and guidebook in my pocket, let the joy and spirit of the walk be free to speak.

Before me lay 800 kilometres that would bring me simple delights each day, wonderful country to admire, hazards to overcome and sacred places to discover. I was grateful that rain, though threatening, did not eventuate. Instead, fog enveloped the valley, but lifted in time for me to look back and see the basilica dominating the country. What a fantastic range of stories that building could tell! Soaked in history (and blood), it could relate the tale of individual pilgrims and of events that shook the medieval world.

The first day's journey was short because I wanted to embrace a slow rhythm of walking to appreciate the calm and the beauty of my surrounds. I needed to take my time. I was conscious of the lessons learnt two days previously. Be wary of hazards such as oak roots that seem to leap up and do their worst to entwine the unsuspecting pilgrim. At least, in those two days, I suffered no brain damage and at the moment was of clear mind.

I made my first pause at Saint-Père-sous-Vézelay, just 2.6 km. The first basilica dedicated to Saint Mary Magdalene was here but was moved up hill to Vézelay after its sacking by the Normans in 887. Shortly after Saint-Père, a flock of noisy sparrows joined me as I walked along country lanes winding up and down gently sloping hills. They flew before me, just keeping ahead, and as I caught up, they flew on for a hundred metres or so and settled on the trees and hedges as if waiting for me. I enjoyed the company of those small friendly creatures and felt in their chirping they were wishing me well. Who's not to say that they weren't the spirits of pilgrims long gone to God bidding me *'Bon Chemin'* or *'Bon Courage'*.

I passed through the small villages of Pierre Perthuis and Domecy-sur-Cure, along ancient Roman roads. I left the open countryside and walked through forests (Bois de l'Epenay and Bois de Bazoches). I passed by the gates of the Chateau de Bazoches and shortly after mid-afternoon arrived at the town of Bazoches where I was to spend the night. At the entrance was the church of Saint-Hilaire, which was open. Outside was a plaque erected in 1933 celebrating the tricentenary of Vauban, a famous local lad. Inside was his tomb. Sébastien Le Prestre de Vauban was a Marshall of France under the reign of King

## 4.

Louis XIV. He was a genius military engineer who specialised in building fortifications and in penetrating them. The church presented an opportunity to light a candle for Maris and for peace. Above the candles was a familiar notice :

> *Je ne sais pas prier Je ne sais pas que dire Je n'ai pas beaucoup de temps ... Alors ? La Lumière que j'offre est un peu de mon bien, un peu de mon temps, un peu de moi-même que je laisse devant le Seigneur, devant la Sainte Vierge, devant un Saint. Cette Lumière qui brille symbolise ma prière que je continue, tout en m'en allant...*
>
> *(I don't know how to pray I don't know what to say I haven't much time ...So? The light which I offer is a little of my being, a little of my time, a little of myself which I leave before the Lord, before the Holy Virgin, before a Saint. This light which shines symbolises my prayer which I continue, while going.)*

Bazoches was quiet; no one was around. I found my resting place *Chambre d'hôtes-Restaurant La Grignotte* (which means 'Snack'), a neat two-storey building half-covered in ivy, yellow walls, maroon doors and window frames. The lunchtime crowd had left, and I found the place closed. The proprietor Francine let me in, showed me to my room on the first floor, a small dining room opposite and left me on my own with dinner and some wine. I had the whole place to myself. I didn't mind. I had made the day short (15 kilometres) to allow my body to adjust to the rhythm; I was happy to rest.

Later, I explored. Bazoches is a neat village with lots of signs, making it difficult to get lost. Back at La Grignotte, I microwaved my dinner and drank the wine while watching TV. I switched to the World Athletics being held in London. The commentary was in English, and I found myself cheering when Australian Sally Pearson won gold in the Women's 100 Metres Hurdle. Later, as I came to stillness within myself and drifted into sleep, I offered a prayer of gratitude for all that was this day and for arriving safely in this quaint *Chambre d'hôtes*.

The next morning the dining room was open, and I had breakfast with the company of some locals having their morning coffee fix. The previous day, the Chateau of Bazoches was hidden by the high gate and fence and foliage, but this morning I had a clear view as I left the town. A large building with four towers and an inner stronghold around an interior courtyard, a feudal castle began in the 12th century by Jean de Bazoches and modified by Vauban and still in private hands. It nestles in the midst of forests and presents a magnificent spectacle across the fields, revealing itself at a lingering human pace, details apparent that would be lost if I had flashed by in a car.

I was on my own in beautiful countryside, yet I had a feeling of being in safe hands. I took my time with frequent stops just to admire the views. I passed through the village of Neuffontaines, past wayside crosses and two forms of signage. One was the familiar red and white bars of the Grand Randonnées (GR), the other was a yellow and blue arrow with stylised shell symbol and the name of the local 'Friends'- *Association des Amis et Pèlerins de Saint-Jacques de la Voie de Vézelay*. At the tip of the arrow was the word *'Compostelle'*. At this stage, the two forms of signage followed the same route although, to my cost, I was to find that sometimes they diverged.

Several times, I passed a notice on trees and fences referring to a lost cat (*'Loustic'*) which went missing on April 9th, 4 months previously. As well as a photo, it included a phone number, a thank you from the owner *('Lulu')* and a final comment – *très chagrin! (very dejected)*. I hope Lulu found her pet.

I arrived at the village of Anthien. Although I had only

## 4.

covered 11 kilometres, it looked a nice tranquil place, so I stopped. After inquiring of a young local who introduced himself as Andrew, I found the *Accueil pèlerin L'Esprit du Chemin* (Welcome Pilgrim the Spirit of the Camino). I was welcomed in English by Hennie, a tall man with grey hair and beard. He offered me a beer, and we chatted about my day. We were joined by his partner Anna. They told me they were hospitaliers, volunteering for a few weeks. The owners were Arno and Huberta. They once ran a refuge in Saint-Jean-Pied-de-Port but decided that the town was too crowded and moved to Anthien. Hennie showed me my bed, upstairs in a large expanse under the roof, which was once two rooms. There were four beds, one in each corner with screen provided. In the space in the centre they could have fitted quite a few more.

After a shower, some washing and a rest, I explored the building and the village. It could have been hundreds of years old. The ancient stone walls enclosed a large open space of lawn with a vegetable garden at the end. Only a few buildings equally ancient, the hamlet took a minute to inspect. Indeed, hamlet could be too grand a word. Farm buildings holding machinery and fodder, an ancient well and quite a splendid ornate calvaire (wayside cross) and a few houses, it's definitely the place if you want to get away from it all. Yet everything looked well cared for, as if the people were proud of their tiny spot in the world.

I met the other guest, Martin from Holland. The four of us had an excellent meal together in the garden prepared by Anna. We lingered over wine and shared our stories. All conversation was in English. Hennie was Dutch, and Anna was French. They met on the Camino 25 years previously and had been together since. Martin was 49 years old. When he married, he told his wife that he wanted to walk to Santiago before he was 50. He had walked out of his home in Holland and was planning to continue until he arrived, which he estimated would be about his birthday. His wife was aiming to meet him on some weekends and walk with him. I told some of my story. All were intrigued that I had come all the way from Australia at 84 years of age. They were interested in my being an author, and both Hennie and Martin asked for my website address.

That evening was wonderful, the first time on this pilgrimage that I had company for dinner. I am convinced that a refuge offers a meal for more profound reasons than nourishment. It is over food that people bond, that hearts are opened, people relax their suspicions, fears are revealed and love is expressed. My old friend Fr. Peter McGrath, who founded the Family Group Movement, always said that sharing stories over a meal is just as spiritual and sacred an activity as attending a church service.

Martin occupied the bed diagonally opposite. We chatted for a while, but I settled down first and was quickly asleep. I vaguely remember hearing some movement, and in the morning, I noticed that Martin had moved to the bed on the same side. He was concerned that his light might disturb me. I thanked him for his thoughtfulness. Hennie joined us for breakfast. Martin wanted my photo in case we didn't meet again. I was to find that everyone wanted to take a photo with me. I was a bit different, I suppose; an eighty-four-year-old Australian walking on his own. Martin was keen to press on in order to reach Santiago on time. I had no such demands and would probably lag well behind him. I left before him, but he caught up and vanished over the hill.

This Sunday August 13th was overcast. Rain was threatening, so I had my wet weather gear at the ready. I did not have to extract them, and by the end of the day, the skies had cleared. I

## 4.

made Corbigny in good time. Corbigny has had a troubled history. A monastery was established in 864 and later received the (so called) relics of St. Léonard, becoming a place of pilgrimage well frequented by those on the road to Compostelle. Fires and pillaging eventually destroyed the monastery despite the town's fortifications. Later, it was caught up in a war between Armagnac and Bourguignons, while the Wars of Religion were equally disastrous for both town and abbey.

This Sunday was peaceful; an extensive market filled the main drag and spilled into the side streets. Stalls were selling everything including food, and lovely aromas filled the air. Restaurants' tables spread out on the road were full of diners, a regular shindig. I heard my name. 'Noël!' I looked around to see Hennie and Anna beckoning me to join them at their table. I had already eaten a nondescript roll, but I sat with them. We chatted. Anna had looked up my website and was keen to talk about my books. She wanted to know more of Maris. Her direct questions saddened me. Sometimes, an unexpected reminder can arouse nostalgic memories of what might have been; although I know I would not be in this small town bustling with a Sunday market and speaking to this couple if she were still with us.

It would have been lovely to settle down for the arvo to a few red wines with Hennie and Anna. If I drink alcohol during the day, that's as far as I'm likely to get. I pressed on, not too far, about four kilometres to Chitry-les-Mines and Chaumot where I found a camping ground on the edge of town. *Camping L'Arsan* was located by a small stream and the Canal du Nivernais, a pleasant shady spot. The owners were Dutch, and in fact, everything about the place was Dutch including the guests. I heard no French. At first, I was told the park was full, but then I was given a small caravan to myself. Well decorated not very tastefully with flowers and birds, even the number plates were Dutch. I imagine someone would have had a fun afternoon, armed with paint brush and a little imagination to create this scene. Outside were two blue plastic chairs. I enjoyed sitting in one watching the campers walk by and admiring the waters of the canal and stream beyond, the trees gently dipping their branches into the water.

The camping ground had a restaurant, which according to the blurb, provided gourmet meals. Dining was like eating in Little Holland; all I heard was Dutch. I sat on a small table on my own, but a couple at the next table invited me to join them. Marion and Pierre were Dutch but preferred to speak in English. They were touring around in their own caravan and were parked in a shady spot down the back. They told me that *Camping L'Arsan* was very popular and well-known in Holland for its welcome. They were intrigued that I was a pilgrim and was planning to walk to the Pyrénées. They did not know much about the Camino and seemed astonished that such numbers should follow it. As we parted company, Marion kindly insisted on giving me a banana.

I left my happy campers early, about 7.00 a.m., for I knew I could have a long day. The morning was crisp, and the day was full of sunshine. According to my guide book, Prémery should have been my destination, but that was 33 kilometres. My anxiety about such a long distance threatened to grey the whole sky like cloud cover. I stopped at Guipy for breakfast, about six kilometres. As I enjoyed the moment and sipped my coffee, I thought it would be nice if a bus came along and was going my way. No bus came, so I put on my backpack and continued. As I walked out of the town, I noticed a taxi parked outside a house, and I could see through the open door that someone was home. Lights flashed in my brain. I heard two

## 4.

voices. *'Noël, here's an opportunity to shorten your day. Take the taxi to say, Saint-Révérien, about seven kilometres. That will save you two hours,'* said one. The other, a sterner voice, replied: *'Noël, you're a pilgrim, you should walk the whole way.' 'But mate, you don't have to be a hardcore pilgrim anymore. You've already proved yourself. Act your age and take advantage of whatever's available. Providence has sent you this taxi.'*

I heard that voice and knocked on the door. Out came the occupant in his house painting clothes. Although he said it was his day off, he disappeared inside and soon returned in more appropriate work dress. That grey cloud cover vanished. I'd made a good call. We arrived at Saint-Révérien in no time. For the remainder of the day, I walked in sunshine along a boring asphalted road, but the highpoint was meeting Martin. I was having a breather on the roadside, and along he came with his wife Rianne. She had joined him for the weekend. I had met him only two evenings previously, but it was as if I was meeting an old mate. That's the Camino. He thought I had made good time. I didn't tell him about the taxi ride. He told me of a new gîte opened a few months — *Un Pas á la Fois* (One step at a time) at Le Breuil. He rang ahead for me. He and Rianne would not stop there. They would push ahead. I saw one other walker that day. In Moussy, I passed a young dad pushing a crying baby in a pram. Had he been sent out to settle the babe?

The afternoon was hot, and I was thankful for that taxi ride, brief as it was. I arrived in Le Breuil, just a few houses, and found *Un Pas á la Fois*. My host was working in the garden, and as I walked through an archway covered in roses spanning the path, a wild thorn caught my thin skin and sent a stream of blood flowing down my arm. Not a good way to greet my host. I always carry my first aid kit at the top of the pack and have become adept in quickly finding a band aid and applying it to the wound. After that, I was able to say G'day (*Bonjour!*). Fortunately, I stopped the blood flow before it found my clothes. Chantal showed me to my room. I was the only guest and I dined with her, her sister and brother-in-law. They had visited Australia, so we chatted about the places they had seen. Our conversation was a mixture of French and English. They were planning a fourth visit, so they were keen to practise the language and to gain my impressions on what there was yet to see.

I was content I'd come so far in one day although I hadn't walked all the way. Time to worry about the next day. August 15th was a public holiday. Over breakfast, I discussed my concerns with Chantal. She recommended aiming for Nevers (about 34 kilometres) and offered to drive me to Guérigny; that left me with 14 kilometres of walking. In the old days when I was a hardcore pilgrim, I would have declined, but age and common sense ruled the day. I accepted gratefully. I am overwhelmed by the generosity of the local folk who go out of their way to support and help their pilgrims. Hospitality is a long-standing custom, centuries old. It's nice to think that my actions bring out the better side of people.

Despite an easy walk, the day was hot and I was ready to stop by the time I reached the outskirts of Nevers. Walking under the hot sun through built-up areas, some of them rather ugly and uninspiring, is always tiring. Nevers is a large town with lots to see. This was my seventh day, so a rest would not be out of the question. I was surprised by the number of people who greeted me. It was not difficult to guess that, with backpack and shell, I was a pilgrim. Was I going to Compostelle? They followed my reply with '*Bon Courage!*' or '*Bonne Continuation!*' Perhaps I was sagging with weariness and looking my age. Two young men were just coming out of their house and invited me in for a refreshing drink. My water bottle was not

## 4.

empty, but the water was warm, and their ice-cold water was delicious. They were intrigued by my coming all the way from Australia. I told them many young French people go backpacking in Australia and visit my mountains for the ski season. Perhaps I roused their interest for a trip down under.

I was aiming for *Gîte l'étape La Bonne Dame* at 21 rue du Plateau de La Bonne Dame, which was on the other side of town, so I had to traverse the whole city and the River Loire. After a pleasant walk by the river in the shade of many large trees, I found my hosts Martine and Xavier. Their garden was dominated by a large cherry tree, overloaded with fruit. I liked the leafy shade, ideal for a hot day. I liked the feel of the place, ideal to pause and refresh my spirits. Could I stay two nights? No worries! (or the French equivalent). I found my way through the green and leafy garden to the second set of stairs. The first set was the home of Martine and Xavier. My home was small but adequate. A kitchen and dining area led into a bedroom with two sets of double bunks. Through the wall I could hear the TV and some conversation, but mostly the place was quiet and peaceful. As I came to peace and stillness within myself, I reflected with gratitude that I had arrived thus far. I reconnected with the last 7 days, what had happened to me, what had been asked of me and how had I responded. I heard myself responding; give myself time. Be gentle, be patient.

In the morning, I asked Xavier: where are the pilgrims? The gîte was full earlier in the season, he replied, but later in the season the numbers dwindled.

One of the changes I had noticed since my first Camino lay in accessing the internet. Once upon a time, internet cafes were available in every town. Refuges and gîtes had a computer in a corner for the use of pilgrims and guests. I had a regular address book to whom I sent emails every few days.

People told me how they enjoyed reading them. Now, everyone (Well, almost everyone!) has a smart phone to access the internet and their emails. Before I left home, I'd tried to set up my travel phone to access emails, but I was a fish out of water. Technology defeated me, and I gave up. I've come a long way in mastering technology, but not far enough. I hadn't accessed my emails since I left Australia. I mentioned this to Xavier, and he loaned me a computer. I mucked around for a large slice of the morning, but no luck. My service provider was in maintenance mode. Try later! When I did, I got the same result. I gave Xavier back his computer. He introduced me to his friend Henri who had come for lunch. Henri had spent a year in Sydney selling French Champagne. Whereas Xavier was a white-bearded homely old chap, Henri was the smooth sophisticated man-of-the-world, a fraction patronising of an ancient pilgrim but nevertheless genial. I left late morning to explore Nevers and passed Xavier, Martine, Henri and his wife sitting at a luncheon table in their garden, a lovely setting for a leisurely afternoon in the company of old friends.

Nevers is at the confluence of two rivers, the Loire and the Nièvre. The town has its origins as a regional centre in Roman times when it was an important depot for Julius Caesar. It is now a lively, active modern town but has historical monuments, which were my destination that warm afternoon. I walked along the river back to the bridge. On the other side, the town climbed the hill to the monuments beyond. I looked along the river to a beach (*Nevers plage* in large white letters) covered in white peaked tents and multi-coloured umbrellas and litters. I climbed up the hill to the 15th century Ducal Palace, an attractive chateau with a main façade that includes towers at either end and an ornate open staircase in the centre that incorporates many statues and decorations. The palace

## 4.

was built by a local count and reminded me of some of the Loire Valley chateaux to the west, which I visited while I was studying French in Amboise back in 2010.

Nearby is the Cathedral of Saint-Cyr and Sainte-Juliette. Its tower dominates the Nevers skyline, and I'm sure there's a great view to be had across the roofs of Nevers and the Loire river. The cathedral has ancient origins and parts date back to the 6th century. The main church is medieval and partly Romanesque and partly Gothic. The outside features delightful detailed carvings and gargoyles. Inside are many statues, paintings, frescoes and furnishings. More modern are the stained-glass windows, effective in adding light and colour.

My surprise was the shrine of Saint-Bernadette of Lourdes fame. I visited Lourdes back in 2006 at the end of my bout of learning French at Chambéry. At Grenoble, I joined a train full of pilgrims destined for Lourdes. We were part of the Pèlerinage du Rosaire, organised by the Dominicans. Trainloads of pilgrims arrived from every part of France. The theme for that 2006 pilgrimage was *Lumière du Christ (Light of the Christ)* – passing from the darkness into the light. As I had been without much light in the two years since Maris died, those four days were memorable as an opportunity to renew my spiritual resources. The experience was extraordinary, not only for the time in Lourdes but the train journey back and forth. The ceremonies were moving; the music and singing were excellent, and the devotion of the people was profound. Several times, I visited the grotto where the apparitions appeared to the young Bernadette. I felt a definite presence.

I met people, not the ones the average tourist would meet in hotels and restaurants, but ordinary everyday folk. People are the same everywhere. Once you reach out to them and try to speak in their language, they accept and trust you and want to talk about their families and the major burdens of their lives. In turn, they want to know about your family and your life. Maris would have loved to hear their stories, too. I'm sure, had she known French, she, too, would have found these conversations the most stimulating part of her journey.

I should have known about Bernadette and Nevers, that she became a nun and came to live in the convent at 22 years of age. I visited *Espace Bernadette*, the shrine of Saint-Bernadette where her body is enclosed in a glass cage. The convent has a recreation of the grotto and a statue of Mary exactly the same as the one at Lourdes. Nevers is now a pilgrimage destination. Dallying in Nevers was like travelling back in time in search of the sacred in places where the saints shone forth, on holy ground that blazed with meaning.

There were other monuments, but being a tourist is tiring, so I walked back across the river to *Gîte l'étape La Bonne Dame*. On the way, I noticed a pilgrim laden with backpack and looking as if he needed a bed for the night. He was slow moving and in constant consultation with his guide book. I guessed he was looking for *La Bonne Dame* and I would have company that night. The friends were still at the luncheon table although on the point of departing. Two young children (grandchildren I guessed) were pestering Martine for cherries, so I saw them shaking the tree and heard their shrieks of delight as the leaves and fruit fell, Martine following with a basket to gather the fruit. I joined in to help fill the basket. Such a picture of family bliss reminded me of my own grandchildren on the other side of the world.

Shortly after, our pilgrim arrived. Marcel looked laden indeed. His bag, he told me, weighed 15 kilos and included a tent. He'd been walking for two weeks, but today he got a lift from Avallon on the back of a motor bike — both scary and

## 4.

exhilarating, trying to maintain his balance on the curves. I suggested to Marcel that instead of getting in each other's way preparing the evening meal and eating separately, that I cook and we share the meal. He agreed but insisted on helping in the preparation and sharing the cost. Over a dinner of fish soup, egg and tomato salad, steak, mushroom and potatoes we shared something of our lives. Marcel lived in Dieppe. He had just retired from his job as an electrical engineer on a ferry that ran between Calais and Dover and was now figuring out what to do next with his life. Even though the majority of passengers were English, he had never learned the language. He was intrigued that I had come all the way from Australia at my age. He had not met many Australians. We discussed food preferences. The French are always interested in food. He wanted to know what Australians eat and did they have a national dish. I explained that, due to successive waves of immigration, Australians are very diverse in their tastes. One of his preferences was the *'feuille de chêne'* salad for which there are a variety of recipes. By the end of the evening and a bottle of good French red, we were old mates.

You can't beat the power of a meal in developing trust and confidence. If you could get antagonists together over a meal where they are prepared to share a little of themselves, I wonder how many of the world's conflicts could be resolved.

*Anna and Henni, Noël and Martin at L'Esprit du Chemin*

4.

*Xavier and Martine at lunch with friends
Henri and wife at the Gîte d'étape La Bonne Dame*

# 5.

*I'm slowing down the tune*
*I never liked it fast*
*You want to get there soon*
*I want to get there last*
*It's not because I'm old*
*It's not the life I led*
*I always liked it slow*
*That's what my momma said*
*I'm lacing up my shoe*
*But I don't want to run*
*I'll get there when I do*
*Don't need no starting gun.*
Leonard Cohen

The sun had not long surfaced as I left *Gîte l'étape La Bonne Dame* and walked along the River Loire back to the bridge. It cast long shadows along the water with sunshine peeping through the arches onto the water cascading the rocks. The town climbed the hill, the strong silhouette of the cathedral rising as if emerging from sleep – a beautiful peaceful idyllic dream, looking as if nothing had changed for centuries, a scene that could have escaped from a painting. The spell would not last. It would soon be in full sun and lively with people and traffic.

I admired the beauty of the moment – a wholesome start to my ninth day of pilgrimage. The pilgrim looks for the good and the true, but beauty is not always so highly valued. Beauty has an authority of its own, an authority to which everyone responds. It inspires. I remember studying the poet John Keats and his poem Ode on a Grecian Urn;

> 'Beauty is truth and truth beauty,
> that is all ye know on earth and all ye need to know.'

As a seventeen-year-old, I did not appreciate the full implication. As a pilgrim, I've been walking through a countryside full of beauty and wonder. Through this beauty, I am enticed to think beyond myself and be open to what is around me. Perhaps this is God's way of stirring the spirit to see the beauty in everyday life, in the people around me and what they have to say. May this gift of awe and wonder stay with me when I return home.

Marcel passed me. For a time, I walked along a canal, but I left it to go its own way while I tread on asphalt roads, fortunately not too busy. I stopped for lunch at Magny-Cours, which was very quiet, for everything was closed. It would be lively sometimes, for here is the Circuit de Nevers Magny-Cours, a motor racing circuit that has staged the Formula One French Grand Prix, the 24-hour Bol d'Or motorcycle endurance events, the French motorcycle Grand Prix, the Superbike International Championships and several other international events. Nothing much was happening that day.

I passed the Circuit and heard the distant rumbling of vehicles. My destination was Saint-Parize-le-Châtel, about 19 kilometres from Nevers. Approaching the town, one of the few cars stopped. The driver welcomed me and said that I would meet his wife who looked after the *refuge Accueil Pèlerin*. He wished me *Bon Chemin* and drove off. I was feeling tired and would have appreciated his turning his words into action by offering me a lift. Fat chance! I still had a kilometre or so to go. At the entrance to the town was a sign of welcome:

## 5.

*Pèlerins, Saint-Parize-le-Châtel vous accueille*

and announced its 12th century Roman crypt, complete with photos of the main street and the crypt. The town was quiet; shops were closed, and people were absent. The *Accueil Pèlerin* was open, in a decayed building, tacked onto a deserted barn leading on to a yard with not a single shrub or plant apart from long grass. The interior had been renovated and recently painted. Marcel was already installed. Furnishing was of the hand-me-down variety but comfortable. The bedroom had three beds. The living area was spacious and included a television. The refuge had the feeling of someone who cared about it. Soon that carer arrived. Mme Riberolle knew everyone and everything about the town. She booked dinner for Marcel and me at a restaurant and told us about the church (Saint Patrice) and its Roman crypt, which was just opposite the refuge. Mme Riberolle already knew of me — the eighty-four-year-old *Australien*. Martin the Dutchman whom I met at *L'Esprit du Chemin* had stayed there the night before. She showed me his entry in the diary:

*Hi Noël! Just keep on walking!!*

Martin's a good bloke. I wished we had spent more than one night together. I hoped I'd meet him again.

Mme Riberolle left, but M. Riberolle arrived, the chap I'd met on the road. His job was to lock Saint Patrice for the night, but he offered to take us on a tour. The church was first constructed in the 12th century on the site of a monastery but was largely rebuilt in the 19th century with the exception of the crypt, the walls of which were traced back to the 11th century and the pillars and capitals to the 12th century. We looked around the church first, then descended down the steps to the crypt into another world illustrating the mentality and fantasies of another age. The six pillars are topped with capitals decorated with animals and vegetation, both fascinating and grotesque by our standards – a greedy bearded person attacked by a demon with a serpent's tail, a siren with two fish tails, a helmeted centaur killing a deer, a diabolical cook, a pig playing a harp, a monkey playing a viola, monsters vomiting foliage. M. Riberolle took us from capital to capital, explaining the sculptures in detail, at pains to stress their significance. The recurrent theme of the Middle Ages, he said, was the struggle between vice and virtue with a strong insistence on the evil. I must admit I found these sculptures depressing. They illustrated a world of darkness. Just as well that subdued reflected lighting gave us some refuge. Those lights had a spiritual as well as practical purpose.

After thanking M. Riberolle, Marcel and I sought out our restaurant. We seemed to walk around in circles with no one about to ask. We finally found *'La Reception'* just around the corner from our gîte. We were the only diners. We discussed Saint-Parize-le-Châtel. It had a rich history, but nothing much was happening at the moment. Back at the gîte, we took advantage of having a television at our disposal. We were jarred out of the fantasies of the Middle Ages into the realities of the modern world; the dominant news was the terror attack in Barcelona where one man drove his truck into a crowd killing thirteen people and injuring one hundred.

Marcel left early, but I stayed on until 9.30 am, as I was planning to walk 12 kilometres. I lingered over breakfast and watched the TV, full of Barcelona. I felt for the victims and their families, people whom I never met, and as I set out walking, I said a prayer that the survivors would somehow find the

## 5.

courage to keep pressing on. In contrast to the city in turmoil, I found myself in a land of peace. The day was overcast with the threat of rain. I passed through a forest, then moved into open land populated with white cows. They stopped their grazing to stare at this passing intruder while the young calves ran to their mothers for safety. Geese and ducks waddled around ponds and jumped into and out of the water, the serenity in sharp contrast to the horrors of terrorism.

I stopped to admire an ancient windmill. Lovingly restored, it had been built in the 19th century to grind wheat into flour. Its roof was pivoted to allow the sails to face the wind. I wanted to look inside at the different levels, but it was firmly padlocked. Even the long pole which controlled the sails' orientation was bolted to the ground. As I reached Saint-Pierre-le-Moûtier, the rain fell. I sought shelter in the supermarket by the side of the freeway. A kind customer helped me with my poncho, and I set off in heavy rain through the town. My refuge *Accueil Pèlerin* was in Marcigny about two kilometres off route. When I reached Marcigny, I couldn't find my refuge. At that stage, the only people I had seen all day were the few customers at the supermarket. No one was strolling around in this heavy rain just waiting for a lost pilgrim to ask them the way. I noticed a taxi parked outside a house. Someone was home, I thought, so I knocked on the door. A chap with a large belly hanging over his shorts answered. *Désolé de vous deranger (Sorry to bother you)* was my usual starter. He knew nothing about a pilgrim refuge. He stayed behind his wire door, but he did grudgingly allow me to shelter under his porch so that I could remove my poncho and backpack and find my phone. My guide book was in the pocket of my shorts, by now damp from the water running off my poncho which was not quite long enough. The pages were stuck together, but I managed to find the right entry and rang. Mme Marie-France Arbez-Seguin answered. I was in the right street, she said. Her number was 74, which was just opposite. By now, the chap had shut his door as if the sight of a damp and confused pilgrim was too much, so I could not thank him for his generosity of spirit. I returned my sodden guidebook to my pocket, replaced my phone and donned my backpack, somehow managing to get my poncho on unassisted. I crossed the road, stepped in the gushing stream, which had filled the gutters, and approached what I thought was Number 74, a shabby run-down building, which looked as if it hadn't seen paint for decades. An old man who looked as run-down as his house answered the door. *Désolé de vous deranger.* I had difficulty explaining myself for he was deaf. Eventually, he worked out what I wanted. I should go next door. As I walked back to his gate, I noticed his number – 74b, not 74.

I must say, I was relieved to be at the wrong house. I could not imagine what the inside might be like. 74 was a short walk along a hedge. Mme Marie-France heard the gate click and came out to greet me with a large umbrella. By now, the rain had eased, but I dripped over the floor. The pilgrim refuge was a wing jutting out from the main house in good condition, with two bedrooms, living area, kitchenette, and bathroom. Mme put me in an alcove beyond which was another bedroom. She said a couple was coming later.

I peeled off my wet gear and spread it around. I looked at my sodden guidebook. Already dog eared enough and grimy from frequent reference, its pages were stuck together. My guidebook had been a faithful companion. As I referred to it, I found myself loving it, hating it, ignoring it, puzzling over it, scribbling in it. I imagined it would find a treasured place in my bookcase back home along with the guidebooks from previous pilgrimages. I tried to separate the pages. I would be

## 5.

needing it, as I still had lots of walking. I was thankful for the towel dryer in the bathroom.

While resting on my bed, I heard Mme bringing in other people who went to the other bedroom. I met them later. Jerome and Valerie were from Paris. They had arrived by train and taken a taxi. They were not pilgrims but were planning to spend 15 days walking in the region. They were warm generous people as was Mme Marie-France. She brought in our meal and stayed with us for a long chat. They were keen to include me. They were intrigued by my presence – all the way from *Australie* and at my age. The topic swung around to the people we knew who were young in their eighties and nineties or old in their twenties and thirties.

The weather cleared, and I woke to a fine day. I lay in bed for a while and heard Jerome and Valerie creep past and out the door. They left a note for me. They enjoyed meeting me and wished me well. I left at 9.30 a.m. as I was planning another day of 12 kilometres. I took my time as I walked back to Saint-Parize-le-Moûtier. No need to rush. I was walking slowly because that's my way. I've always walked slowly, and now I'm older.

I stopped for lunch in the tiny village of Livry, which was no more than a church and a few shops. As I was sitting in the shade of the church, Kurt arrived. He was German and spoke excellent English. He knew about me, as he had stayed at Saint-Parise-le-Châtel and Mme Riberolle had raved on about me – the eighty-four-year-old Australian walking on his own. Kurt wanted to press on, not before taking my photo. Our meeting was no more than 5 minutes, but he left an impact. Where ever people gather, they love to gossip and tell stories about each other. The Camino is no different.

I crossed the river L'Allier into the Région Auvergne and La

Veurdue, and although it was only 3 pm, I stopped, enticed by their welcome sign:

*La Veurdue vous souhaite la bienvenue.*

The *Accueil Pèlerin* mentioned in the guidebook was no longer available, but a neat sign in the main street pointed to the *Gîte du Pèlerin de Saint-Jacques*, which was housed in the *Maison du Patrimoine* (Heritage House). I rang a phone number, and shortly after, a lady arrived, checking my pilgrim passport and let me in. As well as providing shelter to pilgrims, the building served as a community centre where various groups met. After a brief rest, I went exploring the town and found the church of Saint Hippolyte open. Saint Hippolyte was a saint of the early church, the patron saint of horses. The building began in the 11th century, a tower was added in the 15th, a statue of Saint Ann in the 16th, and the main altar in the 17th. Nothing much has been added since. The walls needed attention, but someone was caring for the church; vases of fresh flowers were distributed around the interior. I lit a candle for Maris in a side altar and sat there, reflecting on the depth of our love. There is a special place in my heart that will always be reserved for her.

Just down from the gîte was a gift shop, La Fontaine des Merveilles. Outside was a fountain, which wasn't working. The shop had a great array of local craft work. I was tempted to buy a souvenir as a gift for someone back home. Buying gifts in the middle of your walking and adding weight to your back pack is not a good idea. How many great opportunities have I let pass because of that demand? Travel lightly was and always will be the first lesson of the Camino.

The well-equipped kitchen invited me to cook for myself. In the middle of my meal, a woman turned up looking for a bed, she said. She made me uncomfortable; she avoided eye contact and seemed too interested in looking around the place, as if noting what was worth souveniring. She was reasonably dressed but was not a walker and had no pilgrim passport. I had already noted the rules that only pilgrims with passports were allowed to stay. Rather than let her in, I gave her the lady's phone number. She went away and said she would come back. Her presence was too creepy; she gave out the wrong vibes, so before I went to bed, I locked the door. As I drifted into sleep, I vaguely thought I heard the door rattle. Was it the wind or the woman returning?

I felt like a local buying bread at the boulangerie at 7.30 a.m. The French buy their bread early morning. Mind you, that's the time to buy and eat a baguette, for by the end of the day it's stale and hard. Eating a stale baguette is an invitation to break your teeth. Over breakfast, I rang my daughter Jacinta back in the Snowy Mountains. The main news from home: a metre of snow had fallen the week before, so the ski season was in full swing.

I enjoyed my visit to La Veurdue. The town had a nice feel with neat compact streets. Nothing remarkable seemed to have occurred in its history although in 1940 the invading German army found the town no pushover. La Veurdue was on the dividing line between Occupied and Free France.

I was finding my backpack too heavy. At the bottom was a small fold-up-into-nothing day pack that I used in towns, so I tried wearing it in front to distribute the weight. It helped a little to ease the weight on my shoulders, but my silhouette was decidedly odd as if I was pregnant. Who cares about appearances on the Camino? I'd seen some quaint arrangements like umbrellas sticking out of packs or packs adorned with a series of plastic supermarket bags carrying all sorts of oddities.

Although the way was flat and fine, I was tiring. Old age creeping up? Why was I doing this? I wished I didn't have to challenge myself all the time. When things are too comfortable, why do I get bored and need to introduce something extra to spice things up? Back home in the mountains, my High Country gym's walls are lined with one-liners such as:

*Life begins at the end of your comfort zone,*
*and Good is not good enough when you can do better.*

Why do I push myself beyond my comfort zone with this long-distance walking? Why couldn't I go in for some sensible, gentle pursuits like bowls or short strolls in the park? Why aren't I on a cruise like other people of my age? I'm afraid sitting around in deck chairs would bore me witless. No spring chicken, do I need my head read? Am I stark raving mad?

I paused for a breather in Petit-Beaumont (I had just passed through Grand-Beaumont) by a shady slimy green pond covered with weeds and searched for the frogs in the muck. There was quite a community of all sizes. I wondered about the social life of frogs. They didn't seem to interact much; they just sat on the water as individuals blowing the odd bubble. Some had their heads, eyes and mouth poking through, others had only their mouths visible. I was tempted to throw something into the pond, even a scrap of food, to stir up some activity, but I chastised myself for wanting to make trouble in such a tranquil world.

I rested in a ditch and watched a beetle struggling to find its way up the bank. It kept falling back, sometimes rolling over, but it picked itself up and continued the climb, encountering further obstacles until it reached the grass at the top and disappeared. I felt like helping with a gentle nudge but decided no. Let it find its own destiny. An allegory for our human journey! A change from watching frogs! I'm not sure what was their destiny.

I recalled a vintage Leunig cartoon, one of my favourites. Under the heading: A Man Meets Twelve Great Spiritual Leaders, a man meets a bird, a flower, a dog, a fish, a duck, a cat, a tree, a baby in a pram, a goat, a lizard, a butterfly, and finally bends down to meet a beetle. That cartoon has profound meaning on many levels, ranging from what can man learn from these creatures to a deeper connection with nature, creation, God, or whatever your spiritual being wants to name it.

At one point, I read a sign pointing up the road *Big Forest Camp Hébergements Atypiques* complete with sketches of a covered wagon and a wigwam. I was curious and tempted to walk the 1.7 kilometres to find out more, a white donkey watching me all the while. He bid me goodbye with a bray. I passed another sign informing me they bred donkeys here and were available for sale. I was in donkey country. I had seen pilgrims with donkeys; they'd be handy to carry your pack.

Valigny is indeed donkey country. Apart from the *Hôtel-Restaurant Relais de la Fôret*, the only shop was a Savonnerie, selling cosmetics made from ass's milk, and as well a place of education for the breeding of donkeys. In the window was a poster advertising a Fête aux Anes (festival) the following Sunday on August 27th complete with market of second hand and antique goods and entertainment. Pity! I was six days too early.

There is a sad side to donkeys. On the page devoted to Valigny, my guide book relates a story about the pilgrim donkey. A rough translation follows:

*I have faithfully carried baggage, I have borne the bad moods of my master, I have eaten inedible stuff. In the event by not*

> returning from this pilgrimage, here are my last wishes: I, Ferdinand, of healthy body and mind, wide in stomach and tall in ears have written thus so that none of it is ignored: I bequeath my bag of oats, my share of hay and my salt lick to my companions of the field. I bequeath my halter to the Foundation which will perpetuate my memory and tell the story of my suffering. I bequeath my tether to the Museum of Slaves. I bequeath my ears to Science so that the voice of reason may be at last heard among men.

Perhaps my guidebook writers may have taken their inspiration from Robert Bresson's cinematic masterpiece *Au Hazard Balthazar*, which tells the story of a saint-like donkey, ruthlessly victimised by human greed and folly, a moving allegory of sacrifice, suffering and redemption.

As well as providing meals and accommodation, *Le Relais de la Forêt* was the hub of Valigny. It was the bread depot, sold some groceries and even provided candles for the church opposite. My bedroom upstairs was west-facing — hot from the sun, but at least my washing dried quickly. I bought a candle and visited the church. The pigeons in the tower were noisy, but the ambience was peaceful and the building well cared for. Notre Dame is a 14th century church with statues of the Virgin of the Annunciation, Sainte Marguerite and Sainte Barbe added in later centuries. An interesting notice about Sainte Marguerite read:

> *According to the legend, Saint Marguerite, Virgin and martyr of the 3rd century, endured all sorts of torments. The devil, disguised as a dragon, would have penetrated her prison in order to dismember her, but Saint Marguerite, had no need to arm*

*herself, like Saint Michael, with a lance to put the beast to flight. She blessed herself and that was enough.*

Back at *Le Relais de la Forêt*, a meal was available from the Menu du Jour. The couple who ran the show were quaint. He was gruff and of few words. She was bent over, frail and looked a battler who had endured a life of hard work. I'm sure she was tough underneath, for she gave the directions to her grumpy husband. I hoped the bloke treated her well. I was the only guest although the bar was the local watering hole and had plenty of patrons.

This was my thirteenth night on the road. So far, I had only four nights in the company of other pilgrims. I hoped that would change.

*In the crypt at Saint-Parize-le-Châtel*

*Gift shop La Fontaine des Merveilles
(the gîte is behind on the left)*

# 6.

*What then? Shall we sit idly down and say*
*The night hath come; it is no longer day?*
*The night hath not yet come; we are not quite*
*Cut off from labour by the failing light;*
*Something remains for us to do and dare;*
*For age is opportunity, no less*
*Than youth itself, though in another dress,*
*And as the evening twilight fades away*
*The sky is filled by stars, invisible by day.*
Longfellow – Morituri Salutamus
(Quoted in a blog by Margaret Meredith)

I didn't sleep well. The church bells began at 3 a.m. and continued until 7. The cock started crowing before dawn. Le Relais de la Forêt was astir early with deliveries in the yard below my bedroom. Locals arrived for their morning coffee. I joined them for breakfast. The bread was delivered. I tried to buy a baguette but was bluntly told every loaf was ordered. The old bloke also had the job of opening and closing the church, and while I was sipping my coffee, I noticed him wander across the road.

I rang my destination for the day, which was the refuge at Ainay-le-Château. I was surprised to be told they were expecting my call. They had heard about the ancient Australian walking on his own and were waiting for him. I guessed pilgrims who had slept where I stayed were the informants. Gossip and the grapevine work well on the Camino as they do whenever people talk to each other.

The lady took my card for payment. Good! I was almost out of cash. She seemed happier too that morning and had lost her burdened look. She even smiled as she wished me *Bonne Continuation*. I bought another candle for Maris and visited the church. The pigeons were just as noisy, but the atmosphere just as calm. I offered thanks for the time that Maris and I shared our lives. I offered thanks for the gift of my age. Walking at my age means I have to tackle the Camino in a way different to the younger pilgrim; I need time to adjust and to figure out how to translate the fire burning in my heart into action that was not beyond me. I offered thanks for the day and that, apart from the rose thorn, I had come so far without mishap – always a blessing. I hadn't been lost once. So far, so good.

The day was fine; the going was easy, and the French countryside was lovely just as it had been the day before and the day before that. I walked for a time along a canal and a road, which was not too busy. Late morning, I passed a large field where a tractor was busy at work dragging a scarifier. Up and down the tractor went on the far side of the field, and I enjoyed watching its progress, for, apart from cows, it was first sign of activity for the day. It lifted the scarifier, moved across the field and stopped just ahead of me. The driver jumped off and approached the fence. It was a lady with a weather-beaten face, a legacy of a life lived out-of-doors. She introduced herself as Catherine. Was I walking towards Compostelle? She became animated. She had left her farm two years previously and had walked to Santiago. It was a wonderful experience, and she would love to do it again, but had the routines of her farm to attend to. She was intrigued that I had come so far. *Australie? C'est loin.* I told her something of my journey, her tractor quietly popping in the background. Across the fence, she wished me *Bon Courage, Bonne Continuation,* climbed back into the tractor and away she went to continue the job. Amazing! A five-minute conversation can open up a whole new world.

I left the farmlands and moved into woodlands. At first, the noise sounded like a car boot being shut, but I realised I was hearing gun shots. I was uncomfortable. I had come across hunters before, and I reckon hunting and pilgrims don't mix. I heard later that the forest was popular with wild pig hunters.

I arrived at the *Refuge Pèlerin* about 2 p.m. No one was about, so I left my pack around the back and went to explore the town. Ainay-le-Château is a medieval town. The city was enclosed by walls and boasted a castle. Remnants of the fortifications, which include a clock gate and enclosure with walls and towers, are classified as historical monuments. The ancient and the modern blend well. In the modern part, I found an ATM that worked and provided relief for my cash drought. On a hot afternoon, I enjoyed a beer at a nearby bar before returning to the refuge.

The *Refuge Pèlerin* is run by the *Association des Amis et Pèlerins de Saint-Jacques de la Voie de Vézelay*. Inside I found the hospitalier, the volunteer who looks after the pilgrims. Bernard was the hospitalier; in fact, he was the president of the association, one of the heavies. A big jolly man, he welcomed me warmly and introduced me to the others – Cornelius, a Dutchman, and Valerie, a French lady and her young daughter Lila, aged 9 years. At last, I will spend a night with others, and I was looking forward to sharing a meal. The refuge was well-equipped, and Bernard cooked us dinner. We told our stories. Cornelius had taken 12 months off work and was planning to reach Santiago. Valerie and Lila lived in a tiny albeit expensive apartment in Paris. She had taken a few days off to get away from the confines of a big city, was due to catch the train back to Paris the next day and wanted to walk in the morning. Bernard had been president for some time and worked as a hospitalier every year, sometimes more than once. They tried to man their refuges with two volunteers, but that didn't always work out. He pointed to a poster addressed to pilgrims. *Now that you have walked la voie de Vézelay, consider volunteering.* I mentioned that I had worked as a hospitalero at Rabanal del Camino in Spain and knew some of the ropes. I mentioned I was a Camino addict, and, despite my age, this was my fifth.

Valerie was to catch the train at Saint-Amand Montrond about 20 kilometres away. I was planning to stay at the Association's *Refuge Pèlerin* at Bouzais five kilometres further on. Valerie did not want to walk 20 kilometres, and I wasn't keen on walking 25, which would have doubled the distance of the last few days. She decided to take a taxi to a point on the Canal du Berry beyond the next towns Charenton du-Cher and Saint-Pierre les-Etieux and walk from there into Saint-Amand Montrond. I suggested I'd accompany her and share the cost. Cornelius was going to walk and would stay at Bouzais too.

Next morning, Bernard gave us fried eggs for breakfast – a 'bonus' he called it. It certainly was, a change from the usual French breakfast of bread and jam. Bernard's hospitality was exceptional, a lovely example of just how wonderful the Camino can be. Such a contrast to others' indifference. I'll forget the names of the places I visit, but I'll remember always the generosity of my hosts whose welcome is genuine and whose hospitality comes from the heart. Bernard gave me his card and said they were always looking for volunteers. One of these days, perhaps. The taxi arrived on time, and when Valerie explained, the driver said he knew exactly the place for us and dropped us on a bridge crossing the canal.

The three of us walked together – lots of chatter, laughter and photos. No hurry, just hanging out and enjoying each other's company and finding a way through the grass. The

## 6.

day was overcast, and the canal was peaceful. We had it to ourselves until we neared Saint-Amand Montrond where the canal's surrounds changed into parkland with seats and a gravel path. Just the place for the townsfolk to walk, jog or just sit, a few of whom we met doing those same-said things. We were only together for a few hours, but what a lovely bond we developed. Valerie was the age of my daughters and Lila that of my grandchildren. To the observer we could have been a family unit – grandpa, daughter and grandchild. I felt like we were just for that short time, a change from my usual silence and solitude. Valerie thanked me for my company and for the few days of walking. They were like an escape hatch from her usual hectic cramped life in Paris. She was determined to put her phone aside and not consult it every few minutes. She believed she was addicted and was pleased that she had managed to avoid its pressure. She was sure she could live without if she really tried. In town, we embraced each other, exchanged addresses and said goodbye. Another Camino parting! You meet people you never want to say goodbye to. Another sacred moment! You form such a bond with people you have just met as if you have known them for years. May I meet other pilgrims in the coming weeks. May we enjoy each other's company and develop that precious camaraderie that I love.

Apart from checking a computer at the tourist office for emails (some success), I did not hang around Saint-Amand Montrond and struck out on the five kilometres to Bouzais. By now, the clouds had vanished, and I walked in a hot sunny afternoon. Just a tiny village, there did not appear to be any shops. I passed a small chapel (locked) and found the *Refuge Pèlerin*, which advertised its presence in French and German. It was only 2:30 p.m, and as the *Refuge* opened at 3:00, even though it was physically open for the breeze, I waited in a park-like open space, removed my pack and rested. Outside the house next to the *Refuge* a chap was tending to his climbing rose, a vivid splash of red on the white wall. He saw me and over he came. Dressed in shorts, singlet and flip flops, he sported a large droopy white moustache, like Father Christmas without a beard. Very jovially, he asked if I was looking for the *Refuge* and pointed. I thanked him and replied I was just having a rest, and back he went to his roses. Cornelius arrived. He had walked the entire distance from Ainay-le-Château. I had 'cheated' with the taxi ride. We had a brief chat about how nice walking along the canal was, then together approached the *Refuge*. We were welcomed by the hospitaliers, a German couple. Gerd and Gisela offered us cold drinks, and we sat around the table and talked. Outside Cornelius and I had spoken in English, but now the conversation was in French. Gerd said that because he was in France at the moment, he should focus on French, but every now and then, he lapsed into German, as Cornelius understood the language. The chap from next door joined us. His name was Gerard and seemed to be the unofficial Mayor of Bouzais. He was custodian of the chapel and had the key; he invited us to inspect it any time. Another pilgrim arrived. Much younger than the rest of us, Etienne was French. We were crammed into a small space for the *Refuge* was in sympathy with the village and just as tiny. The kitchen, dining and living areas was the central room. On the left was the door to the dormitory with five beds, a single and two bunks. On the right was the room for the hospitaliers, the bathroom and toilets. No room to swing a cat, or as the French would say, we were *écrasés comme une boite de sardines (squashed like a can of sardines)*.

    While Gerd and Gisela prepared the meal, the three of us washed and rested. I shelled the peas; otherwise Gerd and Gisela had everything under control. We were served salad and

# 6.

a chicken casserole with plenty of red wine, and afterwards sat outside and chatted. Cornelius had taken a year off; I wanted to get to Saint-Jean-Pied-de-Port by September 30th, and Etienne was walking until September 2nd. He had covered over 30 kilometres that day and was troubled with a sore tendon. I offered him my 'Deep Heat' cream. Gerd and Gisela were finishing their stint Friday in two days and on Saturday would drive to Germany. Gerd told me he was looking forward to getting home. 'Would he return for another stint?' I asked. He thought he would. He would appreciate the village where he lived more than ever and fall in love with it all over again. He would enjoy speaking his maternal language. Yet, after a while the daily grind, the political circus and all that would have him yearning to be back on the Camino. He showed me photos of his own Camino, which he had walked the previous year. Incidentally, I can't remember whether we spoke in French or English. Once again, we made a nice family for the evening – German, Dutch, French and Australian – with enough common languages to communicate. The night was warm, but I slept.

The Deep Heat seemed to have relieved Etienne's pain, and he was off very early. Cornelius and I left about 8 a.m. after lots of photos and farewells. We more or less walked together for the day. He would go ahead, and I would catch up with him. I had aimed for 12 kilometres to stop at Loye-sur-Arnon in an Accueil Pèlerin, but as I couldn't raise anyone, I decided to go to Le Châtelet, another 11 kilometres. At Loye-sur-Arnon, I found Cornelius enjoying a coffee, so I joined him. He told me some of his story. One of the joys of the Camino is the preparedness of people to open up to strangers, that is, once trust has been established. I had known Cornelius for two days, but he must have thought I was a decent bloke. I offered him my encouragement.

I left Cornelius to finish his second coffee. After the open fields, I found a delightfully shady spot by an ancient mill. A weir had been built to establish a pond and waterfall. Just below was a ford and a footbridge, an ideal spot for lunch. A footbridge, perhaps, was too grand a word to describe the log thrown across the water. It was just as easy to wade through the water. That did not detract from the serenity of the spot. The sound of running water is therapeutic and healing. I was content to sit on the bridge dangling my feet in the water. I had just settled down to lunch when a pilgrim arrived. A young man in singlet and no hat, he said he was German and had taken time off from work, as it was getting too stressful. He had left his phone and watch at home and didn't know which day it was. He was on for a chat – an affable charming young bloke with good looks and physique. He hadn't met many pilgrims either and enjoyed speaking to one, the first person he had met for the day. He had a tent in his backpack, preferred to camp and go when and where he liked. He wasn't sure if he would reach Santiago. I admired him for the free spirit he was allowing to blossom. We spoke in English, the preferred language of Germans in France. He had only left two minutes earlier when Cornelius arrived. He did not dally but continued on.

With reluctance, I extracted myself from this haven and took to the open road, eventually arriving in Châtelet. This town, as the name implies, started as fortifications in the 11th century built on a hill overlooking the town site, now replaced by gardens. Cornelius had already arrived at the *Gîte Rural* run by M. and Mme François. He had visited the supermarket and bought enough to cook dinner for both of us. The *Gîte Rural* was on three levels. First, a kitchen, bathroom and living area. Steps led up to a bedroom and from there another set of steps (rickety and squeaky) led up to a bedroom in the roof. Cornelius had

## 6.

already settled into the first bedroom. He offered to move up into the roof, but I could see that he had already unpacked his bag. M. François arrived to see that we were settled in happily. A big man with beard, he kissed and embraced me with an exuberant bear hug. It was a pleasure to meet me, he said. He had heard about the eighty-four-year-old Australian who was walking on his own. He prised open my eyes, but I'd be lying if I said I wasn't pleased with his enthusiasm.

I walked to the supermarket to buy red wine. A simple enough trip, somehow, I took the wrong turn and had difficulty finding my way back. I had ignored one of the basic lessons of the Camino. Always check for landmarks for a return trip. Eventually, I found my way and enjoyed the wine. We had a good evening. I enjoyed Cornelius's company. He had a relaxed easy manner, and he told me about his home town. In turn, I told him about my home in the Snowy Mountains. I took overseas two photos of my house. One showed a clear blue sky; this was my house in summer. In the other the ground was covered in snow; this was my house in winter. Both looked picturesque. Europeans think Australia is a 'wide brown land', hot all over and are surprised to learn that Australia has alpine regions and winter sports. Holland has no mountains, but most Dutchmen I met were proficient in ice skating. I told Cornelius that my neighbour represented Holland at the Olympics. Carla had married an Australian athlete and settled in Jindabyne. I did not know Carla's maiden name, but Cornelius worked it out and knew of her.

Next morning, I was tired after the 23 kilometres of yesterday. Cornelius was pressing on, but I decided on Chateaumeillant, only 12 kilometres. It was a struggle. I passed through the tiny village of Saint Jeanvrin, an area of lakes and farmlands. One of the neatest and tidiest, its grass was being mowed. But for the popping mower, a calm and peaceful spot where nothing much happens in a day. I paused outside its church (Saint Gorges) with origins in the 11th century. It was not open. My movements were observed, for a lady stepped out of her house opposite and gave me some prayer cards with photos of the church. She addressed me as *Pèlerin* and wished me *Bon Courage*. Perhaps she sits in her house all day waiting for pilgrims to pass.

The church at Chateaumeillant was open, and I lit a candle for Maris and for our love. Saint Genès, origins in the 12th century, is built in pink sandstone and inside its columns are striking, capped with chapters adorned with carvings of people, fantastic animals and vegetation. I found my refuge for the night, a *Chambre d'hôtes*. My first impressions were not favourable. The place was run-down and its garden overgrown. Both needed tender care. Mme Meillet seemed uninterested in me as a person and, after showing me my room upstairs, left me to it. Chateaumeillant didn't seem too friendly a town. After a rest, I found my way back to the main centre for dinner of a hamburger. On the walk back a lady leaned out of her window and asked if I was lost, the only person who took an interest in an old fart passing by. I was happy to say I knew exactly where I was and where I was going. I spent a quiet night, reflecting that for the first time in a few nights I was on my own. I was lonely and would have loved company.

Next morning was Saturday, never a good day. My mood was tinged with blue, both from the lonely night and from memories of the day of the week that Maris died. Grey clouds threatened to drift over my clear sky and even turn into fog, but the mist lifted completely over breakfast. Mme Meillet was animated and enthusiastic, in sharp contrast to her tepid reception. She was keen to talk about the spirituality of the Camino. I even told her some of my story. As I left, she waved me goodbye. I was much brighter and better equipped for the day.

The previous afternoon, I had arranged for a taxi to pick me up at 8.30 am. Back at Le Châtelet I had tried to book a bed at La Châtre, but everything was booked out for the weekend because of a big wedding. La Châtre was 17 kilometres, a reasonable distance. Consequently, I had to go well beyond the town and booked a bed at Neuvy Saint Sépulchre, 37 kilometres, which was far too long a day for me. I asked the taxi driver, a lady, to take me to Sarzay 26 kilometres, leaving me about 11 kilometres to walk. She dropped me at a bus shelter/tourist information booth, 53 euros poorer.

The château dominates this small village. Built in the 14th century, it comprises 38 towers and three drawbridges, and several furnished rooms have retained their authenticity. The castle withstood the English invasion and emerged intact from the Hundred Years War, the Wars of Religion, the Fronde and the French Revolution. The deep moats give the chateau an imposing aspect. It's open to the public and takes its place in the literary world, as it is the setting of one of George Sand's novels, *Le Meunier d'Angibault*. A faded poster in the tourist information booth/bus shelter told me about this connection. George Sands was a French romantic writer and a dominant figure in 19th century literary life, much published throughout Europe. Her work was an important influence in the spread of feminine consciousness.

The day was full of interest and beauty. I passed the ancient abbey of Varennes, and a notice in French, German and English told its history. Founded in the 12th century, it belonged to the Cistercians and was a stopping place, as was Neuvy Saint Sépulchre for pilgrims on the way to Santiago. The abbey enjoyed two centuries of prosperity. Then followed precarious and troubled times. The Hundred Years War, the Wars of Religion and the Frondes began the decline and the French Revolution finished the job. At the beginning of the 19th century, the abbey was put to farming; the church became a stable and a barn. Since 1980 the whole place is being restored by its owners, and in 1993 the site was declared an historic monument.

A swathe of history that fires the imagination dominates the towns in this region, but present day life goes on in the form of a farmer parking his tractor dragging a water tank in the middle of a shallow river and drawing water with a noisy pump, his thirsty cows grazing in the adjacent fields, a pack of motor bikes going who knows where, a gang from Paris escaping the confines into open air.

Neuvy Saint Sépulchre reeks with history but was throbbing with life and action when I arrived on a Saturday arvo. Through the bustle of the main street, I found my way to the *Gîte de groupe Le Relais de la Vieille Route* in rue de maréchal Foch. To get to the gîte you went through an enclosure, which according to my guidebook, was suitable for my horse. Inside was a large kitchen, living room and two bedrooms. Quite comfortable! As soon as I showered and washed my clothes, I returned to the main street to join in the action. First, I visited the church which was unusual because it was round. It was built after a pilgrimage to the Holy Land and was modelled on the circular church of the Holy Sepulchre in Jerusalem. Over the centuries, it decayed from neglect and other vicissitudes but was restored in 1850. Always an important stage on the Chemin de Saint Jacques de Compostelle, it had a relic of the blood of Christ. Nowadays, it's the parish church. I read the Mass times for Sunday. The main Mass was at midday. I could have a late start in the morning and go to church. Back home, I go most Sundays, and although I'd visited a few churches to light a candle for Maris, I hadn't attended Mass since arriving in Europe. Before leaving, I lit a candle for her.

Down the road a spruiker on a loud microphone was busy telling everyone about his market, inviting them to join him, extolling the attractions of each stall and insisting that the parents take their kids to the sideshow attraction — jumping castle and carousel. He drew me in. As I approached, he asked me in his booming voice where I was from. I told him I was a pilgrim from Australia on the way to Compostelle. He echoed my reply and boomed it to the world and told everyone to welcome me with a *'Bon Courage'*. Nice to be so heartily welcomed. Lots of vintage vehicles were driving down the street; some were parked, their owners enjoying the hospitality of the bars. I joined the Bar Restaurant *Le Luché*. The afternoon was hot, the western afternoon sun blazing down on this ancient yet modern little town. I noted that the bar served dinner. I would come back later. Back at *Le Relais de la Vieille Route* in rue de maréchal Foch, I found Cornelius. We left Bouzais together two days ago, and although I had caught a taxi part of the way, he had walked all the way. There was a French couple, but they were walking from the south. The French couple ate their dinner in the garden, but Cornelius and I went back to the bar. We sat outside on the street until the sun began to set. Against a background of busy waiters, chinking glass, laughter and passing motor bikes, he told me more of his story. His father was a resistance fighter. He hid young Jews for which other resistance fighters were shot. After the war he suffered trauma, which had its impact on the family. Cornelius mentioned he was a non-believer, but, at the same time, he said humans are more than just flesh and spoke of a 'universal energy'. Another description of God?

The French couple were still sitting outside in the cool of the garden, and we joined them. They asked about places where we had stayed. Before retiring to bed, I said goodbye to Cornelius in case we did not meet again.

Everyone left early, but I indulged in the luxury of sleeping in. Out in the garden, I found the spruiker and his wife. They lived next door. He was just as loud and larger than life without his microphone. His voice needed no amplification. I cooked myself fried eggs for breakfast and had time to grab a coffee at our bar before attending the midday Mass. I was early, so I lit a candle for Maris. She was with me on this pilgrimage and celebrating this Mass with me. Her light will always shine. I think of her every day. She walks with me. Maris is a part of me. She goes wherever I go, never more than a heartbeat away. She infuses every breath with her love and her influence in my life. I'm still married to Maris and continue to wear my wedding ring. I wear the cross she wore. She is my partner albeit a silent one.

I placed my backpack against the wall. The altar was surrounded by pillars, so I chose my seat carefully to have an uninterrupted view. Everyone seemed to be local and know each other. Although I knew no one, I felt I was one of them. When you attend Mass said in another country in another language, you know that the Catholic Church is really Catholic and universal. What's more, the priest was black, the only non-white face in the congregation. His French was fluent and melodious, his manner solemn. Celebrating Mass was a serious business, no laughing matter, although he relaxed and showed his human side afterwards when the people came up and spoke to him. The music was beautiful. The choir was supported by organ, horn, flute and bagpipes. The people joined in – overall a happy, joyful community celebration.

Why did I attend this Mass? It fitted into my day, I suppose, but that's not enough. You'll have to do better, Noël. Some of my fellow Catholics go to church because they have to. Sunday Mass is a matter of obligation; they're fearful of committing a grave sin if they don't. My religion is not about enforcing laws and rules made at a particular point in history. In my childhood, obeying rules and avoiding sin were paramount. The Mass was said in Latin, and the priest had his back to the people. That changed. Now the ritual is in the vernacular language, and the priest faces the people as an attempt at communication and interaction.

There's a difference between religious practice and faith. Faith is not static; it evolves and grows. For example, in his teaching, Jesus uses parables and a language of growth and development. He relies on metaphors such as the seed, the ripening ear of corn, weeds and wheat growing together. Jesus was on about finding, discovering and being surprised. He was on about change. What is acceptable and life-enhancing in one time or situation may not be appropriate in another. Without such an evolutionary worldview, we can't really understand, let alone foster, growth and change, or have a clue about where history is heading. We are in evolution all the time. Creation is constantly being recreated. Think of the enormous growth in knowledge just in my lifetime in all fields of human endeavour.

I think of my faith journey as a pilgrimage, an adventure. Since my first Camino walk, I've taken the time to reflect on all my values and belief systems. The walk has been in itself the destination. I'm not clear where it is heading. Staying on the path, trusting that I'm getting somewhere, knowing that I'm moving and hopefully to somewhere better is a way to describe faith. It's joyful, positive, apprehensive perhaps, but never fearful. I have to be patient that my awareness changes with time and thankful that the Camino has given me the opportunity. Attending Mass is joyful and positive, and I go because I want to. I'm not concerned about breaking the rules if I don't. I want to feel closer to God. I'm not sure who or what God is, but that's part of my search. Perhaps, he, she, it is a 'universal energy'.

Before I left the church, one more candle for the road! Keep pressing on, Brother!

*Cornelius, Noël, Valerie and Lila*

*Gerd and Gisela (hospitaliers) and Gerard ('lord mayor') of Bouzais)*

*Cornelius, Gisela, Etienne and Noël at Bouzais*

# 7.

*Forgiving releases us. Until we forgive, we're imprisoned.*
*It allows us to look ahead. It empowers us.*
*It gives us positive energy. It opens up the future.*
    Patrick Lindsay: *It's Never too Late*

The afternoon was uncomfortably hot. No shade! Although only 12 kilometres, I was frazzled by the time I reached the small village of Cluis after passing castle ruins dating back to the 12th to 14th centuries. Often the toughest job is finding the place where you are staying, but this time the friendliest of grocers (*un épicier*), standing outside his shop (*La Petite Epicerie*), shouted a greeting and pointed across the way. In fact, he left his shop and took me, talking all the way, past the church the hundred metres or so to the *Refuge pèlerin* run by *Association du Refuge Pèlerin de Cluis*, a narrow-fronted building right on the street. A window jutted out of the tiled roof indicating a second floor. Inside was a small kitchen and table. Judging by the mess of unwashed pots and plates in the sink, and clothes thrown over the chairs, someone was already in residence.

I showered, washed my clothes, hung my washing on a rack, which in the absence of a back yard I placed outside on the street, and made myself a cup of tea. In came the other pilgrim. He introduced himself as Frère Michèle. A brother of the Jesuit order, he had been gathering chestnuts, which he dumped on the table. He didn't have much more to say, but he pulled out his phone and said, or rather sang, his Office. He seemed to have an app, which would be far more appropriate for a pilgrim to carry than a heavy breviary. On and on he went, chanting his prayers and replying to himself. I admired the Jesuits for introducing a modern touch to an ancient practice. I left him to his noisy ritual, visited the church and performed my own ritual of lighting a candle. This was the first time I had heard music playing gently in the background, a kind of Gregorian chant which gave a beautiful and peaceful ambience. I sat in front of the candle and listened. Across the road to the friendly épicier where I bought some fruit, milk and eggs for dinner. It was Sunday evening, and I didn't expect any of the restaurants, if there were any, to be open.

Back at the *Refuge pèlerin*, I found Frère Michèle cooking the chestnuts. I placed my purchases on a bowl in the middle of the table and went upstairs to the bedroom. Earlier, I had opened the windows because the room was hot and stuffy, but they were closed. I opened them again just to let in cool air and returned downstairs. Frère Michèle had helped himself to an egg and apple, and was cooking a blend of chestnuts, egg and apple. I assumed he lived in a community where everyone shared their goods. Besides, it seemed the pilgrim thing to do, to share with one's fellows. He finished his meal, and while I was cooking an omelette, he sewed a button on his jacket, one of the items he had thrown over the chair. I offered him a glass of red, which he happily accepted. He helped himself to another. Upstairs he went, and I heard him chanting again. I couldn't make out the words, but I could distinguish the readings from the response. Eventually, I heard no more, so I assumed he had gone to bed. He had taken the bedroom near the window, which he had closed, and I had the other in an airless corner. Why he kept the windows closed, I never found out.

I was woken at 5:00 a.m. Frère Michèle had resumed his prayers, chanting as he read his Office. I was still half asleep.

## 7.

His voice was quiet, and I was lulled back to sleep. At 6 a.m. however, he woke me with a loud *'Bonjour Noël.'* and asked if he could have my banana. Downstairs, I asked him about his Office. He said his prayers three times a day every day. He left before 7, wearing everything he had. He had no backpack but carried his stuff in a side bag, like the medieval pilgrims with their bourdon and stick. I guess he was undertaking his pilgrimage like the ancients, taking little with him and relying on the generosity of the locals. I visited the boulangerie for a freshly cooked baguette and the épicerie for another banana. I left about 7:45 a.m. The épicier spotted me, and out he came of his shop. He was not going to let me escape without wishing me *'Bon Chemin'* and showing me the way out of town.

Cluis stands out for the lessons I learned about sharing, tolerance and forgiveness in meeting such an eccentric as Frère Michèle. At first, I was cheesed off and resentful of his intrusion, but his presence was an opportunity to grow and to learn about myself. One should forgive before allowing resentment to take on a life of its own. Our encounter was a gift, sacred in its own way, disguised as a minor disturbance.

Cluis stands out for the friendly grocer. I have never met before or since a more welcoming shopkeeper.

The two routes from Vézelay join at Gargilesse, and I was now following the common route. I was intrigued by the village of Chambon because its story is similar to that of my home town Jindabyne. The village sits by a lake that was formed when a dam was constructed in 1926. Part of the village, several mills and the bridge into Chambon from Fougères were flooded. Phantom traces of buildings appear when the lake is drained. The bridge, 29 metres under the lake, is perfectly preserved. Old Jindabyne lies at the bottom of the lake formed by the dam built as part of Snowy Hydro Scheme in the 50s. The entire town had to be relocated up the hill, and whenever the water level is low, some buildings appear like unhappy spirits evicted from their graves.

At Crozant I had difficulty finding my way out of the town and had to retrace my steps to ensure I was descending the right path down to the river. Eventually, I set off, and for a time, I followed this beautiful stream, shaded with large trees and indulged in the small pleasures of listening to the birds and to the plonk of acorns falling into the water. Occasionally, one struck me. Along the stream, small dams created waterfalls and mills that could have been there for centuries.

Once I left the shade and water, the day was dry and hot. At Chapelle-Baloue a sign offering coffee enticed me out of the heat into an overgrown garden, still beautiful, cool and calm in its wilderness. Having to brush through the plants to get to a table just added to its charm. Through the foliage I saw the other customers, a young couple with backpacks like me. I guessed they were walkers, so I ventured over to speak. They were pleasant and friendly, a little guarded as if not used to being approached by an elderly gentleman and a foreigner at that. Yes! They had begun that morning and were walking four days. They introduced themselves as Liliane and Baptiste. They had no English, so we conversed in French. I wished them *'Bon Courage'* and left the cool shade to continue on to Saint-Germain Beaupré.

I seemed to lose track of where I was heading. I was following a roadway in accordance with the map in the guidebook, but I was plagued by an anxiety that I was not following the right one. Should I just push on and hope, or should I ask someone? But the road was quiet and no one was around to ask. I had to wait awhile until a car turned in from a side road. The driver stopped at my request and assured me that I was on the right road. The sign at the entrance to the tiny village of La Maisonbraud, which was on my map, reassured me that I was on the right track and was not lost. I knew I did not have long to go.

At Saint Germain-Beaupré I stayed at *Accueil pèlerin* where my host was Alain Malberg. A young man, he told me the house was his grandfather's. It was definitely old and showed signs of generations of living. Alain did not know when it was built, but probably early in the nineteenth century. The family hadn't decided what to do with the old building, so they gained some income from sheltering pilgrims on their way to Compostelle. The furniture was of heavy dark wood, all of which would have looked well in an antique shop. The bed was a high poster with a deep sag in the middle.

Alain told me I would have company that night as a lady was staying. Alain returned to his own home, and shortly after Liliane, whom I'd met at lunchtime, arrived. Baptiste arrived too, but it appeared he was not booked in. Only Liliane had been booked in. I was intrigued and began to wonder about this twosome. What was their relationship? They sat together in the kitchen until dark, and he wished her good night and went outside. It looked as if he was sleeping outside *á la belle étoile*. The night was mild, so sleeping under the stars would have been pleasant. The key was in the door, but I did not bother to turn it. I wondered if he crept inside during the night.

In the morning, I found him sitting in the kitchen. I offered him a cup of tea, and shortly Liliane appeared and off they went, leaving me to tidy up and pack my bag. Alain turned up. He wanted to know more about Baptiste's presence. He questioned me, but I said as far as I knew, he did not sleep in the house. He looked at me directly as if he thought I knew more, but with a shrug he let the matter go.

Every morning brings new possibilities. What will I do today? The answer is infinite and unknowable. What will I do today? Anything. Everything. Experiences and adventures. I will marvel, wonder and delight. What challenges and frustrations to be overcome? I enjoyed this day, for the walking was off road in beautiful rolling hills interspersed with open farmland and patches of bushland. The continually changing scene helped me to see more deeply and to hear more attentively. The only other living companions were brown steers and bulls with rings in their nose. They stopped grazing to stare at me as I passed. Later, in a patch of woodland, I came across Liliane and Baptiste sitting on the side of the track eating breakfast.

Shortly after in another patch of woodland was a rest area complete with seats made out of logs. I could not resist the invitation. Many times, on earlier Caminos, I had longed for the opportunity to rest, but no suitable spots appeared. Nowadays, whenever I see a seat, I ask myself if I should linger and accept the seat's request to be sat on because there may be no other places for yonks. Nailed to a tree was a letter box with a shell on the side and in faded letters 'Ultreia'. I wondered if the intention was to write a note while resting and place it in the box. Which is what I did, as well as a few notes on the previous day. I tried to discipline myself to write every evening, but I missed the previous night. While engaged in this scribble, along came Liliane and Baptiste. At first, they were looking ahead and missed me in the gloom, and I called out to them. A few words and they continued. I finished my journal, including a mention of our encounter, and then I tore a page from the back and wrote a short note for the letter box. I wrote a thank you to the person who build the seats and to the person who looked after the area, for it was tidy and no hint of rubbish. Too often I was saddened by the rubbish lying around rest areas, plastic bottles being the most offensive. Would a true pilgrim spoil his or her environment? A true pilgrim would have great respect for nature and believe it needed care and nurturing. A true pilgrim would believe they are part of creation and creation is part of them. They would leave nothing of their passing except their footprints.

Just as I was packing and getting ready to move, another pilgrim arrived. Bernard was Dutch and had begun walking from his home. So far, the Dutch whom I had met preferred to speak English, so we soon left French behind. What's more, he had heard of me. I was gaining the impression that everywhere I stayed and everyone I'd met told everyone else about this elderly Australian who was walking on his own and to look out for him. We walked together for a time, but I invited him to move on. He was a quick walker and planning to cover over 30 kilometres that day, and I was slow and content with my puny 16.

I left Saint-Germain Beaupré in fine weather and blue sky, but clouds rolled over during the morning, and rain descended when I reached La Souterraine. I knew that the town was worth a look, but the rain was falling steadily, and I could find no shelter. In hindsight I should have persisted and removed my rain gear in order to study my guidebook (in my pack) on the best way out of town. Up to now I had been following two sets of signages. One was the white and red markers of the GR system (Grandes Randonnées), the other was the blue and yellow arrows pointing towards Compostelle. For the most part, the two ways coincided. If you followed the GR signage, you usually got to where ever you wanted to go. I found the red and white markers but not the yellow and blue. I followed them out of town and into a deep forest. After a few kilometres I knew I should have retraced my steps back into La

Souterraine. The name places were not in my guidebook, and none of the guidebook's were on the ground. The thought of losing so much time frustrated and angered me, so I pressed on, hoping that miraculously the yellow and blue would appear and all would be well. By this time the rain had ceased, and I happily removed my poncho.

I left the forest and walked a road through open country. No houses, no traffic, no people! Not even an animal in the fields! At 4 p.m., 3 hours later, I arrived at a crossroads, feeling fatigued and frustrated. I should have arrived by now. I had run out of puff. I had run out of water. The maps made no sense. I didn't have a clue where I was. I was lost. There was not even a post or rock to sit on. I had visions of having to curl up for the night under some tree, on damp grass, hungry, thirsty and exhausted.

At first, I heard the sound of a car engine. Over the hill came a small panel van, popular among the French farmers, big enough to bundle a few hay bales or a couple of sheep in the back. I hailed the young driver. He stopped, and I told I was aiming for Saint-Priest la-Feuille and how far. His earnest young face peering up at me, he told me it was about ten kilometres to the east. He pointed down the road, gave me a maze of directions (*á droite, á gauche, tout droit etc*) and drove off, leaving behind a bewildered pilgrim. Here I was, abandoned in remote central France. My only consoling thought was that I still had about 6 hours of daylight to find my shelter somewhere.

I had collected my thoughts and baggage enough to start heading in the direction my young friend had given. I remembered him saying to go straight ahead (*tout droit*) and then turn right (*á droite*). After that, I hoped that I would meet someone else. I had walked for less than 5 minutes when I heard the sound of a car engine, and he was beside me. He pulled up

## 7.

and from the driver's seat he yelled above the popping engine: '*Montez! (Hop in!)*' He handed me an ice-cold bottle of water and drove at a hectic pace, chatting all the way, pointing out his parents' farm and that of his grandparents. Probably in his late teens, his name was Florian, and he had lived on his farm all his life. He enjoyed throwing his van around the many turns, and, in no time, he dropped me off outside the church at Saint-Priest la-Feuille, reversed and disappeared the way we came.

That afternoon stands out as a highlight of my pilgrimage. I could not thank that young farming lad enough, going out of his way to help a distressed old pilgrim get back on track. Probably, Florian led a lonely life with few things to entertain him or offer him diversion from his hard work on the farm. Perhaps there were few people in his life, so a lost pilgrim brought him company for an instant or two and made him happy. He gave to me, but I wanted to give to him as well. I was not sure how. I was glad to spend a brief time in his company and in his van with its strong smell of the earth. I was so happy he went out of his way. It was as if I was meeting Jesus, well disguised, mind you. His caring mix of kindness and youthful exuberance made it obvious that we were brothers (frères). I will never see this good young man again, but I hope he will have a happy life, marry a nice girl, raise a family, earn a good living from his farming, make a solid contribution to his community and handle his adversities with resilience, compassion and courage.

It was time to move on and find my accommodation for the night. The *Chambre d'hôtes* was on the way out of town just after the football ground. At the entrance was a small cabin with couch, shells, flowers and other signs of welcome, and a life-size cut out of a pilgrim. The grounds were spacious with a large house and a series of cabins. Mme Marjorie showed me mine. Painted light blue, it contained a room with couch, microwave, TV and two small cubicles each with one bed. The cabins fronted onto lawn and a vegetable garden. Overall, a lovely place to rest.

After a shower and some washing, I consulted my guide book. When leaving La Souterraine, the instruction was explicit. *Ne pas suivre le GR*. (Don't follow the GR!) Silly Noël for not consulting the book when in doubt. That should have been a lesson learned long ago. When in doubt, read the directions. I was thankful that I was now rested and refreshed. And dry because the clouds had rolled over and a fierce rain squall battered my cabin. I could have still been on the road where the soaking rain would have added to my misery. Another round of thanks for meeting my young 'Jesus'.

At dinner, I met another pilgrim. Ferdinand was Dutch and spoke English and French. The other guests, two couples, were not pilgrims. They had arrived by car and stayed in the house, paying tourist rather than pilgrim rates. I would have liked to spend more time with Ferdinand, but the conversation over the table was in French. Back in my cabin, I enjoyed watching TV and listening to the light rain on the roof. I thought, it looks like I'll spend the night on my own until Liliane and Baptiste arrived. They were soaked. They had to struggle out of their wet gear and spread it around in the small space in the hope of getting it dry. It seemed they had difficulty, too, in finding the way but had no kind Florian to help them. Liliane took the bed in the other cubicle. Sleeping outside was out of the question, so Baptiste settled on the couch. I wasn't sure if he paid this time, but although suspicious at first, I was beginning to find him a pleasant young man. We chatted, and he often corrected my pronunciation although always respectfully. It's quaint how first impressions can be misleading. Some people impressed well on first meeting but turn out a disaster; to

## 7.

others you warm up slowly. I thought Baptiste was a freeloader at first, and although I didn't know much of his story, I liked his caring and solicitous manner with Liliane. She seemed a little helpless and dependent on him. She spoke to him softly, and in a French that I didn't understand. He, in turn, seemed to reassure her. We settled down for the night, Liliane and me in our cubicles and Baptiste on the couch, the rain falling gently on the tin roof. Though we couldn't see each other, we were quite close. The night was restless for there seemed to be a lot of movement in our confined space, and somehow the slightest noise was amplified.

The morning was cold, but the rain had ceased. I left Liliane and Baptiste gathering up their gear, which was almost dry. A much cooler day than others, the touch of autumn weather made for good walking. I had planned to stop at Bénévent l'Abbaye (about 14 kilometres) but decided to continue on to Marsac (another five). Bénévent l'Abbaye was an important stage on the Chemin de Saint-Jacques and boasted a large abbey and church built in the 12th century. The town drew its name from the Italian city of Benevento from which were transferred the relics of Saint Bathélemy.

I arrived in Marsac about 4 p.m. and soon found the *Gîte-Accueil pèlerin Chez Bernie* in the main street. It looked as if it was once a restaurant and had a large yard around the back. There I found Ferdinand waiting for Bernadette (Bernie) to open the door. We chatted about our backgrounds. He told me he was a missionary priest, a White Father, on sabbatical from his work in Africa. Bernie arrived with the key. A lively young woman, she did not stop talking, showing the various features. Indeed, Chez Bernie was a restaurant complete with commercial kitchen, bar and dining room. Upstairs were the bedrooms. She left us to clean up and said she would return later to collect the money. Ferdinand and I each took a bed in the one room. We continued our chat. He gave me a brochure outlining the work of the White Fathers. There are about 1250 *Missionaires d'Afrique* from 36 nationalities living in 215 intercultural communities in 42 countries of which 22 are in Africa. I found Ferdinand a cultured and intelligent person, quite a contrast to Frère Michèle. Frère Michèle was set in his ways whereas Ferdinand seemed flexible and adapted himself to his company. His English was perfect, and he probably spoke the dialects of the African people he served as missionary. Downstairs we inspected the kitchen. It was well-equipped while the bar and restaurant had everything needed to run a business. Liliane and Baptiste arrived. They seemed to be in discussion for a few minutes tossing up whether they would stop. They came inside, and so the language switched to French as they had no English. I was a little disappointed, as I was enjoying a conversation in my maternal tongue. I admired Ferdinand for his keenness to include everyone.

We began to think about the evening meal. I proposed that, instead of each of cooking our own meal and getting in each other's way, that we eat together and that I cook the meal. The others thought that was generous on my part, but I replied that it was practical. So, while Liliane rested, Ferdinand, Baptiste and I walked the three hundred metres to the *supermarché*. I had worked out a rough menu, so we more or less bought to that, including wine. We split the cost at *la caisse* (check out). Back at Chez Bernie, we fell to preparing the meal. I banged around a few pots and pans; Baptiste peeled the vegetables, while Ferdinand set the table. He found the restaurant's paper tablecloths, its silver service and laid out the cutlery and condiments as if the cardinal were coming to dinner. He even found some artificial flowers, which he set in a vase as the

## 7.

centrepiece. Our table looked high class, as good as the best in Paris. Ferdinand, I said, you have done this before. Was that part of your religious training? I hoped that my cooking would live up to expectations.

In the middle of these preparation, Bernie arrived to collect the money. She was amazed at our efforts. She was used to her pilgrims muddling through makeshift meals, feeding rather than dining. Not so, I said, with such beautiful facilities available. Usually, we find just the basics at other pilgrim refuges. She asked me how come I spoke French so well. I always think I struggle with the language of Molière, but it seems to come out well enough. I told her of my times at Chambéry, Amboise and Montpellier when I enrolled at French language schools and was totally immersed in the language and culture – a sound preparation for walking the Chemin in France. Ferdinand invited her to join us for dinner. I agreed. We were pilgrims offering back something to the people who looked after us, but she declined as her husband had prepared dinner at home.

We sat down to our dinner. Ferdinand began with a grace, not too long, for he did not know whether Liliane and Baptiste were church people. I wished I had taken notes of what we actually ate, but the others thought it was great. They were probably hungry by now and would have eaten anything. They demolished each course with gusto. I was pleased, for I had accepted the challenge of cooking for French people whom I thought revere cooking and eating as an art form. Over that meal, we bonded. Sharing a meal is a wonderful experience. You get to know the other, and they get to know you. One of the delights of the Chemin! Ferdinand told us stories about his mission work and the people he served. Liliane and Baptiste were family — cousins. Not lovers — my first impression. They lived not far. Liliane wanted to walk and asked Baptiste, as a favourite cousin, to support her; she was not confident she could handle it on her own. They finished their walking in the morning. Another family member would pick them up. Ferdinand was planning to take the detour to Rocamadour and would re-join the Chemin later on his way to Compostelle. Baptiste took on the role of my teacher and would correct my pronunciation or word choice.

Unlike Frère Michèle, Ferdinand did not chant a noisy Office in the middle of the night. He seemed to do nothing out of the ordinary in his preparation for bed and rising in the morning. He said his prayers silently, which I took as another sign of his respect for others. I suspected a certain depth in Ferdinand, a contemplative side that I would know more of through discussion on some meaty spiritual issues.

Over breakfast, we said our farewells and took lots of photos. The Camino is a series of good-byes. How often have I parted from people with whom I have formed a fraternal bond in the short time I've known them. It's both joyful and sad. I will most likely never see these good people again. It's the passing parade of the Chemin, I guess, to *salut* new brothers and sisters in the one *instant* and to say *adieu* in the next.

*The Friendly Grocer of Cluis*

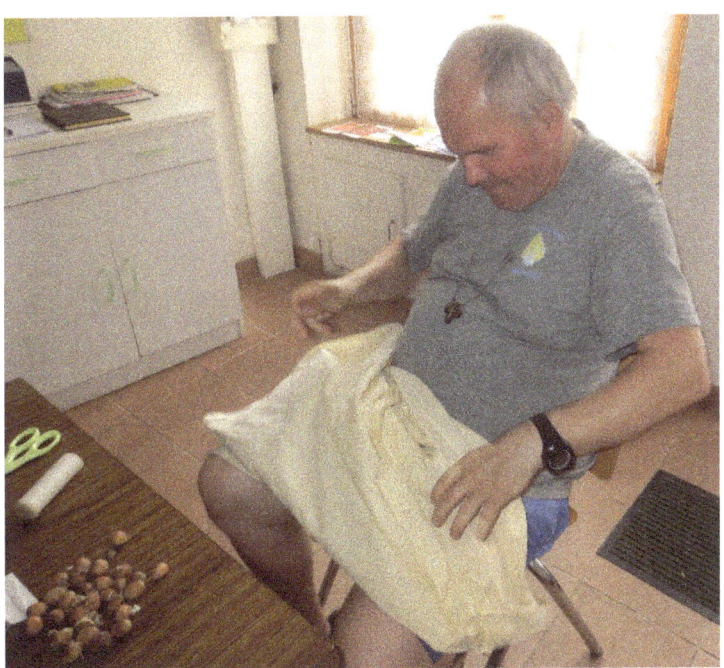

*Frère Michèle mending his shirt*

*Ferdinand, Baptiste and Liliane*

# 8.

*Hope*
*I am not an optimist*
*Because I'm not sure that everything turns out well.*
*Nor am I a pessimist,*
*Because I am not sure that everything ends badly*
*I just carry hope in my heart.*
*Hope is not a feeling of certainty*
*That everything ends well.*
*Hope is just a feeling that life and work have a meaning.*
Vaclav Havel – Czech Playwright and Politician

Leaving good friends always produces a sadness, an emptiness, and that morning was no exception. The hollow feeling was not helped by a dark overcast day and an encounter with the first killer hill of this pilgrimage, a steep and steely climb through forest. My mood lightened, as always, when I met another pilgrim. Libby was French. She had heard of me because she had met both Bernard and Ferdinand, both of whom told her that I would be coming along. I climbed further out of my pit at Saint-Goussard where I expected to find little as the guide book mentioned no facilities, but in reality, *Le Relais de St Goussard* faced the church. I first sought shelter from the rain in its entrance but decided to enter for lunch to enjoy a thick pea soup. Outside, a group of four walkers were eating their lunch among the tombstones of the church, but they showed little interest in talking to anyone but themselves. I was ignored rather than knocked back, so I left them to their own company and continued on to Châtelus-le-Marcheix. God was on my side that afternoon; it ceased raining; the sun came out, and I walked downhill through delightful chestnut forests and a soft damp carpet of autumn leaves. The area felt untamed, and I half expected to meet a sanglier (wild boar) on the path. Eventually, I returned to civilisation in the form of the tiny village of Châtelus-le-Marcheix. *Gîte Maison Blanche* was a large white house, formerly a hotel. I had spoken on the phone to the lady who managed it. Sarah Leith had a strong North England accent. I rang her when I arrived, and she ran me through the procedure of finding the key in a small safe by the front floor. Sarah arrived shortly to collect the money. She used to own the building but sold it recently. The new owners asked her to continue managing, as they planned to retire there.

I was the only guest. The building was shaped like an arrow head, the tip being the former entrance to the hotel. Downstairs were a kitchen, dining room/lounge room, large side entrance hall used for storage, the former hotel foyer and upstairs five bedrooms and bathroom, all comfortable and homely with lots of books, CDs and DVDs, just the place to stay for a few days, particularly if the weather was inclement. Although large, the place was cosy. A large stack of firewood in the storage was waiting to warm the house in the coming winter. On the side road behind the gîte was a sign pointing to Rocamadour. Ferdinand would have passed by earlier that day.

The sole enterprise in the village was the bar. In between showers, I wandered the short distance up the road and found the bar full. The locals gave me a casual glance as I entered and returned to the serious business of drinking, but the lady behind the bar was attentive and welcoming. On display were some grocery items. I bought a few from her limited stock including a bottle of wine and, as the bar didn't serve a meal,

## 8.

returned to the Maison Blanche to prepare dinner. I would have enjoyed company in my cosy refuge. I thought of the people I had shared a meal with and wondered where they were now. Liliane and Baptiste were probably home, and Ferdinand was on his way to Rocamadour. Cornelius would be well ahead of me by now. I didn't mind too much being on my own, but I hoped I would meet others on the road. The presence of other pilgrims stimulates. We support each other. We are brothers and sisters (*frères et soeurs*) on the same journey, following the same *destin*.

I slept soundly and woke late. I could have stayed longer. I had a leisurely breakfast and left about 11.15 a.m. The weather was cool, and a cloud of fog continued to hang over Châtelus-le-Marcheix, a beautiful village among forests, farming, lakes and streams. The main points of interest were the church dating back to the 14th century and a Lanterne aux Morts (lantern to the dead). They are curious monuments of ancient origin, usually found in cemeteries, built of stone, a small tower of 8 to 15 metres at the top of which a fire could be lit. Their original purpose is unclear, but it's thought they are survivors of a Celtic rite. The light was to ward off evil spirits and to guide the souls of the departed to their eternal repose. Later, they were incorporated into Christian practice. Their symbolism has been adopted in the modern practice of an eternal flame on the tomb of an unknown soldier in Paris and elsewhere. Perhaps my regular habit of lighting a candle for Maris could have had its origins in these ancient practices. It's a nice thought that I'm continuing to light up the way for my beloved wife of 42 years.

Death is such a mystery. It puzzled the ancients, and they developed rituals such as the lanterns to the dead to guide the departed on their way. It puzzles the moderns too. Is there life after death? I can walk by a tombstone of someone I've never known or loved and think: gone for ever. It was another thing to gaze at the body of my beloved wife, Maris. I could not imagine that this beautiful person and our love could just slip away into nothingness. I like to think that she exists beyond my memory. I continue to talk to her and to believe that she is on another journey somewhere, clothed in complete mystery. She has been a continuing presence in my life. I cried out against her death. That she was here one Saturday morning and absolutely gone by lunchtime was impossible to comprehend, too grotesque, too incongruous to the sense of our enduring love. I was driven by her death to believe that there is more. She was just too lovely, too good, too real to simply disappear, to be gone forever, to be dead, dead, dead! Before she died, I followed my Church's teaching and believed with my head in life after death. Now I feel it in my heart. I hope we are more than flesh. One day, my body will join hers in our grave in the Frenchs Forest Bush Cemetery. Our spirits, souls or whatever we like to call them, will be joined, too.

The fog cleared, and although bright and sunny, walking in the shade was cool. The wind rose and stirred the forest. At first, I mistook the sound of the wind in the pines for traffic. Flurries of autumn leaves filled the air and settled gently as I passed, adding to the carpet beneath my feet. My boots never trod a softer surface. This was feral France. The only signs of human endeavour were the occasional stacks of wood, preparations for the coming winter. No wood cutters were to be seen today although there were signs by the roadside indicating they were around. Perhaps God's unseen little creatures, too, were making ready for the change in season, busily storing food for the bleak times. Creation was at work.

My destination for the evening was the *Gîte-Chambre d'hôte*

8.

*Ferme de la Besse.* I liked the idea of stopping on a farm away from any built-up area. I left the pilgrim route and took a side road, but I was unlikely to get lost, there being regular signs advising the traveller how far to go. La Besse was a few houses and the gîte was beyond. The building looked new, surrounded by a garden with a large thick hedge, so I didn't see much of the farm. They had a dormitory with five beds and three rooms. Sylvie and Yann were the hosts. Sylvie explained that they had closed the dormitory. It was late in the season and the number of walkers/pilgrims had dwindled. She offered me a room. I didn't mind paying the little extra. The room was in the roof, beautifully panelled in wood, with skylight and sloping ceiling. The bathroom gleamed with new shiny fittings and towel heater, very useful for drying my washing. I enjoyed resting on the bed and through the skylight gazing at the blue sky and passing clouds. I heard the twittering of birds perching on the roof, the occasional cheeky one peering into my room. They seemed to be in conversation: perhaps they were, warning each other of dangers and of good food supplies.

A restaurant was attached, and a meal was provided to pilgrims as part of the package. I descended from my lofty bedroom about 7 p.m. and was shown to my table. Yann was in charge. He greeted me and explained proudly that the food in the kitchen came from the farm. Three other groups arrived so that twelve other diners shared the evening. They seemed to be locals, a good place for a Saturday evening night out. I enjoyed the meal; in fact, I enjoyed everything about this gîte. It catered for a wide range of clientele. As well as a farm-stay, it hosted weddings, baptisms, retreats and seminars, definitely a multi-purpose resource for the local community. I could have stayed a few nights and participated in the farm-stay.

Instead, I was up early, as I was planning to walk about 22

kilometres. Being Sunday morning, the restaurant opened late, but Sylvie left me a breakfast in the room at the bottom of my stairs. This room was a lounge for the pilgrims who would have stayed in the dormitory. My companion was a large Alsatian. He greeted me on arrival and seemed well advanced in doggy years. He padded around and turned up at the restaurant the previous night. He slept on the couch and ignored me, as if he was accustomed to pilgrims eating their breakfast in this place. The door had been left ajar so probably this was his regular resting pad. It felt very homely, accepted without fuss by the family dog.

The sun was just emerging as I said goodbye to my canine brother. As I left, I said a quiet prayer for my hosts, that their entrepreneurial efforts would be a success. The morning was calm and still. I tapped my way along the road back to the route and found the tiny settlement of Les Billanges. No traffic! I walked through forests down to the Pont de Dognon. The water in the river was flat and still, a perfect mirror to the surrounds. No one was about, but there were many boats and places for camping. Such a calm, peaceful Sunday morning to reflect on the beauty of creation. I had been apprehensive about this day, as I was hoping to cover a longer than usual distance, but these charming surrounds calmed me, too.

I stopped for lunch in Le Châtenet-en-Dognon and bought a sandwich at *Chez Claudine*. In all, I walked 22 kilometres. Despite my earlier apprehension, I felt in reasonable shape when I arrived in St Léonard de Noblat. It took 7 hours. *Le Petit Miaulétou* was a bar behind the Office de Tourisme. The bar, like everything else, was closed, being Sunday afternoon, but I managed to rouse the owners, Gigi and Christophe, who let me in through a doorway to the left of the bar and showed my room above the bar.

St Léonard de Noblat originally developed as an important

medieval pilgrimage centre, the pilgrims being drawn to the tomb of St Léonard. St Léonard is a very popular saint in France and other Christian countries where he is invoked as a liberator of prisoners. I like reading about his story.

*A nobleman in the court of Clovis, he converted to Christianity at the end of the fifth century. He requested from Clovis the privilege of liberating whatever prisoners he might find worthy of freedom at any time he deemed fit. He later became a monk and settled here, where he eventually founded the abbey around which the town grew. Legend says that prisoners who called upon the monk's intercession would have their chains miraculously broken, which the grateful ex-prisoners would then carry to the sainted Léonard as testimony to his mercy.*

Léonard's story has many lessons. Many people are made prisoners by metaphorical chains. They may have not been forgiven for past wrongs. To forgive them, that is, to release them of their chains, is an act of mercy that gives both the forgiven and forgiver freedom. It can mean new life to the forgiven. The forgiver is released, too, from the chains of resentment and anger and gives hope to both for renewal in their relationship and enables them to start again.

Léonard's prestige was immense when he died in 511, and his remains were venerated in this town. The present Roman-style collegiate church had its origin in the 11th century. As one of the destinations on the Chemin from Vézelay to Santiago, it is officially listed as a world heritage site. Saint Léonard is popular today. Many churches around the world are dedicated to his name. Indeed, while I lived in Melbourne in the seventies, I attended the church of Saint Léonard's in the parish of Bulleen. The kids attended Saint Léonard's school.

After a rest, I crossed one of the boulevards that broadly define the town's historical centre. These have replaced the moats and walls that were once part of the town's defence. I wandered through the narrow streets. Many of the houses are half-timbered while the grander ones are made from stone, many with interesting little features. On the Place de la Republique are two houses with towers, one square, the other round, both built in the 17th century. It was easy to get lost as I wandered from Place to Place — Place de la Republique, Place Gay-Lussac, Place Noblat. Everything was closed, but I found a small pizza bar. The Pizza Coquille folded its pizzas to look like a shell — a nice way to honour the town as an important stage on the way to Compostelle. I would have spent more time exploring, but rain fell, heavily enough for me to beat a retreat back to my room in *Le Petit Miaulétou*.

Saint Léonard de Noblat is about 22 kilometres from Limoges. This noble city of the French Chemin should have been my next destination. Fourteen gîtes were listed in my guidebook. I rang everyone, and all were full (*complet*). Every bed in Limoges had been booked because a new bishop was being installed; everyone had come to town for the show and were hanging around for the celebrations. I had seen notices on church doors that on Sunday September 3rd, Monseigneur Pierre-Antoine Bozo was being ordained as the 107th bishop of Limoges. If there was no room at the inns in Limoges, I might as well give the town a miss.

I found a card for a taxi in my room, but the number did not answer. In the morning, I joined the locals for coffee and breakfast. Just the smell of coffee revives. I mentioned my difficulties to Christophe. He rang another number, and the taxi arrived in 20 minutes. What would have taken hours, we traversed in minutes. I was happy to miss the many kilometres of ugly suburbs. Even my guide book regarded this section as very difficult (*Grosse difficulté*). In comparison to the large urban areas already encountered in other cities such as Nevers in this Chemin and Bourges and Leon in Spain, with their dreary interminable outskirts before reaching the old quarters, my guide book regarded Limoges as the longest and most confusing. Tackling the way on foot in the confusion and pollution of the traffic was heroic, it told me, so take the bus. I would have caught the bus, too, had I known where to find it. My taxi did the job. A far cry from the peaceful rural lanes that I loved. The one advantage my guidebook claimed was the presence of comfortable gîtes, which I had already contacted and found them *complet*. My guidebook told me that Limoges is a ford on the river Vienne, and its abbeys were first established in the 4th to 9th centuries. The monastery housed the relics of Saint Martial and became a place of pilgrimage and also a stage on the Chemin de Saint-Jacques de Compostelle.

My driver was ready for a chat. He told me he had been in taxis for 25 years including a spell in Paris. By the size of his stomach, he hadn't done much walking in that time. He dropped me off at the church in Aixe-sur-Vienne. The church of Sainte-Croix was built in the 13th century. Legend has it that a pilgrim carrying a thorn from the true cross chose the site as a resting place.

My destination was Saint-Martin-le-Vieux, only nine kilometres. There was nothing to hurry for, so I dawdled so as not to arrive too early. What a joy to take one's time! So much of our lives we are dashing hither and thither. The road led me through shimmering green fields where sheep with a daub of red on their fleece grazed in peace. The day was worth a linger to absorb its untainted beauty. I thought of nothing in particular and just listened to the rhythm of my footsteps and to the tap, tap, tap of my pacer poles. My body was enjoying the movement; no part of it was hurting; it was at peace. So was my spirit, as if it were experiencing the deeply real that lurks beneath the stereotypes and other images that prevent us from truly seeing places, people and other times. At times like this, I sense a presence. Someone's walking with me, keeping me silent company. Perhaps it's Maris, perhaps it's Jesus. I tell others, on retreats and other appropriate places, that Jesus is my mate and he talks to me in an Aussie accent.

A number of chateaux lay along the route. They looked unoccupied yet reasonably well maintained, although none had the faint suggestion of a garden. Weekenders? The only people I met were three pilgrims, a girl named Lidi and a middle-aged couple, all of whom were making for Flavignac. They had no time for chatter other than a greeting, so they passed me while I continued on to Saint-Martin-le-Vieux where I was planning to stay at the *Chambre d'hôtes*. I received a very warm welcome from Martine when I arrived and was offered a beer. Three of the rooms were upstairs in the main house, while I was shown to a building out the back. Up a flight of stairs was my room, all newly built or renovated. My room was comfortable indeed with its own ensuite. Martine offered to do my washing, so after a shower, I returned to the main house with the clothes I'd worn that day and inspected the garden, well maintained with a number of fruit trees. Playground equipment and some bicycles pointed to children in the household. A large hedge surrounded the property, and beyond were the open fields of farmland.

I was the only pilgrim guest. I dined with another guest. Christophe worked for an Italian company that designed spiral staircases. He was responsible for sales and installation and was travelling through France. We shared a carafe of wine,

## 8.

and I learned from him that evening the workings of his job. Strange what one learns on the Chemin! Next time I climb a spiral stair, I hope I remember enough of Christophe's lesson to appreciate the intricacies of its design. It's amazing what you learn when people let their guard down and embrace the possibility of human connection, instead of sending texts or emails on their phones.

I mentioned the following morning at breakfast that I was planning to walk to Châlus, about 19 kilometres. My host mentioned the *Hôtel du Centre,* run by an Englishman and lots of English gathered there. It seemed a good idea to stay there and spend an evening speaking English rather than French. For most of the day, I walked along quiet roads, past calvaires decorated with flowers. I stopped for a sandwich at Flavignac. The origins of the town go back to pre-historic times, I read in my guidebook, but it was a certain Flavinius of Gallic-Roman times, who owned an important villa, who gave his name to the town. I found the church and entered, hoping to light a candle for Maris. Although there was a light before the statue of Our Lady, I couldn't find any candles. The church was dark and uninviting. On the way, I passed more wrought iron crosses, or *'calvaires',* as the French call them. They were more inviting than the church, so I stopped before them for a short breather and a prayer of thanks that I had got this far – four weeks on the road.

For the afternoon, a misty rain settled on the way. I met two other walkers, Carol and Christophe. I heard them coming, for Christophe never ceased to talk, at a machine pace at that. They were lively and warm hearted. I appreciated their company for the brief time we chatted as a relief from the gloom in the weather. Near Les Cars, a lady invited me to rest on the seat in her garden, but her dog, a black poodle, was not at all happy with the arrangement, so I thanked her and moved on.

On the outskirts of Châlus, I ran into Carol and Christophe at the *Supermarché*. Christophe was still talking incessantly but paused long enough to greet me. I hoped Carol had both the fortitude for her walk and for the ceaseless ear bashing. She seemed content in his company. When I arrived at the *Bar-Restaurant Hôtel du Centre*, naturally enough in the centre of town, I found the door locked, but I was intrigued by the notices: 'English Spoken Here' and 'Bière Anglaise' and 'English Beer'. I knocked, and Dave emerged. The bar didn't open until 5 p.m, but he let me in. I'm not familiar with English accents, but it sounded northern. He hailed from Manchester. He took me to my room across a bridge to another building. My room was comfortable enough but not inviting, nothing much more than a bed and bare walls. At least there were no notices forbidding me from doing this or that. After a shower, I hung my washing on the bridge rails – very public as a thoroughfare passed underneath that saw the occasional pedestrian or vehicle.

When I crossed the bridge back into the hotel, the bar was open. It was the watering hole for expatriates, for all I heard was English. One was complaining long and loud about the problems he had with the French authorities to get his car registered. Others arrived, all English. It appeared that a number had settled in the area, and this was where they gathered. Only one Frenchman was in the bar. He was the local butcher. His shop was opposite, and when he saw a customer enter, he'd cross the road, attend to them and return to his drink. I met Mick and Barry; both kept up a steady pace drinking their English beer. I steadfastly refused to keep up with them. Their accents were strong, and sometimes I had as much trouble understanding them as I did the French. I asked them what impact did they think Brexit might have on them, and they thought not much at all. I wondered if they had their heads in the sand. I also wondered if they bothered to reach out and appreciate the French culture; none of them, apart from the owner, Dave, had learnt French. I have heard people walk into a shop and speak English as if expecting everyone to understand. I'm afraid I was not impressed with my company.

At dinner, I noticed other guests. They were English. In the morning they were given the full English breakfast (bacon, eggs, sausages), while I was given the French version. I left Châlus in similar weather conditions as I arrived, overcast and misty rain. On the building next to the hotel was a sign announcing that Thomas Edward Lawrence (1888-1935) at the age of 20 stayed in this building, a former hotel, on 16th August 1908. Following in the footsteps of Richard the Lionheart, he toured France by bicycle then wrote his thesis: 'The influence of the crusades on European military architecture at the end of the 12th century', before accomplishing his destiny as Lawrence of Arabia.

I passed castle ruins. Châlus earns its spot in the pages of history as the place where the English king, Richard the Lionheart, was mortally wounded in 1199 during the siege of the Châlus castle. The remainder of the day, I walked along tracks through quiet and peaceful forests. There were no facilities until I reached La Coquille, about 17 kilometres. The town's name evokes the Chemin de Saint-Jacques, as the word *Coquille* means shell. It was an important stage for medieval pilgrims on the way to Compostelle.

My destination was the *Refuge associative des Amis de Saint-Jacques*. At first, I could not find my refuge, but a kind old chap directed me to a specific laneway. When I arrived, I couldn't see any building that resembled a refuge. I passed a building that looked like a hall. I heard music and assumed a ballet dance class was in progress. At the end of the lane were two houses.

I walked up the path of one. I could hear the television, and I knocked. No response. I knocked again. I knocked again during a brief pause in the sound. I heard a response, and an elderly lady appeared, a little flustered at my intrusion. I explained I was looking for the pilgrims' refuge. She recovered quickly and told me I had just passed it. She came out and took me down her pathway, into the lane and to the hall. She explained it was at the back. I apologised for troubling her. (*'Excusez-moi de vous déranger!'*) She replied 'no worries', or the French equivalent. I was not the first to inquire and would not be the last.

The refuge was tiny indeed and easy to miss, only identified by a set of steps. The only indication of its presence was a small sign by the door, not visible from the roadway. Inside, I was warmly welcomed by the hospitaliers, Anna-Maree and Jacques, an elderly couple. Present were two other pilgrims, Mireille from Belgium and Dick from Holland. Mireille was as petite as Dick was large, a giant of a man in many ways. Everyone was excited and talking at once. In the midst of the confusion, I worked out that a television crew from France 3 had visited. They wanted to make a series of short films on the pilgrims who passed through the region and the people who cared for them. Would we be interested? *Bien sûr! (Of course!)* This was a new experience, being filmed and interviewed in a foreign language. I was really being dragged out of my comfort zone. That's where life begins.

Shortly after, the television crew arrived. Florian, a young man, was the interviewer, and Pascale was the cameraman. He had such an array of cameras of all sizes. He began filming the activities of the refuge, including me washing my underwear. Florian asked the time I'd be leaving in the morning and made arrangements to meet me the following day. In the meantime, I got to know my fellow pilgrims. Dick was a man in a hurry. He was aiming to cover more than 30 kilometres per day, and petite Mireille was much the same. Compared with their distances, my efforts were puny. They seemed to be in competition; whether it was a battle of the sexes or whether the honour of Belgium and Holland were at stake, or both, I'm not sure. One thing was certain. I was not in a race, nor was I in a competition.

Nevertheless, we were brothers and sister for the evening as part of the Camino family. Anna-Maree and Jacques, our hosts, were part of that family, too. Anna-Maree rang for me the refuges at Sorges and Périgueux, both managed by the same association as La Coquille, the *Association des Amis et Pèlerins de Saint-Jacques du Limousin-Périgord*. She cooked a beautiful meal although she was careful in her serving of the food and the wine.

The next morning, Thursday September 7th, my 30th day on the Chemin, I had the usual difficulty finding my way out of the town. Eventually, I made it into open country and forest. The car approaching bore the France 3 logo, the first of three encounters with Florian and Pascale. They wanted to film me in different terrains. Pascale filmed me from every angle, even from a drone. The use of a drone prised open my eyes. Often when watching a film with aerial shots, I used to think that the plane was flying very low and slowly. Now, I understood how often a drone is used in film making. Florian and Pascale left me. I entered a forest. Here I met Jean-Paul and Christophe, fresh, friendly and full of an exuberance and joy for life. They were walking for four days as a break from their life in Paris. Their presence was inspiring and their enthusiasm contagious, as if God or Jesus or Maris had sent them along to spur me on. We passed each other several times during the day, always with the same flamboyant welcome. They made both my steps and my pack lighter.

As I emerged, the France 3 car approached me from a side road. I was impressed that they found me. Florian explained they had a map and they had met Mireille. Dick did not wish to participate, as the filming would hold him back.

Christophe produced his drone and had me walking along a farm track in open country, the drone on my right and then on the left. While the machine was hovering, along came another pilgrim. Josef and I fell into immediate conversation. I explained the film crew's presence, and he was impressed that I was involved. I explained that they picked me, I was sure, because I was from afar, from *Australie*, and that I was an ancient 84 years old. The drone landed; Josef continued on, and Florian led me into the field for an interview. I wasn't sure how my French would stand up for 20 minutes. I was terrified that I would make a botch of things, not understand Florian's questions and have to request repeats. Television interviews always seem to run quickly and fluently. However, Florian was a natural and had me relaxed, which made me feel good, so away I went in my best French telling my story, explaining my motivation and detailing the lessons learnt. Christophe cut the camera, and Florian thought my French was excellent, which made me feel better. Off they went to catch up with Mireille.

I had met and was talking to Jean-Paul and the other Christophe when they arrived for the third time. Christophe filmed my feet for ages, then Florian thanked me and took my email address. When the editing was complete and the film gone on air, he promised he would send me the link. He thanked me and departed, leaving me to walk to Thiviers along a mixture of roads and tracks through fields and forests under an overcast sky, never far from the hum and traffic of the N21.

Florian's link did not arrive for some months well after I had returned to Australia. The outcome was four short films of about two and a half minutes each. My twenty-minute interview had been reduced to about 20 seconds. I made a significant point in that short time about the camaraderie of the Chemin. I said that I was like a brother (*frère*) to pilgrims who had walked in the Middle Ages, the present and the future. Then in a voice-over, I commented that we pilgrims are all brothers and sisters (*frères et soeurs*) because we are following the same destiny (*destin*). I sent the link to my daughter Angela, and she sent an email around the family with the heading: *Dad is famous in France*. The link is:

https://www.youtube.com/watch?v=FaEWfTucwTM

It was slow work getting into Thiviers. I had to turn left at the gendarmerie and walk a further 400 metres to the *Gîte pèlerin-Chambre d'hôtes Les Conches*. Just as I arrived, rain fell. Mme Cordier was slow letting me in but was warm and welcoming. I had a suite to myself including a television and microwave oven. She left a food tray for my dinner, which I warmed in the microwave. No other guests. I wondered where Mireille and Dick got to that evening. I was not feeling lonely as I had the television, but I must admit I would have happily given the box the flick for company. It was too far into town to find a bar.

In the morning, I joined the family and Chambre d'hôte guests for breakfast. The family included a teenage son in his school uniform. I was late leaving and took a short cut through sporting fields to get back on track. It was overcast all day although there was no rain. Along the way I met Mireille and Dick, as well as Jean-Paul and Christophe. Jean-Paul explained that he disliked the idea of sleeping in a dormitory (*dortoir*). Too much snoring! They stayed in relative comfort in the chambres d'hôtes. I stopped for a rest at Négrondes, just a tiny dot on the map, and sat on the steps of a church opposite the office of Catholic Relief. A lady was waiting for the office to open and when she spotted me, asked if she could join me. No worries! (or the French equivalent – *je vous en prie*). She introduced herself as Annette. Was I a pilgrim on the way to Compostelle? She wished me *Bon Courage* and explained how hard her life was. She was unemployed and had to rely on charities such as Catholic Relief. For the 10 minutes we chatted, we were brother and sister. Amazing how close you can feel to a person whom you have just met. I was saddened for Annette, a pilgrim on another journey through the darkness. I hoped my presence brightened her day and gave her just a little strength and hope to fight off despair and struggle on. The office opened, and I wished her *Bon Courage* back. Keep pressing on, Sister!

I passed through extensive fields of sunflowers, not at their finest under a dull sky. They are at their best in the full sun, embracing the light and standing firm and hopeful. That is what sunflowers do to me. They are a wonderful symbol of renewal. Each of those thousand or so seeds in the centre is capable of new life.

I pressed on to Sorges, another tiny dot on the map. My bed for the night was in the *Refuge associative des Amis de Saint-Jacques*. I was greeted warmly by the hospitalier. Catherine had long black hair pulled over her left shoulder. She was a younger woman in contrast to the hospitaliers and pilgrims I had met so far. She showed me to the dormitory upstairs. After a shower and the usual chores, I took a short stroll. The refuge faces a large square and is next to the church, a massive structure, and I'm not surprised it started life as a fortified church, destroyed a good many times, rebuilt and remodelled down the course of the centuries. The doors were locked. Two shells indicated the role of the church in receiving pilgrims on their road to Compostelle. The village is famous for the truffle, a treasure and often referred to 'le diamant noir' (black diamond). The village boasts a truffle museum and also an *Auberge de la Truffe*. I visited the bar, drank one beer but did not sample the truffles.

Back at the refuge, I met the other guests. I knew Dick and tiny Mireille from La Coquille. Marielle, Josie and François were French. The six of us squeezed into the tiny dormitory meant for five. Two more pilgrims arrived, but Catherine had to knock them back. No more room at the inn! One more, perhaps, for I noticed some spare mattresses. Some refuges have a policy of there's always room for one more, depending how desperate the pilgrim. Catherine prepared dinner, no truffles, but a nice casserole and salad. She presided over her family, noisy at times, for Mireille, Marielle and Dick held the floor most of the time, in competition to tell the best Chemin story. François, Josie and I were the quiet ones. I did not get to know them. François was content with his own company. He was a recluse with his grey hair, white beard and moustache. I sensed that he didn't want questions from a curious Australian. Perhaps he was seeking answers to his existence. No need to question Dick and the others. They were the extroverts. They told it all.

In the morning, I left with the ladies, Marielle, Josie and Mireille, while Dick and François forged ahead. We chatted and took photos of each other in front of a crudely painted sign: *Compostelle. Plus que 1210 km*. The ladies moved ahead and left me content to walk alone. The morning was overcast with a definite feel of rain. I moved out of the open fields and climbed gently into thick forest (*Forêt Lanmary*). I found myself in the midst of a large permanent scout camp. No one was around, not even a caretaker, but there were hundreds of canvas tents, plus ablution blocks, small shelters with notice boards, and a system of roads. Nothing was locked. I looked into one of the tents. On a wooden floor were a number of beds, without mattresses or blankets. I imagined what this place might be. Although forlorn at the moment, it would spring to life with the arrival of hundreds of scouts, full of exuberance and excitement at the prospect of a few days of outdoor adventure.

The camp brought back memories of my ten years as a scout leader, a fascinating stage of my life pilgrimage. For nine years I worked with boys aged from nine to fifteen. When they arrived, they were children, but over the five years I saw them mature and grow into young men. In the final year I was 'promoted' to Group Leader, which removed me from direct contact with the boys, my prime responsibility being the running of the troop, liaison with the committee and the recruitment and care of leaders, etc. I grew tired of this administrative role and quit. I have many memories of friendships, both with the boys and the other leaders, the highlights being the Jamborees held in camps similar to this one.

I was so absorbed with the scout camp and my reminiscing that I did not notice the skies darken. In less than 5 minutes, the rain fell hard, fast and fierce. I scrambled to get my backpack off, retrieve my poncho, and struggled to get it over my pack and myself, wishing all the while that I had dallied that few extra minutes back at the camp where there was more than ample shelter. The rain fell harder and cold water trickled down my neck and flowed down the track in a stream. I should have gone back to the camp, but I pressed on in the hope of finding shelter further on. The bottoms of my shorts were soaked and so were my precious guidebook, socks and boots. At first, the trees gave shelter, but they, too, became sodden and dripped just as copiously as the rain battered the forest, louder than a steam train.

## 8.

I came to a crossroad of tracks just as a car from the side road sent a cascade of mud over me. I cursed the driver for his speed in such conditions. I saw shelter, a notice board under a tiny sloping roof and a seat on either side. The seat was useless to rest on, but if I stood on it, my head was sheltered. Which is what I did, taking care not to slip. I had time to breathe and take stock. This is as bizarre as it gets! The joys of life on the road as a pilgrim! I was thankful that God through the people who managed this forest had provided this shelter. The rain continued to belt down and dimmed visibility. I noticed another shelter on the diagonal corner, and two pilgrims were sheltering, one on each seat. I recognised Jean-Claude and Christophe. They saw me, and we waved. They laughed. My spirits soared, and I saw how ludicrous and absurd our situation was. The stuff for comic films. I laughed, too.

The rain lightened, so I hopped off my shelter and walked across to Jean-Claude and Christophe. Together, we walked along the muddy track until we came to a clearing with an old, open-sided shed, full of rubbish – farm machinery, trailers laden with boxes of magazines and clothes, oil drums, a creeper in the process of covering the structure. But the rain had not penetrated, an opportunity to strip off our wet weather gear, to dry out and to eat some lunch. Jean-Paul produced a bottle of red and some chicken. I broke my rule of no alcohol during the day and accepted a plastic tumbler, and with the old trailer as our dining table, we drank to our pilgrim journeys. Jean-Paul and Christophe's journey was to end that day, for they were planning to take the train from Périgueux to Paris. They said goodbye as they left, and I remained for a time in my temporary home among the rubbish. In the meantime, the rain stopped; the sun shone, and wisps of steam drifted from the wet grass and foliage. I would have happily settled for the night in the rubbish and made a bed on one of the trailers among the old magazines. I had plenty of reading material to pass the time, but I had no food, and my destination was the refuge at Périgueux.

The *Refuge associatif des Amis de Saint-Jacques* took a long time to find. Like all the bigger towns along the Chemin, busy streets, traffic lights and gawdy shopfronts were a shock after days of wondering through France's quiet and leafy regions. Périgueux was no different. Its busyness was intimidating. It made me feel small, old and awkward with my backpack and pacer poles. I seemed to walk forever through hostile, or at best indifferent, streets. My mood changed to that of a grumpy old man. Eventually, I found the refuge by finding the railway station. The warm welcome of the hospitaliers was in sharp contrast to the mood of the streets and did wonders for me. Dominque couldn't be more helpful in settling me in. He shared his duties of care with his wife Marie Therese. They lived in Biarritz and were due to finish their shift in two days. I knew the other pilgrims from Sorges – Dick, François, Marielle and Josie. Marie Therese prepared a beautiful casserole dinner, and Dominique produced copious amounts of red wine that kept the conversation and the camaraderie flowing.

*Jacques and Anna-Maree, hospitaliers at La Coquille*

*Noël, Mireille, Catherine, Marielle, Dick and François at Sorges*

# 9.

*Of course, you can also do without hope.*
*But life without hope*
*Is an empty, boring and useless life.*
*I cannot imagine that I could live*
*And strive for something*
*If I did not carry hope in me.*
*I am thankful to God for this gift.*
*It is as big as life itself.*
*Vaclav Havel – Czech Playwright and Politician*

I tossed and turned more than usual in my comfortable refuge. The night was warm. Dick, my roommate, took the bed under the window, which he wanted left open to capture the breeze. It also captured the traffic of Périgueux. Cars were frequent enough, but the occasional heavy truck penetrated my sleep as if it had driven right into our room. Dick was restless, too. His snoring was as loud as the traffic outside, like the traffic intermittent but nevertheless penetrating. I gave up trying to sleep and turned to my situation.

Sunday September 10th was my thirty-third day on the way; I had come 545 kilometres since leaving the train at Avallon, well below what I had covered in my earlier Caminos. By now, the fatigue had penetrated my bones, and I felt in need of a rest, not just one day, but several. I was feeling my age, really feeling my age. Most eighty-four-year-olds don't walk across a country carrying a backpack that increases in weight as the day advances; they sit at home, or the more adventurous might go on cruises where everything was taken care of and the main adventure for the day is which beer to try tonight.

Back in 2010 when I walked from Le Puy-en-Velay to Saint-Jean-Pied-de-Port, I passed through the city of Figeac. There I saw the detour sign to Rocamadour. It was possible to walk to Rocamadour and return to the route further on. I knew little about the shrine and its reputation as a pilgrimage destination, so I pressed on. Later, I met pilgrims who had taken the detour and they told me of an outstanding experience, the highlight of their pilgrimage. I felt a touch of envy at what I had missed. 'One of these days...,' I thought.

A visit to Rocamadour was never far from my mind, and here at Périgueux I was not far away. Why not detour now? I could walk, but there could be a bus or train. I could take four or five days off, travel to Rocamadour and return to the Voie de Vézelay and continue my walk south to the Pyrénées. First things first. I will ask if I could sleep another night, and during the day, work out the details. The decision made, I slept soundly until dawn.

Dominique was happy for me to stay. Bookings were light, so I would not be taking another tired pilgrim's bed. I was saddened to say goodbye to my fellow pilgrims. Dick, Mireille, François had been my Camino family for the last few days, and now we were splitting up, so frequent on the Camino. You just feel you're getting to know someone and they are getting to know you, and then you part and never see each other again. The farewells were touching, particularly with Mireille. I discussed my change of plan with Dominique. I could walk, he said, there were refuges on the way, but I could also take the train. I would probably have to travel first to Bordeaux and take the train along another route to Rocamadour. I visited the railway station and consulted the routes and timetables. The situation was as Dominique guessed.

## 9.

I booked the train to Bordeaux for the following day. I had never visited Bordeaux, reputed to be one of the beautiful cities of La Belle France, so it occurred to me that I should stay a day to look around. Down the road was an Ibis hotel, and through their system I booked two nights in Bordeaux.

That gave me the rest of the day to explore Périgueux. A town of about 30,000, it had its origins in Roman days and grew around an abbey sanctuary containing the body of St Front, known as the Apostle of Périgord and the first bishop of Périgueux. The town has had a rough time. It struggled against the English through the Hundred Years' War and suffered under Protestant occupation during the 16th century Wars of Religion. I visited the cathedral of Saint-Front, built in the 12th century on the ruins of the abbey. One of the largest in this area of France (the south-west), it is built in the shape of a Greek cross, topped by five domes and numerous colonnaded turrets. I attended Mass, and during the service I reflected on the lives of the multitude of medieval pilgrims who sought sanctuary in this cathedral on their way to Compostelle. I was reminded of the bond that binds pilgrims down the ages into one large fellowship.

Back at the refuge, I worked out a plan of action for my remaining time in France. I listened to the two voices chattering in my mind. The one almost screamed so loud that I imagined the whole of Périgueux would hear: '*Noël, take it easy. You don't have to prove anything. You've already walked 545 kilometres. Isn't that enough for an eighty-four-year-old? Give away this pilgrim caper and take it easy doing tourist things.*' The other quieter voice asked me why had I come to France. 'To be a pilgrim!' '*Fine! Take the detour to Rocamadour for that will be a pilgrimage in itself, but come back to the voie de Vézelay.*' I told the raucous voice to be silent.

I made my plans. Train travel in France is excellent, that is, provided the trains are running. Strikes (*les grèves*) are a hazard. I had heard that they were frequent that summer. Fortunately, the unions (*les syndicats*) were giving the public notice of the days they were taking action. My challenge was to weave my travel around these days. Trains would not be running on Wednesday, but it was safe to travel on Tuesday, the following day when I would take the train to Bordeaux, spend two nights, take the train to Rocamadour, spend two nights, and back to Bordeaux for another two nights and then take the train to Mont de Marson where I would resume walking the 132 kilometres to Saint-Jean-Pied-de-Port and the Pyrénées.

One other pilgrim shared the refuge with me that night. Remo was Dutch. He had little English and not much French either, so I didn't get to know him except that he had slept at Sorges the night before. There were five of us when I stayed at Sorges, but Remo was on his own, making it an easy night for the hospitalier Catherine. Once again, Marie Therese cooked an excellent meal while Dominique poured the wine. I had the room to myself as Remo slept in the other. This time, I closed the window against the traffic noise and managed to get some decent sleep after wondering how Dick and Frère Michèle might have got on.

My train didn't depart until after 11 a.m. so I took my time in the morning. Remo discovered he had left his rain cape at Sorges and told Dominique. He was on the phone to Catherine. She had had a quiet evening. She would finish her chores quickly and drive to Périgueux. She arrived about 9 a.m. with the item. Another example of the dedication of the volunteer hospitaliers to their job of looking after their pilgrims. Ask a hospitalier/hospitalière why they have volunteered, and they will reply that, having been on the receiving end of hospitality as a pilgrim, they want to give back in return. In 2015 I was a hospitalero at Rabanal del Camino in Spain for two weeks, so I know something of the care and foibles of the role. One of these days, perhaps, I could be a hospitalier in this refuge and do as good a job, hopefully as well as Dominique and Marie Therese.

I arrived at the railway station, apprehensive that the unions might have called an unplanned strike. At first, I heard silence and was relieved to hear the comforting sound of engines. I was in plenty of time to buy all the train tickets for the week. The journey to Bordeaux was not long, and I relaxed, admired the passing French countryside reflecting that, for a brief time, I would be shedding my pilgrim identity and donning that of a tourist. I felt just a touch of guilt. Somewhere down deep there lurked a thought that I would not return. That voice nagged me: *'Noël, do you still want to tackle the challenges and overcome the obstacles of life on the Chemin? It won't be long before you'll be enjoying the luxuries of life as a tourist.'* I'd be lying if I denied that I listened to that voice. *'Go on, Noël, just be plain lazy. You know that you'd prefer never having to walk with a backpack again.'* But I resisted. *'Get behind me, Satan! I am committed and will return to the challenges of the road, whatever they might be. I will overcome my doubts and return to the job that I came to La Belle France to do. After a few days I will put aside the mantle of tourist and take again that of pilgrim.'*

At Bordeaux, I was thrust into the confusion of a big city. Outside the huge railway station was a place bustling with trams and traffic and masses of people darting hither and thither. Across the busy roadway was an Ibis hotel, not the one I had booked, but I reckoned they would know where mine was. With eyes everywhere, I accepted the first challenge of Bordeaux: to get across the road alive. Ibis Bordeaux Lac is too far to walk, the young ladies on the desk advised me. It's a good 25 minutes by tram. Back to the tram stop outside the station, the second challenge was to coax a ticket out of a vending machine. I have to say I've dealt with some pretty user-unfriendly vending machines in Europe, but this one was near top of the anguish list. I joined the queue of frustrated travellers. After several attempts I succeeded. *'Persévére, Frérot! Keep pressing on, Brother.'* Next challenge. Which tram to take? A tourist's life has as many challenges as a pilgrim's. With a sense of triumph, I settled into my seat and watched the passing parade of Bordeaux. The sixth largest city in France, its buildings reminded me of Paris. The streets were graceful and clean. The buildings looked to have been renovated back to their 19th century elegance. Once rather seedy, the town has benefited from massive investment to make it one of the most attractive in France. I noted plenty of sauntering tourists, tiny packs on their backs and city maps in hand. I would probably join them on the morrow.

The tram swung around a corner to follow the broad River Garonne and then along leafy boulevards into not-so-elegant suburbs, more recently built in modern angles and shades of grey. The Hotel Ibis Bordeaux Lac was by a lake surrounded by other hotels of the luxurious kind. There was nothing luxurious about the Hotel Ibis, all white, uniform and soulless, not a single painting or image on any wall.

Tuesday September 12th, mainly fine although showers were forecast, was my day in Bordeaux as a tourist. Although the unions wanted the day to be a 'general strike', the trams and buses were running. Perhaps the drivers belong to a renegade union. I had decided I couldn't see all Bordeaux in one day and would return for a few days after my visit to Rocamadour. Consequently, I did not rush around trying to fit in all the monuments. I got off the tram at the Place des Quinconces and sauntered the short distance to the River Garonne and walked along the broad esplanade flanking its banks. Impressive buildings abound. I wandered through the streets. I joined the queue at the tourist bureau for a map and spoke to couples from Wales and New Zealand. I passed a hairdresser and had a ten-euro haircut, which made me feel less scruffy. I visited a bookshop and found a number of Australian authors whose works had been translated. Perhaps, mine will be too, one of these days.

The next morning, I took the tram back to the station for my train to Rocamadour with changes at Toulouse and Figeac. I was back in familiar territory, for I had passed through Figeac in 2010 and stayed in Toulouse in 2013. Coming into Moissac, I recognised the canal path along which I had walked. The walkers were out that day, complete with their backpacks and poles, and the same barges seemed to be moored along the canal bank. At Figeac, I changed into a one carriage train and was the only passenger. I felt as if I was leaving the modern world behind, the world of train strikes and masses of tourists, and entering into a deep remote France. At the unmanned station, I could have walked into Rocamadour, but the lady in the bar opposite ordered a taxi for me. Only 5 minutes away, I arrived in rain at my hotel *Le Relais Anadourién*. I dumped my pack and, despite the rain, ventured out to see the village.

Rocamadour is spectacular. Perched on the side of a limestone cliff, it towers majestically over a valley, the Alzou canyon. I walked the short distance to the top of the cliff, and from the ramparts of the ancient fort, I had a breathtaking view of all Rocamadour, the Alzou canyon and the wild, unspoilt surrounding landscape, part of the Regional National Park of the Quercy Limestone Plateau. Amazing! The setting is beautiful and dramatic, as if the village had climbed up the cliff face and managed to just hang on. I had a bird's eye view. Because the village hugs the cliff so closely, it mainly consists of one street lined with medieval houses. By now, the rain had ceased; the sun emerged from the clouds, and the light glistened on the rooftops and trees. Apart from its natural beauty, Rocamadour has been an important pilgrimage destination for over one thousand years. Built on the site of a shrine to a Black Madonna, the shrine became famous for its miracles and healing powers and was a stop on the path to Santiago de Compostela (Chemin de Saint-Jacques de Compostelle). No wonder Rocamadour is one of France's most important tourist destinations and receives up to a million visitors a year. Not many around just now, but I reckoned I would see lots the next day when I descended and inspected the village in detail.

As I prepared myself for sleep, my mind continued to cover old ground. I was pleased I'd made the decision to take a break from my walking and visit Rocamadour. Should I give away the walking completely? Once again, the two voices argued with each other, but I managed to reaffirm that I would resume walking once I had finished with this tourist business.

The next morning, it rained steadily until 11 a.m. I emerged with the sun and spent the day outside. I spurned the escalator that disappeared into a tunnel and, instead, zig-zagged down the cliff face along the *Chemin de la Croix* (Way of the Cross). The 14 Stations were in reverse order as you are supposed to start at the bottom and work your way up. The Way of the Cross was blessed in 1887 according to the marble monument. Down the bottom the tourists had emerged with the sun. I walked down the main street, the Rue de la Couronnerie lined with impressive medieval houses, to the stone fortified gateways at the end, then walked back past many shops and bars to a series of monumental steps, known as Le Grand Escalier. These led up to a small square surrounded by eight significant religious buildings. There are 216 steps in total, which many medieval pilgrims climbed on their knees. I had visions of millions of tired pilgrims working their painful way slowly upwards and upwards as an act of penance before entering the presence of the Blessed Virgin. The main draw was a small statue of the Black Madonna housed in a chapel, Sanctuaire de Notre Dame de Rocamadour. A sign outside announces: *Vous êtes au Coeur du Pèlerinage* (You are at the heart of the pilgrimage) and invites you to *admirer* (admire), *contempler* (contemplate) and to *prier* (pray). Millions have prayed to the Virgin over the centuries. I felt a definite presence and prayed too. At the back was a wall of candles, and I lit one for Maris and for the family back on the other side of the world. A crude sign written on a blackboard told me: *Cette Lumière porte vos prières et laisse le signe de vos espoirs, de vos désirs.* (This light conveys your prayers and leaves the sign of your hopes and wishes.) I thought of the light leading Maris along her current journey, whatever and wherever that is.

Many legends are associated with this Black Madonna. The chapel has a miraculous bell reputed to ring when a miracle occurs at sea and a sailor's life is saved. This Black Madonna seemed to specialise in saving the shipwrecked. A notice announced these miracles down the centuries and the chapel is adorned with ship models made by grateful sailors. Other buildings include the basilica Saint-Sauveur, the Saint-Michel chapel, the palace of the bishops (Palais des Eveques) and several chapels. As I stood at the entrance of Saint-Michel chapel, I was intrigued at the small space that these buildings had been squeezed into, all the time the cliff face towering above. Inside the basilica Saint-Sauveur, the interior walls were covered with inscriptions and paintings recalling the pilgrimages of famous persons – kings, bishops and nobles. A young man was playing a grand piano. Rather than sacred music, his piece sounded to me like Chopin's. A notice told me that a priest was always on hand for confessions, but I spotted none. Perhaps they were at lunch.

After a visit to one of the many cafes, I walked down the leafy path to the valley floor, crossed a small bridge and along the road for more spectacular views of the village. By now, the afternoon was fine and the sky was cloudless, which brought out the tourists by car and busloads. The Rue de la Couronnerie was a throng by the time I returned. I was happy that I had already visited the religious site known as the "Holy City" (another Jerusalem?). Instead, I climbed the Way of the Cross, starting at the First Station Jesus is Condemned to Death. The Stations of the Cross is a Catholic ritual commemorating the last day of Christ's life. It's a mini-pilgrimage, and through prayer and meditation, you move from Station to Station until the last Jesus is Laid in the Tomb, which in this instance was at the back of a cave. These Stations were very conducive to prayer. Even a non-believer would find them restful and beautiful, a delightful example of how nature has enhanced a man-made structure. It winds its way up the cliff face with a place to rest at each Station. The gradient is gentle, and at all times the Way is leafy and the trees are full of bird song. The sun filters its way through the canopy above, and the ground sloping down to the path is covered with ivy. At the top is a large iron cross (La Croix de Jerusalem) placed on a cairn of rocks by pilgrims in August 1887.

After dinner, I went for a brief walk along the cliff top and was in awe of the way in which floodlights added a new dimension of beauty to the valley.

My train did not depart until the afternoon, so I had plenty of time to walk around the top of the cliff to l'Hospitalet, once a place which welcomed and took care of the medieval pilgrims after their arduous journey into Rocamadour. After many weeks or even months, pilgrims could rest and be treated here for their injuries and diseases, hence the name Hospitalet. They could then complete the last part of their journey to the shrine of Notre Dame de Rocamadour only 700 metres. There was still 1268 kilometres to go to Santiago.

The view all the way back was just magnificent, overlooking the valley to the hills beyond, an appropriate way to wind up my visit. Houses above the stream, churches above the houses, rocks above the churches and a castle on the rocks. A medieval village clinging to the rocks, a great place of pilgrimage on the way to Santiago where people came to pray to the Black Madonna.

My curiosity led me to take this detour. Where does this curiosity lead me now? Perhaps a slight hunger to return one of these days, not as a tourist, but as a pilgrim? Coming back to this place and walking along the same path as the ancient pilgrims would bring home to me, as with all pilgrimages, that I was part of a continuum, linking past, present and future, an enlightenment that stirs me emotionally and spiritually. This same revelation stirs me when along the route I see in the dust the footprints of those who have walked just before me. I think of those millions who have followed the same path for over a thousand years. Each has left something of their essence, just as my footprints will for those who follow. If I return as a pilgrim to Rocamadour, I will be pursuing a sacred journey with gratitude for all that is.

It was a big weekend back at Bordeaux. My weekend, September 16th-17th, coincided with the *Journées Européennes du Patrimoine*, (European Heritage Days), an annual event celebrating cultural and heritage values when historic edifices not usually available to the public are open and entry to museums is free or at reduced prices. The first *Journées du Patrimoine* were held in France in 1984, and since then the idea has spread to 50 countries, allowing visitors to learn something of their common heritage, stimulate their interest and sensitise them to the richness and diversity of European culture. As a flow-on, it is hoped that the public, governments and decision-makers will be more aware of the necessity of protecting cultural heritage and be more tolerant of other cultures across Europe, one more step in the struggle against racism and xenophobia.

With these lofty ideals in mind, I set out to explore the diverse *patrimoine* as expressed in Bordeaux. So did many others judging by the milling crowds that had descended on the city. Volunteers were handing out pamphlets listing all the opportunities, far too many to visit in a weekend, so I wandered around with my map. I visited the Cathèdrale Saint-André, not in the same league as Chartres, but nevertheless a beautiful religious monument, unexpected and endearing, especially for its freestanding belltower, which I climbed up the narrow winding staircase to the top and was rewarded with a great view of the city and the river. The Basilique Saint-Seurin was just as awesome. Not as impressive from the outside but inside was quite beautiful with magnificent stained-glass windows. Its highlight was its 6th century crypt, which housed some sarcophagi from the period. The Basilique Saint-Michel was a gothic extravaganza. It, too, has a separate bell tower that tapers to form an elegant, ornately decorated spire, making it the tallest building in Bordeaux. In medieval times, pilgrims on their way to Compostelle made their devotions at these three churches. They continue to welcome them in the 21st century.

I visited La Maison de Pèlerin, a place of hospitality for pilgrims coming from Tours, Brittany or the British Isles. They were also open to the public with lots of displays about the Camino in their foyer. About eight of their people had gathered to talk to visitors, and they greeted me with exuberance when I told them I was a pilgrim taking a few days off the voie de Vézelay. They stamped my pilgrim's passport. I wandered through some of the city's beautiful public gardens, a contrast to the churches although I sensed they were just as sacred. I'm sure the good citizens of Bordeaux enjoyed their gardens – trees, beds of shrubbery, waterways complete with ducks and little arched bridges. One pecan tree had been given the award of *Arbre Remarkable de France*, in recognition of the municipality of Bordeaux for its care. I'm sure the award extended to the gardens as well, for they were a delight.

Bordeaux is famous for its wines. I know you are supposed to visit a vineyard and sample their wines. I visited none, not even a wine cellar. I took no cruises on the River Garonne although I enjoyed walking along its banks and admired the many restored buildings. I was happy that I had made this detour to Rocamadour and Bordeaux. I was happy with what I had seen – the *patrimoine* (heritage) inherent in both places, the wild surrounds of Rocamadour, the cultivated gardens and elegant buildings of Bordeaux.

I was ready to return to my pilgrimage.

*With my friends at La Maison du Pèlerin at Bordeaux*

*Rocamadour*

*Rocamadour from the cliff tops*

# 10.

*Above all, do not lose your desire to walk. Every day I walk myself into a state of well-being and walk away from every illness. I have walked myself into my best thoughts.*
Søren Kierkegaard

The day Monday September 18th was overcast, but at least it was not raining. I was happy to quit the soulless Ibis Budget Hotel and take the tram for the last time. While waiting with a coffee for my train, I heard an Aussie accent. A group of three, they lived in Sydney. We compared notes on our journeys. They seemed impressed with my experience. Walking through France had never occurred to them. They were content with tours and buses to take them around and saw a different world. We wished each other well on our travels and parted for our respective trains.

My destination was Mont de Marsan. Built on the confluence of two rivers, the Midou and Douze, it's very picturesque with promenade walks along the river where small waterfalls and adjacent buildings make for a tidy, attractive scene. After leaving the railway station, I made straight for the tourist office where the friendly and helpful girl gave me a map and directions to get to my accommodation, *Refuge de l'association des Amis de Saint-Jacques des Landes*. Outside the tourist office there was a great view along the river as well as an impressive statue of a diver about to plunge into the river below. (The French word for diver is *plongeur*). I found the refuge. A notice on the floor told me to go around the corner to the Asian supermarket for the key. On the way back I ran into Dick, the giant Dutchman whom I last saw at Périgueux 8 days previously. His greeting: *'I bet you didn't walk here.'* No doubt he had walked the 229 kilometres. He would have averaged about 29 kilometres per day, a pace that I could never have attained. I would have achieved about half his rate. This Dick would have known. Hence his surprise at seeing me just ahead of him. I was never sure of Dick's attitude towards me. Although very helpful, I thought he was intrigued perhaps that an old bloke in his eighties was pursuing the Camino on his own, difficult enough for younger pilgrims. Dick was young, fit, healthy, large, robust, self-assured and confident. His pace was twice that of mine.

Seven pilgrims stayed at the refuge that night – Dick, Carol, Christophe, Denise, Roland, Gilbert and me. I was pleased to be back with a Chemin family. Instead of feeding separately, we dined together on take-away pizzas. As always, sharing a meal breaks down the barriers. We were honourable companions who were gaining access to a truth that unites people. We learned each other's names and countries – French, Belgian, German and Dutch (and Australian!), shared our stories, opened up in conversation and sought to understand each other, to feel for each other and to listen. It was as if we were giving each other the gift of our presence. Nevertheless, I was pleased when the hospitalier, Dominique, opened the second dormitory. Dick decided to move from the bunk above me into the other room. Although he had shared his story, he would not have to share his snoring.

It had rained every day for the last two weeks, so I was hopeful of a fine day on my first day back walking. I bid farewell to my fellow pilgrims, for I expected they would get well ahead of me, particularly Dick who told me he was *'powering on'*. I met Roland and Denise on the way, and we shared a break at Benquet. Roland had a lot to say. Denise was quieter. They were both involved in youth work, and their generous nature made me feel they were well suited to their vocations. I walked through wooded areas, the Forêt des Landes. It felt good to be back walking. Walking has many benefits. It is 'man's best medicine', according to the ancient Hippocrates. It enhances well-being and is supposed to prevent dementia and decrease the dangers of Alzheimer's. It can be counteractive against heart-related illness or stroke. It can expand lung volume and increase the oxygen stream in the circulatory system. It enhances digestion, tones muscle, builds sturdier bones and muscles and relieves back pain. It can induce a calmer mind, wipe out tension, soothe your mind, elevate your spirits and help you to look at the world in a new light.

Such benefits, I'm afraid, did not prevent me from feeling weary after 19 kilometres of such an intensely healthy activity. The day's walking ended with a decent climb, and I was more than happy to find rest for the evening in Saint-Sever at the *Halte jacquaire Cloitre des Jacobins*. I was grateful, too, that no rain fell.

Saint-Sever was an important stage for the medieval pilgrims on the way to Compostelle. After the long passage through Landes and before the crossing of the Pyrénées to Roncevaux, the hospitality offered was appreciated. A reminder of this period is the abbey church of Saint-Sever, founded in the 11th century. It's been beautifully preserved and is an impressive example of the Romanesque style with its many stone carvings. Another is the Jacobin Museum which was the original Couvent de Jacobins, founded in the 13th century, and has had many uses down the centuries. Both buildings seemed to have survived the vicissitudes of the centuries – the Hundred Years War, the Wars of Revolution and the French Revolution, just to name a few.

My refuge was in the same complex of buildings as the Jacobin Museum. I was warmly greeted by the hospitalier, Philippe. He showed me my bed and left me to shower and rest. While I explored the town and the abbey church, I noticed Philippe driving a car that towed a trailer loaded with hay bales. Perhaps he's a farmer, I thought, doing a few jobs in between greeting pilgrims. Back at the refuge, other pilgrims had arrived. I had met Gilbert, Roland and Denise the previous evening. The others, particularly Dick, would have pressed on, regardless. My heart went out to Gilbert, who was young and German. He seemed depressed. When he said in halting English that he needed time and space, I let him be. He was having a bad trot. He needed solitude and wasn't interested in reaching out to his fellow pilgrims. On the other hand, he seemed to appreciate having us around if he did not have to interact. Perhaps our presence gave him hope for a release from his suffering. Roland and Denise were more open, and together we prepared our meals in the refuge's well-equipped kitchen, chatting about our days. While we were sitting down to our dinner, two girls arrived. Lise-Marie was Dutch, and Carmen, despite her Spanish name, was German. Here I found the reason for the hay bales. Carmen had a third companion, a donkey. When she rang ahead, Philippe welcomed her and her four-legged friend, and went out to acquire hay so that he could have as comfortable an evening as his mistress. Carmen had just settled him down in a corner of the cloister courtyard. His name was Prairie. I was intrigued. I had seen donkeys on the Camino but never had an opportunity to talk about them. Carmen told me she was an excellent horsewoman and worked on a farm. When she was thinking about the Chemin, she decided a donkey, rather than a horse, would be a good companion. Prairie was placid and easy to handle. She appreciated Philippe's warm welcome. Other places were not so keen on donkeys. She had started walking on her own, but she met her friend Lise-Marie a week ago; they clicked and decided to walk together.

In the morning I met Prairie. He was settled comfortably in his hay in a corner of the courtyard mushing on fodder, getting his nourishment for the day. Coincidentally, my guidebook Miam Miam Dodo had filled a blank page for that stage with an extract from a book by Jacques Clouteau who walked and talked with his little donkey Ferdinand several times across Europe. Jacques Clouteau is also the author of the guidebook. I imagined the conversations one could have with a little donkey and the likely responses, full of wise comments about the absurdities that humans get up to.

*Hello, little donkey. What are you up to today?*
*I don't know. I'm waiting for my mistress.*
*Your mistress?*
*Isn't that politically correct for you humans? Should I use the term master to cover both a man owner and a lady owner to avoid offending someone?*
*I'm sure you could say master or mistress.*
*Perhaps you should say carer or friend or companion.*

I visited the boulangerie just around the corner. A freshly baked baguette for breakfast was a perfect start for the day. I said goodbye to my new friend Prairie and hoped we would meet on the way.

I walked under a cloudless sky. I met Gilbert but he still needed his time and space, so I said no more than 'Bon Courage!' Although Hagetmau was only 15 kilometres, I was tired enough by the time I arrived in town. I was making for the

*Relais de Saint-Jacques*, but I found the place closed and a notice on the gate told me to *'aller a la cité verte'* for the key. *La cité verte* was on the other side of town, which involved a couple of extra kilometres of walking. It turned out to be a sports complex, complete with gymnasium and swimming pool. An athletic carnival was in progress, children were in sports uniform and teachers/coaches issuing orders in loud voices. At the same time, building work was in progress that required negotiation around the scaffolding. I tried a number of doors, which attracted a security guard's attention. He directed me to the swimming pool's reception, which would have been an obvious place to start. Armed with the key, I walked across town back to the *Relais de Saint-Jacques*, somewhat irritated with the thought that there could have been an easier method to collect the key.

That evening, I shared the refuge with Roland and Denise, Gilbert, Joseph and Remo. We didn't talk much, but I was pleased to have their presence. I still had my Camino family of sorts. I walked back into town to have dinner at a pizza restaurant. The waitress quizzed me about my background. I told her I was a pilgrim. She guessed I was not French from my accent, thought I was German and was impressed that I came from Australia and spoke French. I find that people reach out to you if you know their language. I liked this pizza place. The people were welcoming and friendly. The pizza wasn't bad either.

The next day, Tuesday September 21st, presented a problem. The *Refuge pèlerin municipal* at Beyries was closed. A pity because Beyries was only 12 kilometres, a nice walk. The next place for accommodation was Orthez, a distance of 30 kilometres, too far in one day. The suggestion came, I'm not sure from where, was to catch the bus to Amou, a village a few kilometres away, and to walk from there to Orthez, about 15 kilometres. That seemed much easier to handle, so while the

## 10.

others decided to walk directly to Orthez, I took the bus. After many stops in small hamlets, I arrived in Amou late morning.

The walk to Orthez was comparatively easy; the most difficult task for the day was finding the Office de Tourisme where I could get the key for the *Halte jacquaire Hôtel de la Lune*. Just around the corner, the refuge was unremarkable from the street. The door was closed and looked like the entrance to a derelict house, but once through, you entered a charming courtyard lined with ancient walls, outdoor furniture, flower beds and a set of stone steps leading up to a tower. A beautiful carving of a pilgrim with shell graced a corner. A notice proclaims the Hôtel de la Lune as one of finest examples of the town's patrimoine. It's considered a remarkable example of a fortified house of the 13th century made more comfortable by refitting in the 15th century. You have to climb the steps to the door of the tower, up spiral stairs to the second story, but once inside you found a comfortable space with room for six in two bedrooms. Roland and Denise had already arrived and were resting. Soon after, the hospitalier arrived. Jacques announced he was 83, took our money and pointed out the well-equipped kitchen. He was expecting three more and was impatient they hadn't arrived. He was a year younger than me but seemed much older. Perhaps, he saw himself as the king pin, needing to take great care of his resources, particularly his time. He announced he'd be back about 7 pm. Gilbert and two girls arrived. They kept to themselves.

Shortly after, a local turned up. Guy had been walking the Chemin and was back home ready to start work on the next day. He was hoping to get a final stamp (*tampon*) on his credencial. I found it for him. He was ready for a chat about his experience and sad it had come to an end. I listened to his stories.

I cooked an omelette for myself and had dinner with Denise and Roland. They were still quiet, but we communicated well. Denise was keen to get copies of my books, but I had to explain they hadn't been translated to French. Perhaps one of these days! They were planning to take two days off the Chemin to visit friends in Oloron-Sainte-Marie. I told them I had passed through Oloron-Sainte-Marie and took a rest day there back in 2013. I realised just how close I was to the Chemin d'Arles and that I was not that far from the junction where the French Chemin routes join together as they move into Spain.

I was intrigued at the gîte's parsimonious approach to toilet paper. A notice told us to use two sheets. There was only one half used roll, and I could find no spares. With six people the toilet paper soon ran out. Fortunately, I always stuff a few sheets into my back pocket for emergencies, and this was one. I heard Gilbert pleading from the toilet, and I was able to save him from disaster. I wondered if toilet paper was part of Jacques's regime. I'm sure he would have disapproved of its profligate use. I had visions of him issuing one sheet at a time and making us sign.

In the morning, I descended into the courtyard and before I departed through the dilapidated door, I looked back to admire this fine example of how history had been adapted to meet the needs of the present. Orthez had always been an important stage on the Chemin de Saint Jacques de Compostelle, and still is. Heavy rain delayed my departure in the morning, so I took shelter for an hour with a coffee in a bar around the corner. Eventually, the rain eased, and I ventured out into the elements to make my way. I realised I'd left my pacer poles behind at the bar, so back I hurried. Fortunately, the proprietor had found them and put them aside to await my return. I told him how grateful I was to the local people who look after their pilgrims.

## 10.

Despite the short distance (only ten kilometres), I found the going tough, for I had moved into a series of rolling hills, a prelude to the foothills of the Pyrénées. The rain cleared, but the day was overcast. My destination was L'Hôpital-d'Orion, and the *Gîte Trescoigt* was about one kilometre short of the village. I arrived about 2 p.m. No one was about, so I waited on the patio and had time to look around. The garden was well maintained, and the house was surrounded by farmland – a calm country setting with herds of cows peacefully grazing, the cackle of chooks coming from a hen house behind the house, an elaborate dog kennel, but no dog. I admired a tiled emblem by the wall next to the front door – a brilliant orange multi-rayed sun against a blue sun with the words in handwriting in the corner *'Chez Mireille'*. Mireille loved her house and looked after it.

About 3 p.m. a car pulled into the driveway. Mme Mireille Fauve was warm and welcoming and dressed in oranges and blues, just as colourful as her house. She showed me into the gîte, fresh and modern-looking with crystal chandeliers and different floral wallpaper in each room – two bedrooms and a sitting room. She returned to her part of the house, and I saw her no more that day. I was the only guest. The wallpaper in my bedroom was apricot with bunches of lavender. A nude in an elaborate gilded frame hung on the wall. She was young and innocent, reclining on a marble bench in a garden, fan gently hanging from her hand and a pink sheet draped strategically across her lower body. I liked my nude. I wondered if she was a younger version of my host, but the colouring was different. Mireille was dark while this one was fair; also, the painting suggested to me the Romantic idealised style, popular in France in the 19th century. I thought of a name for her, Chloe, after the famous nude in Young and Jackson's, the pub opposite Flinders Street Railway Station in Melbourne. She'd been there since 1909 and originally came from Paris. There was a nude in the other bedroom, but I liked mine more.

In the morning Mireille sat down with me for a chat over breakfast. She enjoyed her lifestyle and did not feel lonely as she had many guests, pilgrims and others, from all parts. She bought the house only a few years ago and had it completely refurbished. I asked about the dog kennel. She told me her dog had been killed by a neighbour, and she was not yet ready for a replacement. I did not ask for details, as I could feel the loss was still hurting. Outside, she explained that the tiled emblem of the sun had been designed by a friend. She stood at the gate to say goodbye as I wandered down the lane to L'Hôpital-d'Orion.

Saturday morning was beautiful with just a hint of mist hanging over the fields, which the sun would soon dismiss. A few cows paused in their grazing to look at me, a stranger in their land. I seemed to have the world to myself. This was a day made for walking. My spirit felt refreshed; my heart was full of hope. Hope has been my constant companion in all my Camino wanderings. How often have I been lost or unclear where the day would end! I always had the hope that things would turn out well, and they did, although not always in the way I expected. Where would I be without hope? I was ready to embrace whatever came my way.

It did not take long to reach L'Hôpital-d'Orion. The contrast between the town of yesteryear and that of today is striking. As a major stopping point on the Chemin de Saint-Jacques, there were numerous facilities. The hospital no longer exists. Today calm and peace descend on the church and a statue of a pilgrim. Mireille had no tampon (stamp) and thought I might find one at the church, but although there was a table with welcoming notices, a stamp pad, journal and pen, I couldn't find the stamp.

## 10.

I covered about 14 kilometres in a land of rolling hills with constant ascents and descents. The going was tough, but the variety and changing scene helped me to see deeply, to hear attentively and to feel the beauty and sacredness of creation in my heart and soul. On the flats the path was muddy, and I had to work my way around to find firmer ground. The ground was covered with a carpet of moss and acorns, still in their furry casings; the sweetish smell of rotting leaves reminding me I was walking in autumn. The small creeks were crossed by ancient stone bridges. The water rippled softly across the stones. On the top of one rise, a row of fruit trees, mostly plums, bordered the path. The notice announced that they had been planted by *Les Amis du Saint-Jacques Pyrénées-Atlantique* in the Jubilee year of 2010.

The highlight of my day was a wedding. As I approached the small village of Andrein, I could see a noisy crowd dressed in their best emerging from the Salle Communale, the women shouting and laughing, wobbling on their high heels, hanging onto their hats as they threw confetti over the couple, Benoit Sarrat and Sophie Allende (according to the banns posted on the notice board). I found a seat in a small sunny park to eat my lunch and watch the congratulations. The men drifted off and returned with their vehicles. Everyone moved on to the reception, and I was left alone in the silence while I watched the confetti stirred by the wind drifting around the paved area outside the Salle Communale, large red and white circular pieces of paper, much larger than Australian confetti.

I approached Sauveterre-de-Béarn through fields of maize. Maize, according to my guide book, plays an important role in the region's economy. Perched on a gentle promontory above the rushing waters of Gave d'Oloron, this medieval town is blessed with both a remarkable architectural heritage and a wonderful natural environment. The hardest part of the day was left until last; in order to reach the town, I had to climb up a series of tough steps to the terrace outside the church of St André, but my reward was a beautiful view of the surrounding verdant country that I had just traversed and overlooked by the Pyrénées. I could see that the town would attract a range of visitors, those who loved the natural environment for its canoeing, rafting, fishing and hiking, and those attracted by its heritage. Once I had rested, I soaked up the medieval ambience. I entered the fortified church built in the 12th and 13th centuries, admired its tympanum and carved capitals and offered thanks that I had arrived. No opportunity to light a candle for Maris, sadly. Then began my search for my place for the night. The *Maison de la tour* was easy to find, just down rue Léon Bernard from the church, along a street of medieval buildings. I was greeted by my host, Georgina Bishop, an English lady, who led me through a shop front into her home. Georgina told me her story. She had never visited Australia but travelled to New Zealand for family. She had four children and 11 grandchildren, one of whom was staying with her. Georgina showed me my room, very large, big enough to turn into a self-contained flat. The furnishing was old style, relics of a former generation, plain but homely and comfortable. She left me in the house to go out. I left shortly after to explore the town. Being Saturday night, I expected more eateries to be open, but I found a pizza place around the corner. They only had Lambrusco wine, which I found too sweet for my palate.

    I was weary and I slept through the night waking at 6:30 a.m. Georgina was going away for two days, so she gave me some ham, bread and hard-boiled eggs, which I accepted gratefully. I had not far to finish my walking, about 45 kilometres to Saint-Jean-Pied-de-Port. Sunday morning, I descended another set of steps into the valley. At the Legend Bridge (*Pont de la Legende*) I looked back to admire the town profile, a harmonious melange of monuments and greenery. During medieval times, Sauveterre-de-Béarn was not only a stronghold protecting the independent Earldom of Béarn from its Spanish neighbour but also a safe place for pilgrims on the way to Compostelle. The bridge was built in the 13th century, fortified to protect the town. It is called Legend Bridge because it is linked to the legend of the judgement of the Viscountess Sancie who was thrown into the cold turbulent river, accused of baby killing. Despite her hands being tied, she survived the ordeal and was declared innocent.

I was now in the Béarn, and soon I would be moving into Basque country. Climbing was steady, but the day was fine and pleasant. Another day made for walking! I was passing through rich agricultural land devoted largely to maize. Originally from the New World, it was at first cultivated in Spain but spread to other regions. Both animals and humans consume the plant, and it has an extensive use as feed in the dry summer. The plant needs plenty of water, which presents a challenge in drier times.

At Osserain I paused to read a notice in several languages.

*Osserain is a symbol of the friendship and understanding between the Basque country and the Béarn. The bridge at Osserain which spans the river Saison brought the two communities together. A large number of pilgrims crossed it. On both banks there was a refuge and a church.*

I stopped for my lunch in the shade of a church at Suhast. While I ate Georgina's bread, ham and eggs, I watched a farmer harvesting his maize in an adjacent field. The sun was hot, so I moved myself and my pack to remain in the shade. Two pilgrims passed by but did not pause in the churchyard. I met them later. We walked together through Saint-Palais. They were heading for the *Maison Franciscaine* run by the *Association des Amis de Saint-Jacques des Pyrénées-Atlantiques*, while I was aiming for a private gîte, *Gîte Soretena* owned by Ludovic Duployé. The gîte was surprisingly easy to find. I came to a busy street, and there it was on the opposite side. I knocked on a big solid door and out came Ludovic, warm and welcoming. Dark solid wood was everywhere. I gained the impression that Ludovic loved his house. He used to work for the Paris Opera on lighting but needed a change. As soon as he and his wife Isabel saw this early 19th century house, they had to have it.

I spent a stimulating evening with this couple. I was the only guest for dinner although there were other residents, shadowy people whom I did not meet. Isabel retired early as she had to travel 160 kilometres each Monday morning for her work at a school. She was away for the week and returned home Friday evening. Ludovic was the house husband. He was a former pilgrim to Santiago and enjoyed this part of his life, meeting and providing shelter to fellow pilgrims, receiving through them the joy and blessing of giving. I spoke about the camaraderie among pilgrims, and he spoke about *'collective intelligence'*, a concept developed by Frederick Nietzsche, a German philosopher. It's the capacity of humans to engage in intellectual cooperation in order to create, innovate and invent. We don't travel alone. We meet up with others who are also travelling along the path of change. One can learn a lot from each other and together carry more learning experiences. Over a glass or two (or three) of Ludovic's wines, we discussed these ideas. In order to survive, we need to work with each other and pitch our ideas in together. It was a good, intellectually challenging night that I enjoyed thoroughly – a pity that there weren't more of them on this Camino journey.

## 10.

The night was full of creaks and strains as if the house had many memories that its ghosts whispered to each other in the darkness. Isabel had left early, and I shared breakfast with Ludovic. A pity I would probably never see him again, as I enjoyed and felt stimulated by his company. He left me to open his small shop in a corner of his building. I wasn't sure of its merchandise, but it seemed to be crystals and organic produce. I let myself out through his solid front door and continued on my way. At the edge of town, I came across the *Maison Franciscaine*, and I wondered how the two pilgrims I met the day before had enjoyed their evening.

The day was hard yakka, a series of solid climbs. I was in the beautiful rolling Basque country, a patchwork of intensely green fields and forests, white houses with orange roofs, and sheep. I walked along paths surrounded by hills and many times I hoped that the path would stay on the flat, but it always took off up the steep inclines. At one stage, I spied a flock of sheep way up there at what seemed a long distance. *'I hope I don't have to climb all the way up there,'* I thought. Sure enough, I eventually passed those creatures, peacefully grazing. At least, I could look back and down to admire the beautiful countryside I had passed through. This is a region where 250 days of rain is expected each year. It wasn't raining at the moment, but it pelted down later in the day.

The morning was memorable for a plantation of trees lined the walk up one of those inclines. Those who planted these trees had gone to a lot of trouble to educate the walkers passing by. A notice in French and Basque told their intentions:

*On our earth, everything stands together. Without trees there is no life, no humans and no walkers.*

*Along this path they are going to guide you.*

*But let's begin by recognising and naming them before approaching their immense mysteries.*

Walking on a beautiful carpet of leaves, twigs and acorns, I came to the next notice:

*The fine oaks of this path with their network of branches as immense above as the roots below will be here for dozens of years to come in company with their brother trees. No sooner do they aspire to this long-term life are they reborn in a wine barrel or in the framework of a great country house.*

Along the path I found myself in good company:

*All is good in the chestnut community the bark for tanning skins the hard wood for heating or the floor and the fruit of "the bread tree"(l'arbre á pain) to carry in one's basket*

Next a little piece of history!

*The "robinier" or locust tree is almost a native of Navarre. It was Jean Robin, botanist, of Henri IV, king of France and Navarre and thus of Saint-Palais, who introduced it under his reign. He realised its qualities; rot-proof and water resistant. But the "robinier" is also a magnificent gourmand dream for its perfumed fritter-like flowers.*

A profusion of labels in French and Basque were attached to trees and shrub without poetic descriptions, (which my translation has done no justice), such as ash, dogwood, blackthorn, flowering cherry, hawthorn, dog rose, wild cherry, larisco pine.

## 10.

Finally, a lesson in geology completed the morning with a notice on an embankment of rock;

*The 'Flysch' is a sedimentary rock formed at the bottom of oceans. It emerged, far above the waves, when the Pyrénées rose up. Thus have marine sands become rocks on this hill.*

Concealed in this path was a spiritual lesson, as well as a blessing that I had learned that lesson. So involving was the path that I almost, but not quite, forgot its steep incline. Reading the notices gave me a chance for frequent breathers, and eventually, I reached the top and with a sigh of thankful relief, descended into the valley below, equally as beautiful as the ones I had passed.

My next inspiration was a vision. I can now say that I have seen the *'Black Stump'*, not in outback Australia, but in southwest France. I emerged out of the wooden area and came across a field. Inside a small enclosure were three tall black stumps set among a few rocks. The notice said it was *'Le Reflet du Ciel'* (reflections of the sky) by sculptor Christian Lapie, fashioned from the one oak tree and erected on 11th July 2013. The setting was magnificent with the rolling green Basque hills in the foreground and the grand Pyrénées on the horizon. I had to imagine what this monument would be like against a clear blue sky. This day the sky was grey with clouds, and rain was imminent. Amazing how the sky and all its changes can inspire sculptures, poems and songs! Erected on the historical Chemin de Saint-Jacques, the monument had the potential to inspire, to make one pause, to reflect, to ponder on the beauty of creation. Another spiritual lesson and blessing.

Just down the hill was another monument, much smaller, known as the Stèle de Gibraltar. Nothing to do with the British enclave in the south of Spain, the name is derived from a Basque word. A place of significance because here the pilgrimage routes from Paris, Vézelay and Le Puy meet. I was here in 2010 on my pilgrimage from Le Puy-en-Velay. I remember taking a photo after another pilgrim obligingly removed his pack. I could imagine the pilgrims of old from all parts of France merging here, saying 'G'day' (or the medieval equivalent) and continuing together on their march to Compostelle.

I remembered the long hill along a track named the *Chemin de Procession*. It looked no different to when I saw it seven years previously. The rain that had been threatening all day fell, and I scrambled to don my poncho. Looking back through the misty veil of rain, I noticed other pilgrims, in singles and in groups, and I guessed they had come from Le Puy along the route known as the Via Podiensis. I also noticed two figures with a donkey. I guessed they were Carmen, Lise-Marie and Prairie. I paused to allow them to catch up. They recognised me and greeted me like an old friend. Such is the power of the Camino! They were making slow progress, as fast as Prairie would allow. He had added a blue tarp to his back to cover the packs but he looked content. The girls told me they preferred to stay on farms, as they had more chance of getting proper care for Prairie than in the towns. They told me they had arrived late at the *Maison Franciscaine* back at Saint-Palais. They were refused at first but were admitted reluctantly.

At the top of the hill was the Chapel de Soyarza. I recognised this building from my earlier visit, a modern building (1894) by the standards of these parts, replacing a much older oratory dedicated to Notre Dame. It provided a rest area and a welcome shelter from the rain. Six pilgrims were sheltering too. They had begun their journey along the Via Podiensis and were interested in my experience of coming from Vézelay. We

## 10.

ate our lunch together, told stories and signed the book. An Australian couple had signed earlier that day.

Between the Stèle de Gibraltar and my refuge for the night, I met more pilgrims than my whole route. The afternoon involved more solid ascents and descents and dodging heavy showers. I was not surprised to pass a number of pilgrim refuges in Ostabat, being the meeting point of a number of pilgrim routes to Santiago. I chose to pass through the town, finding shelter under the eaves, to a farm on the other side. *Gîte-d'étape-Chambre d'hôtes-Repas, Ferme Gaineko-Etxea* run by Lucie and Beňat Eyharts, was up the final steep incline for the day. This gîte attracted me because their entry in the guide book added *'chants basques au repas' (basque singing over dinner)*. It could be a fun night.

I was disappointed. The welcome was inadequate. The woman was abrupt and cold, as severe as a cranky schoolteacher addressing her dumb students. Was she suffering burnout, having managed so many pilgrims over the season and looking forward to a break with the approaching winter? Her welcome was not the worst I'd received; she did not tap a pencil at me. She showed me to a room with three beds. For a while, I thought I would be on my own but two French ladies joined me. We were polite and respectful to each other, but I didn't get to know them, not even their names. The largest group so far, 25 sat down to dinner. The meal was very good, and later Beňat appeared in a Beret Basque and Pay Basque T-shirt and did his Basque singing in a strong penetrating voice. I was not comfortable; everything I felt was managed, and the evening to me lacked spontaneity. Beňat invited others to sing, but no one except me volunteered. I sang 'Waltzing Matilda', but I felt bad vibes as if it wasn't quite what was wanted. The people were subdued. Perhaps everyone had been scolded when they arrived and weren't game to stick out their necks. Only silly Noël! The meal was structured and ran to a strict timetable like a boarding school; no lingering over the table when the meal was finished. A bit of a damp squib. The evening made me realise the gift I received many times from other hosts for whom the needs of their pilgrims, rather than their own convenience, were in the forefront, and their genuine welcome came from the heart

However, a large community room was available and I met Brian, an American who lived in Germany. He was ex-navy and was walking to Santiago in his retirement.

The next day, the walking was tough enough with lots of small rises rather than steep hills. The rolling countryside was spectacular, the fields an intense green dotted with grazing sheep with red dye brands. The walkers were many, and they came in waves, a contrast to the Voie de Vézelay. The larger the numbers the more impersonal the relationships – no more than a greeting, if that. A wayside farm invited the pilgrim to pause, a place to sit and a stall with items of food to sample. A small pup belonging to the farm made a nuisance of itself and ran among the resting pilgrims wanting to play and to jump. It bit me on the arm and drew blood; the second time I had to find a band aid in my first aid kit. If a rose thorn and a nip on the arm by a playful pup were my only injuries, I had done well.

I was looking forward to my place of rest because I had stayed there 7 years previously. My last night on the road I went upmarket at the *Chambre et table d'hôtes Ferme Etxekonia* at Bussunarits. Mayie was my host, a warm, exuberant and outgoing lady. At that time, I was the only guest and we lingered long over the meal. I learnt so much about the Basque language and culture. Mayie's daughter was also present. I remembered her name as Celeste, but actually it's Celine. She has Down's Syndrome and was 30 years old. At first, I heard her singing, and she sounded like a small child. She talked a lot and called me *'Pèlerin'* (pilgrim). Mayie spoke of the difficulties of caring for a child with disabilities. I remember the strong bond of love that existed between mother and child, which I found so touching.

I knew exactly where to find *Ferme Etxekonia* just off the route. Mayie greeted me, and when I reminded her that I had stayed with her 7 years previously and was keen to stay again, she gave me a huge hug and introduced me to the two other guests as *'a dear old friend'*. Joseph and Danielle were a couple from Lyon. They were not pilgrims but were staying for a few nights and doing some walking in the surrounding Basque hills. We had a pleasant evening over dinner. So much seemed the same, but what was different was the change in Celine, now 37 years old. In contrast, she was withdrawn and had nothing to say. She seemed to have regressed and deteriorated. What had not changed was Mayie's strong love. *'Celine is my guardian angel,'* she said. To Mayie, Celine was no burden, but a gift. We had many hugs and photos in the morning and a final farewell from Mayie to her *'old friend'*. *'Please come back again.'* Last time, Celine gave me a hug and a kiss on both cheeks, but this time, she was not interested. I was sad for her and her mother. I wondered what the future might hold.

To Mayie, Celine was no burden, but a blessing. I received as spiritual a lesson as any in the Ferme Etxekonia. All the tribulations of the Camino, the killer hills, the mud, the intolerant hosts, the aching body, the confusion of being lost, the heat waves, pelting rain, snoring roommates, etc. are blessings, gifts that offer enlightenment and enable me with gratitude to learn more about myself. Trying times are not torments but chances to stretch myself, to press on, regardless. Such trials will pass when I finish walking, but Mayie will always have her burden (gift, blessing). She, too, will press on, regardless. As I passed through the front gate, I was certain that the time that I passed with Mayie and Celine was sacred and that I had arrived at a destination, almost as if I'd had a genuine personal encounter with God. The most important lesson that Mayie and Celine taught me was humility and acceptance. Accept one's burdens and regard them as gifts and blessings. Even Maris's death has brought me opportunities, which I would never have received otherwise. It came home to me that the meaning of a pilgrimage lies not in a moment of arrival but in the journey itself where every sacred step reveals a piece of the answer being sought.

Just as I returned to the route, eight walkers appeared. The same pattern continued all the way to Saint-Jean-Pied-de-Port as wave after wave of pilgrims passed. I had only seven kilometres. I paused at the chapel of Saint Mary-Madelaine where I lit a last candle and gave thanks that I was almost there. That candle was like a lamp that shone forth from all the accumulated wisdom of pilgrims who had walked the path before me. In no time, I was entering Saint Jean-Pied-de-Port through the familiar Porte Saint-Jacques at the top of the cobbled Rue de la Citadelle. This was my third visit. As before, I stopped at the pilgrim information office (*Accueil Pèlerin de l'Association des Amis de Saint-Jacques des Pyrénées Atlantiques*) and had my credential stamped for the last time. I arrived at a lull because the office is usually full of pilgrims about to start for Santiago and keen to get as much information as possible.

There is plenty of pilgrim accommodation in St-Jean-Pied-de-Port. Twenty-five places were listed in my guide book. I chose Chambre d'hôtes Errecaldia because the owner's name was Tim Proctor which sounded English to me. He was. I had an hour or so to wait until the Chambre d'hôtes was open, time to reflect as I sat on the wall admiring the view of the town below and the mountains above, enticing the pilgrim to continue. Would this be my last Camino? I had already visited Santiago twice. I had set out from Saint-Jean in 2011 and was unlikely to cover the same ground. If I returned to the Camino, it would be along another route. Perhaps the Voie de Vézelay was waiting to be completed, the gap between Périgueux and Mont de Marsan. On the other hand, some health problems were waiting back home as well as their treatment, which I'd delayed in order to walk this Camino. Besides, at the age of 84, I was on the home run of my life span. My future was in God's hands. I felt content with that thought. I had done pretty well to get this far.

This Camino had been different from the other four because I'd slowed down and walked far less each day. Conscious of my age, I used pacer poles and regularly caught a taxi or bus when it fitted into my schedule. I was far more tolerant of those who do the Camino the 'easier' way, far more understanding of those who believe their level of fitness or confidence prevents them from doing their pilgrimage in the 'hardcore' style.

This Camino was also different because there were far fewer pilgrims. I spent more nights on my own, which made me appreciate those evenings when I had company. I also saw differences in the attitude of the locals. Many people including children greeted me, asked me if I was walking towards Compostelle and wished me *'Bonne Continuation'* or *'Bon Courage'*. I felt the people were country folk just like those in my hometown. Such a contrast from the big cities where suspicion, mistrust, or at best, indifference are the norm.

Eventually, my host Tim arrived and let me in. My room had an extensive view of the surrounding valley, and each morning the town would slowly rise out of the mist. I spent two days exploring and preparing myself to return home. I bought a box at the post office and sent back my boots to Australia plus a few souvenirs for the family. I had no town clothes. I didn't want to spend 50 euros plus on a shirt, so I visited the local op. shop run by *Secours Catholique* and paid 3 euros for three shirts. The town was busy with pilgrims with backpacks streaming back and forth. I hoped those about to start for the first time would gain as much from the Camino experience as I did.

I met other pilgrims at breakfast and in restaurants. Brent and Brendon were Americans and were about to walk the Camino for the second time. Peter and Irene were Canadian, formerly South Africans, and were finishing at St-Jean-Pied-de-Port. They had joined a group with a support bus. Their baggage was carried and a picnic including wine was supplied each day. They did their Camino the 'smart' way – at ease and in comfort. '*Doesn't everybody?*' I felt sorry for Peter and Irene. All risk had been removed. To me the Camino involves risk, and it is how we accept those risks and the change that results that colour our Camino experience. I am drawn to a quote in the June 2017 Australian Friends of the Camino newsletter, which I read when I returned home:

> *But risks must be taken because the greatest hazard in life is to risk nothing. The person who risks nothing does nothing, has nothing, is nothing. He may avoid suffering and sorrow. But he cannot learn, feel, change, grow or live. Chained by his servitude he is a slave who has forfeited all freedom. Only a person who risks is free.*

I joined a table in a restaurant with two Brazilians, (John and Aura), a Columbian and an American. I didn't get their names but it didn't matter. We discussed the 'spirituality' of the Camino and how everyone interprets its meaning according to their own background and beliefs. I was reminded of the reason I began walking the Camino in the first place – to find meaning and structure following the suicide of my wife Maris. I think this Camino has seen me advance a little more along my road of grieving. As far as I can see, my grief for Maris will never truly end. It has become softer and gentler over time, although occasionally it sharpens up. My grieving will last as my love for Maris does – I reckon forever. She accompanied me every step of the way, and I lit candles for her at every opportunity. Their light allowed the occasional heavy fog to recede. My Camino was an ebb and flow, like a constant dance of sadness and joy, of pain and love.

*Prairie, Carmen and Lise-Marie on the Chemin de Procession*

Denise, Roland and Noël at Halte Jacquaire Hôtel de la Lune, Orthez

Chez Mireille near L'Hôpital-d'Orion

2019

**Act VI**

Voie de Vézelay
Via Gebennensis

## 11.

*'Many believe a pilgrimage is about going away, but it isn't; it is about coming home. Those who choose to go on a pilgrimage have already gone away from themselves; and now set out in a longing to journey back to who they are.'*
L.M. Browning

The decision to return to the Camino was made as I was driving back to Jindabyne from a visit to my cardiologist in Canberra. He knew of my interest in long distance walking. He, himself, was a cyclist and so was his practice partner. He knew something of the manner in which a passion can drag you back with a force like gravity. All wired up, I did the stress test. The incline increased, and so did the speed. It went on and on. *'Just one more minute,'* he said as I was getting near the point where I'd had enough. After examining the results, he said, *'You can pack your bags.'*

Up to that moment, I had no plans. I'd returned to Australia from my fifth Camino in October 2017, content that I had done well, walking in my late 70s and early 80s. The Camino was never far from my mind. I travelled around Australia talking about my Camino spiritual journey and my books. I enjoyed these talks because I had a message to convey, one of resilience and not allowing age to get in the way. These tours were a wonderful means of seeing the country and of meeting the people. They were full of questions and in many cases wanted me to keep going when time ran out.

A common question was: *'When's your next Camino?'* I was vague: *'Perhaps!'* *'One of these days!'* I felt the yearning to resume the pilgrim spirit, but in my 86th year, how would my body handle another. Early in 2018, I was a guest for 8 weeks of the Radiation Oncology Department of Canberra Hospital receiving a daily treatment. I knew about the likelihood of a diagnosis before I left Australia in 2017, but told the specialist, if treatment was necessary, it would have to wait. He didn't seem too fussed about the delay.

Now that my cardiologist was giving me the green light, I thought seriously about a sixth Camino, the selection of a route and what else I could fit into another visit to Europe. A fitting start, I thought, was to fill the gap in the voie de Vézelay by walking between Périgueux and Mont de Marsan, a job unfinished. I considered other possibilities in the east of France, routes less well-travelled – la voie des Piémonts, between Montpellier and Saint-Jean-Pied-de-Port; Le Chemin de Saint-Gilles between Le Puy-en-Velay and Saint-Gilles; la voie de Rocamadour between Figeac and Cahors. One thing was sure; whatever path I selected, it would be rigorous. I would be stepping out of my comfort zone, complete with backpack, and walking long distances. In the end, I chose the Via Gebennensis from Geneva to le Puy-en-Velay, which is where I began this Camino caper. I'd be returning to where I started.

I had already resumed gym work and my regular walking. Once upon a time, the recommendation to cancer patients was to rest after treatment, but nowadays, exercise is prescribed. I would have resumed my fitness routines anyway, whatever was suggested. The pilgrimage begins when you start the planning. In your mind, you have already begun. I wasn't sure of my destination, except that it would be a spiritual or inner site rather than a geographical place. The journey would be one of risk and renewal; a journey without purpose or challenge would have no meaning. My journey would be an act of thanks for coming so far in spite of heart conditions, cancer and age.

Not only is physical preparation necessary, you have to prepare the heart and mind as well, and to relish the seeking of adventure. My mind raced over old slogans to get my heart excited: *Carpe diem (seize the day), Make every day an adventure, Embrace the day with gusto, Take refuge in the present moment.* I was preparing myself to take risks because I was embarking on a journey of awakening, a path of inquiry and self-discovery. 'May the Lord comfort and disturb me.' I was seeking to embrace the pilgrim spirit, however you might define it.

> 'To feel the pull, the draw, the interior attraction, and to want to follow it, even if it has no name still, that is "the pilgrim spirit".' – Kevin A. Codd

In the meantime, my old friend Fr. Peter McGrath died. I attended his funeral in Sydney at my old parish church, St Anthony-in-the-Fields at Terry Hills along with 900 others. He had a great influence on my spiritual development, and his presence in my life has been one of my greatest gifts. He was such a larrikin that you never quite knew what he was likely to do next, but I learned so much from his humility, love and compassion for people. His unholy style of communication broke down barriers, and he raised awareness of the need for friendship, support and love. His great gift to the world was the founding of the Family Group Movement, which spread through many Australian parishes of all denominations and the world. Peter's legacy will live on in that he has lit a flame of love and faith that will continue to brighten the lives of those who suffer the pain of isolation and exclusion. Peter had a special bond with Maris because he, too, had his own demons that sometimes were very busy and created considerable anguish and self-doubt. I valued his support after her death. Up to then, I think that much of my inspiration came from the head; I was too *'intellectual'*. Now, it comes from the heart, and I believe Peter saw that change in me. I think I felt emotions more deeply or allowed their expression more openly. Certainly, every word of my memoir detailing my first years of grieving came from the heart. I was privileged that Peter wrote a forward. His message *'what is in the heart that matters'* hopefully will continue to inspire me and all those who have known him.

My pilgrimage really began when I left my home in the mountains. Before going overseas, I visited my family. I said goodbye to my daughter Jacinta and grandson Brody, travelled to Melbourne to see son Tim and his wife Annika, my brother Tom and wife Robyn. Like a pilgrimage into the past, I visited our first home in Notting Hill; it's been replaced by an ugly McMansion. The adjacent small group of shops is in decay, but the preschool that Maris helped to found is flourishing. I called into my old primary school St Francis Xavier in Box Hill where Vera, one of the office staff, showed me around. It was a small school of combined grades in three classrooms but now 14. About 300 metres from the school was my parents' home where I lived for nearly 30 years; it's now six townhouses. I was happy to quit Melbourne; its reputation of Australia's most congested city was upheld. I thought Sydney was bad enough. Since living in the bush, I've developed an aversion to their demented traffic, I'm afraid.

I left my car at Angela's in Sydney. On the 506 bus on the way to the airport, the driver started just as I found my seat, and somehow, I twisted my knee. I nursed the pain, annoyed that I may have damaged myself before I'd even started. I flew to Brisbane and stayed with my sister Maria. Then on to Rockhampton to see my son Stephen, his wife Anthea and children Abigail, Oscarine, Augustine and Thaddeus. Those four grandchildren were born after Maris died. In fact, the marriage followed her funeral by two days. They missed out on their grandmother, and their grandmother missed out on them. In the 3 days of my visit those kids were so excited to see their Pa; they would not let me out of their sight. The competition for my attention was intense. I lost count of the number of games of draughts I played. My grandchildren had a lot to teach me, especially to embrace life with gusto.

My whirlwind tour of the family was as important a part of my pilgrimage as any. Nothing surpasses the importance of family. My family, spread from Melbourne in the south to Rockhampton in the tropics, gives me meaning and purpose. My roles as parent, grandparent and husband (Maris is there, too) are my identity. My final stop was a visit to the cemetery. The plastic blossom on Maris's grave is still looking good.

In the meantime, apprehension like a despot shouting was on the rise. Was my body fit enough to survive? Will my knee recover in time? I wish I had done more training with my backpack. Had I tied up all the loose ends? What's likely to go wrong? What's the worst thing that could go wrong? News of heat waves in France didn't help. I worked hard on reminding myself that I'd done this before and that things always turn okay. Don't worry! How difficult that lesson is to learn. Seek refuge in the present moment. Be thankful that I have the fitness, encouragement and support from family and friends. Be thankful that my story inspires others. Shut up, Noël! Stop the ruminating. Join the curious and dive into the adventure. Thrive on the challenge. Live for the moment.

A final culling of my pack to render it as light as possible and I was ready. Make each day an adventure; really seize the day. After a sleepless night and early rise, my son-in-law, Guy, drove me to the airport to begin Act VI of my Camino. I was planning to read the guidebook on the plane, but I realised that was only an anxiety reduction trick and bought a novel from the bookshop, The Bookshop of the Broken Hearted by Robert Hillman. Just enjoy the flight with a good read and a film or two. The flight included an overnight stay in Seoul, a comfortable way to take a trip to Europe. At the hotel I meet Linden. A young man, he was from Newcastle and on his first visit to Europe. We had dinner together, the debutant and the veteran. He was planning to meet three mates and hike in Austria. He made me recall the excitement of my first overseas trip back in the seventies. I still have the sense of wonder and am far from being travel weary. The other Australians staying overnight weren't too friendly, although I'm sure that if I made the move like I did with Linden, they would have been more open and discarded their habitual suspicions.

A series of challenges followed landing at Charles de Gaulle airport; finding the railway station, buying a ticket, taking the train and finding my accommodation, but I was successful and felt a sense of accomplishment. I was ready for immersion in the French culture and enjoyed chatting with my Airbnb host, Catherine. The surrounding streets contained a proliferation of eateries, and I dined at the nearest, a Creole restaurant. I was pleased how quickly I adapted and felt at home. After all, I had visited Paris many times.

Next day, I walked to nearby Montparnasse station and took the train to Chartres. As I walked from the station to the cathedral, I felt a strange apprehension. Ancient wisdom suggests that if you aren't trembling as you approach the sacred, it isn't the real thing; the sacred evokes emotion and commotion. The

## 11.

cathedral is one of my sacred places and a worthy pilgrimage destination in itself. I knew Friday as the day to visit because the chairs are cleared away and one can walk the labyrinth. Many are drawn to the cathedral for the beauty of its stained-glass windows, others for the breathtaking manner in which it seems to soar to the heavens. ('Wow!') How did its medieval builders manage that?

I value the labyrinth dating back to about 1200 for the opportunity to walk in meditation and in prayer. The labyrinth beckons you to undertake a pilgrimage following the path within it. There's nothing magical, only the energy within you. The main purpose, both physical and spiritual, is to lead you to a contemplation of what is within you.

Walking the labyrinth, step by step, helps us to comprehend that which is beyond ourselves. The path resembles the human journey – long, exacting with its ups and downs leading to a peaceful confidence in the meaning of our existence.

I prayed for a safe pilgrimage and for the enlightenment to accept all challenges, to recognise that it always turns out well, not to be so dim-witted and worry. Surrendering to the essential unknown of it all was the most positive thing I could do. I lit a candle, the first of many. I lit it for Maris, the family, Peter McGrath, that I would reach a destination, and know when I had arrived.

A tiled plaque set in the footpath outside the cathedral reminded me that Chartres is on one of the Camino routes, 1625 kilometres to Santiago.

## 12.

*Accept surprises that upset your plans, shatter your dreams and give a completely different turning to your day. – Dom Helda Camara*

I arrived at Gare Austerlitz at 7:50 a.m. hoping to catch the 8:29 a.m. but it was full, so I had to accept the 12:50 p.m. and a more expensive first-class seat. I had planned to arrive at the refuge in Périgueux early afternoon, but this setback, minor as it was, nourished my anxiety demons. The lessons of the Camino should have sunk in by now, but I'm still dim-witted. I tried to pass the time fiddling with my smart phone finding internet access. A black lady with two small children and a beautiful baby were waiting quietly. Her patience chastised me, and I accepted the lesson there was nothing I could do except to wait. Once I got going, it was good to see the French countryside, flat farming land. A change in trains meant that I was able to see Limoges. I bypassed this grand city two years previously because the ordination of a new bishop ensured that all accommodation was taken. I left the station for a brief walk in the hot sun around its surrounds and admired the architecture. Another change of trains at Bordeaux and I arrived at Périgueux nearing 7 p.m. The short walk to the refuge was familiar, for I had slept there two years previously. I rang the bell and when the hospitalière opened the door, she gave me a real serve. I had arrived late. I should have turned up between 3 p.m. and 6 p.m. When I explained that I had stayed before and would be a hospitalier myself in two months, Joselyn remembered my phone call. She opened up and revealed herself as a warm and outgoing person. I was planning to leave a few items including a small day pack. Joslyn wrote a note to pin to my pack, showed me a cupboard and the place where the key was hidden. In that action I felt I was accepted, almost making me feel I was part of the inner circle. She led me to the same room where I had slept two years previously. The bed was comfortable, but the traffic noise with the window open just as bad.

Five other pilgrims stayed. I saw them briefly at breakfast but had no time to meet them. Everyone had left by the time I departed at 8 a.m. No hospitalière to say Bon Chemin, for Joslyn lived close by in the town and slept at home. Such a contrast to the last time I stayed two years previously when Dominique and Marie Therese were live-in hospitaliers, and they went to great lengths to welcome and extend hospitality. They provided nourishment, comfort and entertainment and in the morning, escorted their pilgrims out of the refuge, wishing their family a good day. (*Bonne Journée!*)

I was a long time getting out of Périgueux. I walked through parklands along the river L'Isle. I was grateful that on my first day the way was flat and, for the most part, followed a cycle path, *la voie verte des bergers*. Being Sunday morning, cyclists, joggers and strollers joined me, but no other pilgrims with shell and backpack. Most pilgrims make for Saint Astier after Périgueux, but I decided 22 kilometres was too far for my first day. My destination was Razac-sur-l'Isle, which required a deviation from the route and leaving the signage behind. I was pleased to cover the 12 kilometres by 12:30 p.m. The day was getting very hot. At least I had learned one lesson – don't overdo things on your first day and exhaust yourself. I stayed at the *Hôtel-Restaurant le Sorbier* and was in time for lunch. The host had a well-practised charm, fine in a Maître-D of a Parisian establishment, but for a country pub? However, lunch was good, and I enjoyed an afternoon nap of about four hours. I felt relaxed now that my first day of walking was behind. My nerves had settled down and I decided to be positive. Apart from the hotel, everything was closed. I realised it was Bastille Day. The television showed demonstrations in many French cities, but I watched an enjoyable and thoroughly French Concert de Paris by the Tour Eiffel.

In my dreams, I slipped back into anxiety mode and dwelt on how to handle the next two weeks, whether to accept my age, abandon the walking, follow the Chemin path as a tourist and what to do with a heat wave. One lesson I have learned was to dismiss any pre-dawn thoughts because they are always negative. I woke, feeling positive about myself and my second day, this time only ten kilometres. I was in the process of acclimatising myself to the Chemin, to ease the strain on my body in the first few days and then increase the distances as my confidence grew and fitness developed. I hoped my judicious plan would get me through the distances and the heat.

It was good to get back on track and follow the signage; every time I leave, I feel alone. Back on route was like being back home. In fact, for the time being the Camino was my home. The walking was ideal, along level paths by waterways. Occasional panels told me the nature of flora and fauna in these parts. There was much to admire along the river and in the fields covered with sunflowers, plenty of spots to rest in the shade. Shortly before the town, a panel told the story of the arrival of the Industrial Revolution in the form of canals, railways, lime kilns and shoe factories. I came to a bridge that crossed to Saint Astier. The town looked charming; many houses edged the river and the waters were full of bird life. I found my refuge for the night, *Chambre d'Hôtes Les Rives de l'Isle*, by the river's edge. In fact, it was one of the houses I admired as I crossed the river. From my room, I had a view back to the bridge. I couldn't imagine a more peaceful, picturesque scene, the bridge in the distance, the water birds playing among the water lilies in the foreground below my window and the gentle sound of lapping water. I was content to have another restful afternoon, for the day was getting hotter and hotter; a heat wave was not far off. In the cool of the evening, I walked around the town to find a restaurant for dinner. Saint Astier takes its name from a 7th century hermit, Asterius, and a monastery was first built in the 8th century. The town's past beckons you – half-timbered and renaissance buildings, while a statue of Saint Astier adorns the main square. There were not many people around. Only one other ate at the restaurant I chose. *'It's the heat!'* the waiter Emmanuelle told me.

I emerged from sleep feeling well rested, positive and in good nick. Breakfast was a dampener. Two other guests joined the table but were not interested in chatting. It felt strange, eating with two strangers who remained so. I was not going to get company this morning. Breakfast could have been a thousand times more pleasant if we had broken the ice. I ate quickly and left them to their suspicion and reserve.

This was my third day and my body was adjusting to the new routine. I was optimistic. My destination was Douzillac, about 18 kilometres. Before leaving the town, I visited the boulangerie and inspected the war memorial, which had an unusually long list of names of those who had died (*Mort pour la France*). Fascinating to see the same family names in the different generations involved in the various conflicts. So much history. I wondered if their descendants were still around, or had they, like so many others, joined the exodus into the large towns. The route moved away from the riverlands and passed through rolling farming country with splendid views of stubble paddocks with intricate patterns of the path of the mower. I was cautious and paced myself, stopping every hour for a breather. Various parts of my body were taking their turn to ache, and as the heat grew, I found the going tough, particularly as this was my first real taste of hills. I was thirsty, and although I had enough water, I ate a mandarin. I never thought the fruit could be so delicious, such joy from such a simple action. I pushed through the pain, had lunch at a hunters' lodge and arrived at the church at Douzillac by mid-afternoon. Unsure of where to find my host, I rang, and instead of my walking, René arrived by car and took me to their *Chambre et Table d'hôtes* at Niautouneix where I met his wife Liliane. They were a delightful couple, so warm, outgoing and hospitable. Their place was equally charming with the thickest of walls, and I was not surprised when Liliane told me it was built in 1746. My room was in a separate building opposite the main house, equally solid and furnished with antiques – large wrought iron bed and walls decorated with paintings and portraits of a bygone area. Between the two buildings was the garden with lots of gnomes and other antiques. We dined under a large umbrella in the warm barmy evening. Family was also staying, and I met Amanda and Tom and their small children Lou and Lanr. They were equally welcoming, and I felt completely accepted into their family, such a contrast from chambres d'hôtes run primarily as a business where the hospitality is routine. Here I felt a genuine and sincere acceptance as if the family really enjoyed their role as hosts. Amanda was interested in my age and that I had come a long way, and before long, she was asking me why. I shared my story. We lingered late over the meal. I learned that Liliane and René were Flemish and came from Belgium. They spoke Flemish to each other, but to include me, they spoke French. They bought the building many years ago. Its history is varied and was once a refuge for the English during one of the many wars.

We lingered late over breakfast and took many photos. They seemed as reluctant to see me go as I was to leave them. I had given myself a shorter day, only nine kilometres, so I left about 10 a.m. René told me of an alternative way to Mussidan that would save me having to climb back up to the Camino route. He accompanied me to the crossroads to ensure I took the right path. I followed this, a footpath along the railway line, until I came to Saint-Louis en-l'Isle where I paused by the church looking ancient and neglected with crumbling walls, covered with weeds and small bushes. A panel just out of Saint-Front de-Pradoux told something of its history. Occupied since pre-historic times, it was a centre for pottery in the Middle Ages and a rallying point for the Resistance during World War II. I liked the reproduction of a crudely printed leaflet:

*Un seul but la liberation Un seul moyen la resistance. (A sole objective liberation, a sole means resistance).*

Mussidan has always occupied a strategic position due to its natural position, located on the confluence of the Isle and Crempse rivers. Mussidan reeks with history in its well-preserved medieval buildings. At the tourist office, I met the lady who looked after the *Refuge Municipal*. She told me she would be around to open the refuge at 4.00 p.m. I had plenty of time to explore and arrived at the Place Victor Hugo with an hour to spare. I found shelter from the heat under the shade of a huge spreading oak tree, about 21 metres in height and over 120 years old (according to the panel). I passed the time watching a *sapeurs-pompiers* crew in training, using ropes and pulleys to climb the tree. The *Refuge Municipal* was adjacent to the tree, so I kept my eye open for any movement. Came 4 p.m. and 4:30 p.m. but no movement at the refuge. I wandered over and peered in through the window. It looked grubby with plenty of spider webs as if no one ever cleaned the place. About 5 p.m., I rang the tourist office. Where was I, I was asked? Outside the refuge in Place Victor Hugo, I replied. The refuge has moved, I was told, and in a few moments, the lady arrived and led around the corner only about 50 metres to the new refuge. The old one has been closed for 6 months, she told me. The guidebook had not caught up with the new address, on the first floor of a more modern building and sparklingly clean.

The good news was that after four days on the road, I met my first pilgrim. Clementine was French. She had given herself no time limits, just walking and would reach Santiago when she arrived. We bought our own meals at the nearby *supermarché* and brought them back to the refuge where we ate together and talked about the values of pilgrimage and giving yourself time to absorb its message. She was a quiet, reflective lady; she seemed to be at a crossroad in her life and was giving herself time out. What better way than the Camino. What better way to do the Camino than to walk in silence during the day and to enjoy good company in the evening.

Thursday July 18th, my destination was Calabre where I was to stay in a wine chateau, a distance of 30 kilometres. My days of walking 30 kilometres were over, so I took a taxi halfway to Fraise, making the day's walk manageable. On the outskirts of Monfaucon was a notice advising that a picnic area just outside the mairie was available to hikers, so I stopped for lunch. Monfaucon looked to me one of those villages where their moment of glory, if it ever had one, was long past. Nothing seemed to have happened for decades. Even the public toilets were of the squat variety. Along came Clementine. She stopped for lunch too. She had done well, having already covered 22 kilometres. She was aiming for Sainte-Foy la-Grande, another 11 kilometres, so despite the fact that she was taking her time, she was covering plenty of ground. I was happy that I only had about five kilometres to go. We chatted over our lunch. She knew something of Australia and of the Snowy Mountains. She compared our brumbies to the American mustangs. Each has its place in the people's hearts. We talked about the differences between gîtes in the warmth of their welcome.

The afternoon saw a series of green rolling hills covered in vineyards. The route was well signed and, every now and then, included a panel with a shell and a one liner in French and English:

*It does not matter how slow you go as long as you don't stop.*
*– Confucius.*

*Sometimes the heart sees what is invisible to the eyes.*
*– H. Jackson Browne Jr.*

*We all have two lives, the second begins when we realise we only have one. – Confucius.*

*Any fool can know. The point is to understand.*
*– Albert Einstein.*

*A journey of a thousand miles begins with one step.*
*– Lao Tzu.*

Not all the panels were legible. They were well weathered and looked as if they were erected decades ago.

Eventually, I found the sign *Chateau Puy Servain Gîte d'Etape*.

## 12.

My accommodation was in the corner of a machinery shed of a winery and vineyard. Mme Hecquet met me with the keys, and that was the last I saw of her. It occurred to me that running a gîte was just a diversion from the serious business of running a winery. The gîte was comfortable with a kitchen and lounge area on the ground level and upstairs a dormitory with six beds. I was the only guest. Mme Hecquet had left a meal in the refrigerator plus a bottle of the chateau's wine, a Bergerac Rouge. I'm sure it wasn't one of their prize-winning wines, but it was very nice. The winery was about a 100 metres away, so I wandered up, mainly to get an internet connection, but a dapper elderly gentleman in blazer and cravat invited me in, so I inspected their range in the tasting room. The vineyard is very well placed on the top of a hill with extensive views of the sprawling vineyards. This was wine country indeed, part of the Bordeaux region.

I was woken before 6 a.m. by tractors getting ready for the day. I left early and, once again, passed through vineyards stretching to the horizon. Every now and then, the route disappeared into shady thickets, which was appreciated, for the day was warming up. I paused in the town of Sainte-Foy la-Grande. It has a long history as a fortified town, but the modern town is busy. Mid-morning, I walked along the bustling main street until I found the *Office de Tourisme*. I was looking for a taxi. I was aiming for Pellegrue, which was too far for my ageing body to walk. My days as a hardcore pilgrim, walking every step, were long gone and now prudence held sway. I only have one body and I want to take care of it. Since I began walking 6 days ago, my body parts had taken their turn to protest. I was told there were no taxis as such, but private cab drivers were available. (*Les Chauffeurs Privés de Dordogne*). The lady rang for me. The driver was on another job and would be along in 15 minutes. Fifteen minutes became 45, and in the meantime, I inspected the racks of leaflets advising of the multitude of available tourist attractions. I wasn't interested. Tourism offers comfort, predictability and entertainment. That's quite legitimate, but not if you're longing for something other than diversion or distraction, escape or entertainment, but for a taste of mystery and a touch of the sacred.

The driver arrived and took me about 11 kilometres to Caplong, which was no more than a church and a few houses. I ran into confusion getting out of Caplong, but the third attempt was lucky. I looked for someone to ask and found a jovial overweight chap in the briefest of shorts and well-tanned skin. He was English and had retired to Caplong. He was in his garden repairing an umbrella damaged in a storm. He was going to sit under his umbrella, he told me, while I was going out in the hot midday sun.

After 4 hours in the heat, I arrived in Pellegrue. The town is arranged around a central square with a large market hall (*la halle*) in the middle. The chap in the mairie wasn't too helpful, but he gave me the code, and I managed to find the *Gîte Municipal*. The gîte was small, cluttered and grotty, as worn-looking as the rest of town. Another pilgrim was already installed and asleep. He woke later and introduced himself as Bruno from Germany. My visit coincided with a Friday evening market, and stall holders were soon setting themselves up around the market hall, which was furnished with tables, chairs and a stage ready for an entertainer. The music commenced at 9 p.m. as it was becoming dark. In the meantime, people gathered, having purchased their food from the various stalls. Two bars on opposite sides were full of drinkers. In the *Bar-Restaurant Chez Mirelle*, I found Bruno and I joined him. We discussed our Caminos. He mentioned that a heat wave (*canicule*) was forecast for the following week. He knew a little of Australia but was deterred by our country's extensive range of poisonous snakes and spiders. Before retiring, I wandered around the stalls. Outside the other bar, without requesting permission or explanation, a lady jumped up, grabbed me, had her photo taken and returned to her friends. I retired to the gîte about 10 p.m. The music was pleasant listening and continued until midnight, loud enough as it was just outside but not too penetrating. I went to sleep thinking how I should manage the impending heat wave.

Saturday, I needed a short day, so I decided I would walk about eight kilometres to La Ferme. I continued on through vineyard country. I was in the Garonne, hinterland of Bordeaux. At one time, I paused to watch three restless donkeys following each other up and down a hill. At another time a snake slithered across the path just in front of me, the first I had seen in Europe. I stopped for lunch in a shaded field, which I shared with the insects in the beautiful silence of a hot windless day.

The first building you see on arriving at La Ferme is the massive abbey. The church of the Benedictine Abbey of Saint Ferme is spectacular. It was built in the Romanesque style in the 12th century while the nave and façade had to be rebuilt in 1615 following their destruction in the Wars of Religion. I enjoyed wondering about its vastness, admiring its simplicity. Outside a mass of pink geraniums contrasted sharply with the grey stone walls. Inside, I lit a candle for Maris, my first opportunity on this year's chemin. Someone before had handwritten a lengthy tribute to his candle's meaning, shedding light on his difficulties and decisions, its flame burning away his selfishness, pride and other imperfections. I was content to leave a little of myself in my candle and to acknowledge

Maris's continuing presence in my life. I had arrived one week too early, for a notice in the porch advertised a concert of harp and soprano the following Saturday, organised by the Friends of the abbey (*Association Les Amis de l'Abbeye de Saint Ferme*).

La Ferme is comprised of few buildings, and the refuge was easy to find. The *Refuge Pèlerin* is managed by the *Amis et Pèlerins de Saint-Jacques de la Voie de Vézelay*. I was met by Yvette, a quiet and reserved lady, but she did a great job of making me feel welcome. Another pilgrim arrived by bicycle. Wolfgang was German and on his way to Santiago. Yvette provided a meal, and we had a pleasant evening together getting to know each other. Yvette had walked the Camino from her home town of Bordeaux. She was an accountant by profession and spent two weeks each year as a *hospitalière*. Wolfgang spoke about the refugee situation in Europe and agreed with Angela Merkel's policy of acceptance. I can never cease emphasising the benefits of sharing a meal. Pilgrims arrive as individuals and become a family.

Wolfgang and I left together in the morning but not before a round of photos. My destination was Saint-Hilaire-de-la-Noaille, about 16 kilometres. Once again, I walked through vineyards with an occasional field of grazing cattle. The tiny village of Coutures came up quickly, a nice surprise for its clean toilets and benches outside the mairie. The church had a well-maintained cemetery-garden, while panels explained its history and the carvings on many of the capitals. The doors were locked, so I didn't get an opportunity to view the inside. I liked the handwritten note requesting the person who stole the geranium and the bougainvillea to return them at the earliest. Did the church get them back? A column of black ants climbing the walls into the eaves was the only life until I saw two people. A chap was walking and his horse laden with a backpack trailed behind. A young boy greeted me warmly and asked if I was walking to Compostelle. He wished me *'Bonne Continuation.'*

Somehow I took a wrong turn and missed the village of Roquebrune. I knew I was off route because it is well marked, and I hadn't seen any signage for a while. I knew where I had gone astray, but I wasn't prepared to retrace my steps. One of the Camino lessons I have learned is to obtain, if possible, directions from more than one source. Sometimes people don't know, but they try to be helpful. Other times, they're having a bad day and give you a bum steer just to get rid of you. I called at a house where the windows were open; a driver stopped, told me I was off route and directed me; I asked two cyclists riding towards me. Gradually, I worked my way back and was relieved to greet the signage as if they were lost friends.

About 2.30 p.m., I arrived at my destination. *Gîte et Chambre d'hôtes La Peyrière* is about one kilometre off route after Saint-Hilaire de-la-Noaille. Looking like a restored farmhouse, it is set back from the road with a lovely stretch of green lawn in front, which a robot was quietly mowing. All the shutters were closed, which made me think no one was home. I tried one of these doors and I'm not sure who was more surprised, the large black dog or me. In response to the barking, another door opened and out came Serge, my host. He explained that they closed up the house as a protection against the heat, by now, well into the thirties. Out came his wife, Bernadette. Their reception was very warm, indeed, and they invited me in, passing through the thick walls into the coolness of their living area. Their system of air conditioning (*climatisation*) worked. I appreciated the beer Serge found for me. Bernadette showed me a comfortable bedroom with its own bathroom. I enjoyed the shower and a rest. Later, Bernadette showed me her scrapbook. She had devoted a page to every pilgrim who had stayed.

It included a photo and sometimes a card or letter which the pilgrim had sent after their return home. She had few Australian entries, but she thumbed back to 2010 where she found an entry for Claude Tranchant, whom I knew of; she is active in Australian pilgrim circles, wrote a book about her Camino and has regular entries on Facebook. Outside, Serge showed me his domain, the various farm outhouses one of which was an old drying shed for tobacco leaves. Now extinct, tobacco flourished for a time in these parts. He grew a few acres of vines, but his grapes go to one of the wineries.

The table was set for dinner outside under a large spreading tree, and the family arrived, Isabel, Christophe and their three children. The eight of us sat down to a meal and to extended conversation. Isabel was very interested in me, asked many questions including my age. The children knew about kangaroos. I felt a favoured guest, completely accepted by this family, comparable to the family five nights previously – Liliane, René, Amanda, Tom and the three children, just as delightful a family in their warmth and hospitality. Both families made me feel I was not an intruder, nor causing undue extra labour by my presence. I was never more a stranger yet never more at home.

Isabel took an extra interest in me, an elderly pilgrim on his own, far from family and loved ones. She was concerned about my welfare and mentioned the likely heat wave in the coming week. I answered that I hoped to cover only short distances and stop early before the heat became too intense. Next morning, Isabel and Christophe walked with me through a vineyard, a short cut to get back to the route. Isabel insisted on taking her photo with me. They seemed like old friends; I had met them less than 24 hours ago, demonstrating once again, the power of hospitality and bonding over a meal.

I passed through more vineyards interspersed with fields of

maize and peas. I arrived at La Réole and stopped to admire the town and its rich history dating back to Gallo-Roman times with its fine medieval buildings. The church Saint-Pierre has its origins in the 12th century. Like many other churches, it has been destroyed, mutilated and rebuilt and has seen many vicissitudes down the centuries. During the French Revolution it was used as a stable and for storing fodder. La Place Albert Rigoulet tells the story of Albert Rigoulet who was a police officer during the German Occupation and headed the local Resistance. He organised numerous parachute-drops of weapons for the Resistance and arranged for young people fleeing the Compulsory Labour Scheme in Germany and Jewish families whom he hid in La Réole to escape to Spain by forging identity cards. He was caught, condemned, tortured and sent to Dachau prison. After the Liberation, he returned to La Réole but died shortly after.

I admired the silhouette of La Réole as I walked along the riverbank. I heard a toot and my name – 'Noël.' Isabel and Christophe waved as they drove by on their way home.

My destination was Bassanne where I was to stay in *the Refuge pèlerin municipal Moulin de Piis*, an old mill. The day was getting intensely hot. The temperature was nudging 40 degrees. My body was aching; my pack was heavier by the step, and it was with a deep sigh of relief that I arrived at the mill by 2 p.m. and dumped my burden.

The mill was in a small reserve surrounded by open fields. A solid and impressive building, it seeped history from every stone. A canal that was once the race and now full of stagnant water ran by the mill, and the place where the wheel was once located was easily seen. I rang a number, and the lady said she would arrive shortly. A couple were having a picnic lunch on a bench under one of the trees. A young man was sitting on the ground by his van and had all his stuff spread out. While waiting, I went over and spoke to him. He had removed his shirt and footwear, had long black hair and was as skinny as a drover's dog. I wondered if he ever ate. He looked like he had gone through his own mill. He was happy to chat. I said I was a pilgrim, and he replied that he had done the Camino once and it was the best thing he ever did. Mme Loubé arrived with the key. Inside, the cool darkness brought instant relief. Walls more than a metre thick made impressive insulation against the heat and in the past protection from potential attackers; the only light coming from slits in the walls that were once peep holes. Mme Loubé related its history as she showed me around. Her exuberance and passion were contagious, and in no time, I, too, was captivated. Built in the 13th century as a fortified mill, it fell into neglect and disrepair over the centuries but in the last few years has been restored by a band of dedicated locals. Still a work in progress, its first floor is the gîte, consisting of a large dormitory of six beds (it could take dozens), an enormous fireplace, kitchenette and bathroom. The beds were well constructed in wood. Extra were a blanket box at the foot of each and a screen in between. On the ground floor were displays of photos showing the various stages of restoration. It's a fascinating building with a fascinating story, and now its main use is a community centre and a shelter for pilgrims on the way to Compostelle.

She departed as quickly as she arrived. I was the only guest. I enjoyed my silence and my solitude in this vast restored relic of the Middle Ages when even a humble working mill had to be fortified. I wondered what stories these stone walls could tell, and every now and then I seemed to hear stirring of I don't know what. My imagination abounded with some wonderful images of days past. I inspected at leisure the photo boards

## 12.

telling their story of love and dedication to a cause. I read a notice about the following Saturday when the Friends of the mill (*Les Amis du Moulin de Piis*) were organising a walk. Starting at the mill at 9 a.m., they proposed a walk of 13 kilometres in the valley of the Garonne, visiting churches and other mills, returning by 6 p.m. for drinks, a meal and music. I was five days too early for the celebration of their *Patrimoine* (heritage).

Outside, the skinny chap had packed up his van and departed, but another lad had arrived and slung a hammock between two trees. An ideal night to camp out, warm from the day's heat. Mme Loubé had mentioned the next day Tuesday was going to be hotter. I heard a knock on the heavy door. A young man with a beer can told me he had found it, and it should be disposed of. I pointed to the rubbish bin, and he seemed happy. I wondered what was his real motivation. He was part of the mystery surrounding the mill as if there were many things present my eyes could not see.

In bed, I browsed through my guidebook, admirable for the author's quirky sense of humour. An entry opposite yesterday's map appealed. A rough translation follows:

> *Pilgrim Friend! It's possible one evening, exhausted by fatigue, emaciated by hunger, dehydrated by thirst, shrunken by the weighty backpack, shrivelled by the scars of blisters, grilled by the burning sun, soaked by pounding rain, buffeted by piercing winds, stretched out by the side of the route, your head on a stone, and feeling that you are about to die alone and in pain. Don't die selfish, pilgrim friend! Help your brothers! In your last breath, take up a stone and write in the sand your Visa card code.*

*Moulin de Piis*

*Wolfgang, Yvette and Noël at La Ferme*

12.

*Isabel and Noël at Saint-Hilaire-de-la-Noaille*

## 13.

*'Sometimes the bad things that happen to us put us directly on the path to the best things that will ever happen to us.'* – Nicole Reed

Tuesday morning was already warming up by the time I left the *Moulin de Piis*. I was planning to stay at the *Abbaye Sainte-Marie de Rivet* at Auros and hoped I would arrive in time to beat the worst of the heat. I walked through fields of sunflowers and vegetables and the ubiquitous vineyards. A farmer was watering his crop, and as the spray came across the road, I paused for a soaking. I had drunk all my water by the time I reached Savignac but I was able to refill at the small shop (*épicerie*). Back on Sunday night, Bernadette had rung the abbey for me. She received directions not to go as far as Auros, but at Savignac to take the road on the right to Brannens. I check this information with the young shop assistant. She gave the same advice. Take the road to Langon, which was the same. I found the turn off to Brannens just after the town. I was in a quandary. If I turned, I would be leaving the signage and the map in my guidebook did not mention these towns. I would be flying blind, without map, hoping that road signs would lead me to the abbey. My smart phone was of no use, as I had no internet connection. Both directions would lead to trouble. I had an ominous feeling that, no matter what, I was being drawn with a gravitational force into a deep vortex. The road sign indicated that Auros was ahead. I knew I could get there. I decided to follow the Camino signage.

The morning was heating up, I was getting tired and I needed frequent breathers. The roadside trees provided shade, and the way became a matter of dashing from tree to tree. On one of my rests, another pilgrim arrived. The young man was Australian. Ben was originally from France and had taken out Australian citizenship. I was delighted to meet a fellow countryman and would have enjoyed a chat, but he did not stay and pushed ahead at such a pace that he soon disappeared. I struggled and finally reached Auros where I found a bare dried out park with meagre shade. I wanted to stop there and sleep, but I had three more kilometres to cover. I realised the folly of my decision. I had come into Auros from the north-east and now I had to follow the road north. I ate my lunch and looked for more water. Around the corner was a taxi stand with a phone number. I phoned and a male voice replied he was on holidays. *'Désolé!'* (Sorry!) There was no other accommodation within Auros. There was nothing else to do but walk.

The next hour is vivid in my memory as the pits of my Camino. The intense heat struck me with a great scorching wallop and just as much radiated from the melting road surface. No shade provided any relief, and the traffic was heavy and fast, adding to the risk. I wanted to collapse. My thirst was raging, but I could not stop to drink in such a dangerous situation. I had visions of collapsing on the road in front of a speed demon. My will dragged my screaming body. *'Come on! Each pace brings you one step closer,'* I chanted over and over. Walking downhill was the only redeeming feature of the furnace, and I felt I was spiralling down into deep boiling crap. Sheer willpower got me to the abbey turn-off where a bus shelter in full sun provided miniscule relief. I felt weird, disoriented. This is unreal! This is scary! This is getting dangerous! I really am in deep shit right up to the neck! I still had an uphill kilometre. How I managed that last kilometre, I don't know. I was exhausted and dehydrated, just hanging on by the fingernails.

## 13.

I went into automatic, conscious of nothing beyond putting one foot in front of the other. The upward slope was gentle enough and, in other circumstances, could have been a breeze, but at that moment, it was a killer hill of the most lethal variety. I reached the driveway, which seemed to go on forever but probably only two hundred metres. I came to buildings. I was disoriented and seemed to hallucinate. This is a children's camp, I thought. There's no way they'll let an old bloke in! In the shade of a large spreading tree, I threw my pack on the ground with a thwack and collapsed.

I'm not sure how long I was there. Perhaps just a few minutes or even seconds. I just wanted to sleep, but I saw a lady approaching the building, so I left my pack and followed her. Come on! Just a few more steps! The building was obviously an abbey. I followed her into the bookshop, which served as the entrance. A kindly nun greeted me and said she would contact the sister who looked after the pilgrims. She offered me a seat. I flopped on the chair and could not stop myself from microsleeps, waking up with a start and falling to sleep again, managing not to fall off the chair. In came Sister Blandine. I got up to greet her, and she grabbed me as if I was about to collapse on the bookshop floor. She knew I was coming and had a room for me. She chastised me for my lack of prudence for walking in such heat. I said I would go back and get my pack, but she replied it had been taken care of. She led me around the back, past old stone buildings to a new wing built in wood like a row of motel rooms. My pack was in the room, which was simply furnished with its own ensuite. I stumbled through a shower, collapsed naked on the bed and slept for two hours.

I was feeling better and took note of my surrounds. The wing consisted of 30 rooms. Next to me was a large dining room and kitchen, and along the veranda were two meeting rooms. The abbey catered for retreatants who sometimes came in large groups, but they also welcomed pilgrims and others who wanted time-out. My room faced a garden with lawns and trees, just the place for quiet meditation. Beyond were the buildings of the abbey and the quarters of the sisters, a contemplative order of Cistercian nuns.

Sr Blandine came around to check. She chastised me in no uncertain terms for walking in such heat and told me I must not walk the next day, for it would be just as hot. I should stay until the weather had cooled. I did not object. In fact, I was extremely thankful. Heat waves can be lethal for the elderly. I was more robust than many of my contemporaries, but nevertheless, I had ventured too close to the edge. I was thankful for my general health and fitness. I was thankful that I had found shelter in such caring hands. Once again, the Camino (or God), despite my lack of prudence, looked after me. Sister Blandine was right in chastising me. She told me where to have dinner. I dined with about six others. I was still vague and didn't take much notice of my company. They were a silent lot. They were worn out, too, by the heat. The room faced west, and the sun was streaming in, the only protection some thin blinds. Everyone was keen to get out of the oven as quickly as possible. I was in bed before the sun, crashed out and slept a dreamless sleep for 10 hours.

In the morning, it took a while to emerge from the depths. I was feeling almost normal but I did not jump out of bed, relieved to know I was having a rest day. As I was living in an abbey, I decided to follow its routines. I attended Laudes and Mass in the chapel. The priest was one of my fellow diners. About 20 nuns sat in the main body of the church while the public were in a space off the altar. The nuns' singing was soft, gentle and tranquil. They read the scriptures as if they meant what they were saying. I felt safe, at home. The dining room was more pleasant in the cool of the morning, and over breakfast, people were open and chatted. Over lunch and dinner, I got to know them. People came to the abbey on holidays or on retreat. Jean-Jacques was the priest. He was elderly, and I guess the role of abbey chaplain was his retirement job. Jacques was younger. He was thin, quiet and the abbey's gardener and handy man. Janine, an older lady with grey hair seemed to be on retreat, spending a few days in reflection. So, too, was Maylis. She was young, a student. I wondered if she was contemplating a religious life. Anne-France and Didier were a couple. They were on holidays and planning to drive to Le Puy at the end of the week. Phillipe needed a stick for walking. He dressed like a hippy in loose flowing colourful clothing. Sylvie was his carer, an older lady. I wasn't sure of their relationship. The black lady was different. She had twin boys one to two years old, both walking and cute. She was shy and subdued. She was neither a retreatant nor a holidaymaker. I wondered if the nuns had rescued her from a domestic problem.

Sister Blandine fussed around, checking on me and the others. I asked her if I could stay for two days, as the heat wave was forecast to continue for the week. No worries! (or the French equivalent). I used my phone to send a message to my girls to let them know I was in safe hands sheltering from the heat wave, which may have been mentioned in the Australian news. Back came their replies to stay put. Another visit to the chapel at 12.30 for Sexte and lunch at 1.00 p.m. I was surrounded by spiritual books, but I selected for closer study *365 Meditations de Soeur Emmanuelle*, a beautiful coffee-table book full of photos and illustrations. I had heard of Sister Emmanuelle through a television series. She was a religious sister noted for her work with the poor in Turkey and Egypt. The book was a compilation of short extracts from her writings, one for each day of the year.

They express her faith in man, respect for others and for justice. Her views were not orthodox, and she was almost as popular as Mother Teresa. She died in 2008 at the age of 99, four weeks short of her hundredth birthday. She is regarded as a model for hope, compassion and courage that could move mountains and practical spiritual wisdom that was an inspiration to many. I noted an entry for the coming days.

*29 juillet : Je me réjouis de tout ce qui m'est donné, sans regretter ce que je n'ai pas reçu. (29 July : I rejoice at what has been given to me, without regretting what I have not received.)*

The day was equally hot, and the temperature climbed above 40 degrees. I could not believe my good fortune in the shelter of the abbey. I felt I was blessed and that invisible hands had led me to this sacred place. At dinner, Sylvie was interested in the Camino and its history. Anne-France asked many questions and even looked up Jindabyne, my home town. She looked up my books, too, and wanted to know more. The evening passed quietly. I felt myself regenerating, but I was happy to have more time.

Thursday July 25th was another quiet day, forecast to be just as hot but with storms in the evening. It was the feast day of Saint-Jacques, so there would be celebrations at Santiago. The abbey continued with its tranquil routine. A newspaper item was posted on a notice board. Published earlier in the month, its headline set the tone:

*Fuir le tumulte et retrouver la paix á l'abbaye du Rivet*
*(Flee the tumult and find peace at the abbey of Rivet).*

*Peace is the first thing that one notices on entering the abbey.*

## 13.

*The second is silence. The abbey offers a monastic hospitality, a silent retreat in the gentle countryside. It's not a hotel nor a Club Med, warns Sister Blandine. The abbey welcomes all without distinction, believer or not, but one has to obey the rules – discretion, restraint, simplicity, acceptance of the routines of the abbey. No contact with the nuns apart from those responsible for the welcome and the bookshop. The nuns live their lives, the visitors live theirs. There are seven services in the chapel each day, from the vigils at 4:30 a.m. to the compline at 7:30 p.m. None is obligatory but it's good to attend at least one.*

I gave 4:30 a.m. a miss, but I did attend the others. In the abbey, one leads a simple life, stripped of luxuries. There's a place for the essentials, and one realises how one can do without the encumbrances of modern life. One can have lots of stuff, but doing stuff gives you a better chance of getting in touch with the inner self. That's one of the lessons of the Camino too. *Be thankful for one's gifts and don't be envious of what others may have.* That was Sister Emmanuelle's story, and is also a lesson of the Camino: The tourist demands, the pilgrim accepts. I like to think I have learnt that lesson. A notice outside the chapel reaffirmed the message.

*Va, pèlerin, poursuit ta quête; poursuit ton chemin, que rein ne t'arrête. Prend ta part de soleil et ta part de poussière; le cœur en éveil, oublie l'éphémère. Go, pilgrim, follow your quest; follow your way, may nothing stop you. Take your share of the sun and your share of dust. With heart awakening, forget the ephemeral.*

On the way back from the chapel for lunch, I saw one of the sisters unloading cases of wine into a storeroom. I was supposed to have no contact, but she was little; the cases were heavy, and she didn't appear strong. It seemed the right thing to help her. She thanked me and mentioned she knew about me. I daresay the nuns gossip like any other group of humans and discuss those staying in the abbey. I'm sure Sister Blandine tells them so that they can pray for us. Sister Josephine from Mauritius was interested in me because she had cousins in Australia. She mentioned that, although they had plenty of rooms for visitors, not enough were staying this year. She put it down to the economy and the heat. However, she added: *'Things seem to take care of themselves.'* How often had I heard that sentiment! No matter what predicament you find yourself in, the Camino or God or Providence will take care.

I could have stayed for ever in this peaceful haven, but I needed to press on. The next day Friday July 26th was forecast to be cooler, so it was time to leave. I planned to take a taxi to make up the time. I tried fruitlessly to organise the ride myself and rang many numbers. I told Sr Blandine. She had her contacts and, in no time, organised a taxi for the morning.

Friday July 26th was Maris's birthday. Occasionally in my dreams she is present, and I am overjoyed to have her back. Her presence is so strong that for the moment, I cannot locate myself, can't find a way to where I am, when I am. She appears so real, her old self before depression destroyed her spirit, and I am bitterly disappointed when I wake up. She would have been 81. Her fifteenth anniversary was coming up on October 30th. How my life has changed, and how might our lives have unfolded if I had succeeded in preventing her from taking her own life on that Saturday morning! In the first years after Maris's death, no way could I see any benefits coming from her suicide, but now after nearly 15 years I see things differently. I would never have walked the Camino and met such wonderful people as Sister Blandine.

Sister Emmanuelle's entry was: *L'amour vole, l'amour court, l'amour chante. Il donne des ailes. (Love flies, love runs, love sings. It gives wings.)*

Maris is with me every day and walks every step of my Camino journey. The love that we shared gives me wings and the courage to press on.

*Entrance to the Abbaye de Sainte-Marie de Rivet*

*Sister Blandine*

## 14.

*Life is either a daring adventure, or nothing* – Helen Keller

The taxi was due at 8:30 a.m., and by 8:40, I experienced a touch of anxiety. When will I ever learn not to worry and to accept that things will turn out! It arrived about 8.45 a.m., just as rain began to fall. A brand new BMW, Kevin was the driver, a young man in suit and tie dressed for driving a VIP, not a daggy pilgrim. He knew Sister Blandine; I think she pulled some strings to get him here. She saw me depart, telling me that the sisters would pray for me and insisting that I write. I promised I would send a postcard from Le Puy and a Christmas card when I returned to Australia. Her religious name comes from an early Christian martyr who was fed to the lions at Lyon in 177 AD. Sainte Blandine is the patron saint of servants; the name is fitting to one who has devoted her life to serving others. Hats off to Sister Blandine!

Kevin was puzzled at my destination, the Gare du Poteau, a disused railway station on an abandoned railway line. I chose it because the map in my guidebook showed the route passed by. Kevin's GPS had trouble locating such an insignificant spot, and he kept on telling me the trip would cost me money. He set off and stopped by the ATM just to ensure that I had enough cash. I enjoyed the comfort of a luxury car with all the latest technology. Kevin mentioned that a lot of his work involved ferrying executives to trains and airports. His clients, however, were not only VIPs, he had regular commitments to old people, taking them for medical appointments and shopping trips. He helped out Sister Blandine, too. He enjoyed his work because he liked to help people.

We drove in the rain through Bazas and Captieux, both drab-looking towns; I had missed nothing. We picked up the Camino signage and took a muddy side-track until we arrived at the Gare du Poteau, now a private residence, in the Forêt des Landes, the largest man-made forest in Europe. Kevin left me outside a small factory building, and I took shelter to don my wet weather gear. The BMW disappeared, and I set off in the rain and mud on a much cooler day, thankful that the temperature was bearable. I was ready to go full bore.

The route ran alongside the autoroute and then followed the old railway line, now a cycle track. Not a single hill today! The rain fell steadily, and I looked for shelter so that I could remove my poncho and access my pack. Seats were placed regularly along the track, but they were in the open and offered no shelter. On one, a grateful passerby had written: *Merci pour cette petite place a l'ombre. Thanks for this little spot in the shade.* The tree was dripping water on the damp seat. Around a bend I came to a shelter beside a pond. With thanks I entered, removed my poncho and found my lunch and water. How I enjoyed the dryness of my pavilion, a refuge against the elements. The vapour rising from the water reminded me of dancing phantoms seeking release from their submarine world, longing to join me and relish the freedom of my spirit.

I passed a farm swarming with geese; the only living creatures I saw. A small chapel came into view. I read a date, 1748, over the portal. It was open, but I saw no opportunity to light a candle for Maris on her birthday. Rain had ceased by the time I reached Bourriot-Bergonce. The church was closed, but its porch gave me shelter to finish my lunch. In such small villages, the Marie is open a few days per week with limited hours, but it was open Mondays, so I visited and found a helpful young lady in charge. I asked for information on my destination, the church St Loup de Vialotte. The young lady didn't know of its conversion into a refuge, but we poured over a map of the commune and together worked out which church it would be and how to get there. Thanking her, I set out on the road and left the Camino signage. After about 3 or 4 kilometres, the only vehicle for the day stopped. There were two people, a man and a woman. The driver said they were hospitaliers from the *Refuge Vialotte*. He pointed out where to join the route in the morning, a cycle track that crossed the road, and continued on with me aboard about a kilometre to the church.

Once an abandoned church, it had been converted into a refuge by the *Société Landaise des Amis de Saint-Jacques et d'Etudes Compostellanes*. Described in typical French hyperbole as *'a new star on the way to Compostelle'* it looked like an old church, but the interior had been converted. The altar had been left intact, but before it was the kitchen and dining area. A dormitory had been installed in the ceiling, and other rooms and bathrooms were on the ground floor. A radio and CD player were installed in the confessional. Outside, a large marquee with many chairs had been erected, and a large crowd of the friends of the Chemin had gathered the previous day to celebrate St James Feast Day. Opened on April 22nd, it featured in none of the guide books. After three months, I was the 105th pilgrim to stay; word of mouth had done its job. Mikel was a jolly outgoing and exuberant hospitalier with a mop of snowy white hair and cheeky grin. A larger-than-life character, he was also a 'heavy', the president of the Société. Françoise was gentle, lady-like and quiet. She had just arrived for the changeover and was due to take charge the following day. They were equally warm and enthusiastic in their welcome and hospitality. Jacobus was the other pilgrim. He was Dutch and spoke excellent French and English. He started from home and had been walking for 7 weeks, with plans to reach Santiago.

Françoise prepared an excellent meal, and we sat down together in front of the altar. Jean-Pierre, the hospitalier from Rocquefort arrived. He had no pilgrims that evening, so he joined us. I was planning to stay at Roquefort the following evening. We discussed many topics, all related to the Camino. Mikel (a Basque name) liked to quote various one-liners such as:

*Le touriste exige. Le pèlerin remercie. (The tourist demands. The pilgrim is thankful.)*

*On ne fait pas le chemin. C'est le chemin qui vous fait. (One doesn't make/do the Camino. It's the Camino which makes you.)*

I remembered some one-liners from my guide book:

*Les difficultés sont faites pour être abattues, non pour nous abattre. (Difficulties are made to be broken down, not to break us down.)*

*L'optimisme, c'est le seul médicament pour soigner la réalité. (Optimism, it's the only treatment to take care of reality).*

We passed a night full of wisdom and inspiration. We were a Camino family – the three hospitaliers, Mikel, Françoise and Jean-Pierre, the two pilgrims, Jacobus and me. Once again, the power of sharing a meal!

Every now and then, we get an opportunity to reflect on the lessons that the Camino teaches us. They make the discomforts and pain of the daily routine almost insignificant.

## 14.

They make us press on regardless. The Camino calls on us to pause and be quiet, to contemplate, to listen, to be in awe, to welcome, to admire and be grateful for creation, to bless the people we meet and ourselves, to acknowledge a Higher Presence, which we like to call God. They answer the question we ask of ourselves: Why are we doing this?

Sometimes, as we get older, we can slip into a comfortable life that no longer offers challenge. But, as the one liner on the wall of my High Country gym says:

*Life begins at the end of your comfort zone.*

Mikel refused my offer of help with the clean-up. That was the job of the hospitaliers. My job was to rest and to be ready for more walking. Next morning, I was up early to say goodbye to Jacobus. Mikel was leaving too, and he drove me the short distance to the point where the Camino route crossed the road. It began to rain, and Mikel's final act of hospitality was to help me with my rain gear. An old railway and now a cycle track, the route ran in long straight stretches through the Forêt des Landes, complete with railway stations and crossing houses, all recycled as private residences. At times, the forest was thick, at other times, cleared with young trees. Everything appeared to be carefully managed. At some point, notices warned the passerby of fire. The forest is usually silent, but this morning, I enjoyed the sound of rain on the foliage. Nearby was the tiny village of Retjons, and just off the route was the 12th century chapel of Lugaut, known for its 13th century frescoes. I was disappointed to find it locked for the panel by the route told me that *'no one would remain indifferent'* on seeing them. At Retjons, the pilgrim has only 1000 kilometres to Santiago.

At this point, my quirky guidebook filled the blank page opposite the map with this helpful piece of advice:

*If you have nothing better to do than to read this inane stuff, right now sit down on the grass at the edge of the route, get into the lotus position, stare at your backpack and very slowly repeat 1,728 times the word 'Retjons', once forwards and once backwards, articulating each syllable. Why 1,728 times? Because it's the magic number of the ancient Druids, that by which what is, is, and vice versa. When you commence to levitate, when your body is a metre above the ground, stop talking and leave for the astrosphere. If a carload of gendarmes appears, go plonk yourself behind a cloud because it's forbidden to levitate in public on the Chemin de Saint-Jacques.* ( I'm not making this up. It really is in my guidebook!)

As I neared Roquefort, I could just make out two people several hundred metres away standing in the middle of the path. As I neared, I could see they were two hikers with backpacks and umbrellas, facing each other as if they had come from opposite directions. They were a man and a woman, and as I passed, they paused to acknowledge my *'bonjour'* and continued talking. Several hundred metres on just before a curve, I looked back to see them still in the rain in the middle of the track. What gossip, I wondered, held their attention for so long? Apart from a jogger who didn't even acknowledge me, I met no one else.

I arrived in Roquefort at 1 p.m., too early for the refuge, so I took a quick tour around the town. Roquefort was once a fortified town as indicated in its ramparts and its towers dating from the 12th and 14th centuries. Its fortified church (Eglise Sainte-Marie), dating from the 11th century, has undergone numerous transformations down the centuries, its story told in a panel in the grounds. Opposite is the small chapel of Saint-Joseph of more recent origins (16th century). It has welcomed pilgrims on the way to Compostelle, and today is dedicated to Saint-Jacques. In a corner is a statue of St James the pilgrim and on a wall a large medieval style illuminated map of the various Camino routes and sanctuaries. Meantime, a banner in the main street advertised a market of local farm products for the following Wednesday.

The *Refuge des Amis de Saint-Jacques* was an easy find up a side street. Jean-Pierre, whom I met at *Refuge Vialotte* the previous night, welcomed me and showed me the dormitory. Two other pilgrims arrived. Manon and Klaus. Manon was a young French lady and was walking her first Camino. Klaus was older. He was German and also walking his first Camino. Jean-Pierre prepared a very nice meal, *Confit de Canard*. Our discussion was more mundane. Both Klaus and Manon had problems with their feet and their equipment. What you should and should not bring on a Camino was foremost on their minds. Manon, I think, was beginning to realise she had brought too much, for she had her pack's contents spread out everywhere. Klaus mentioned that his son Kevin was planning a visit to Australia for the following year. I gave Klaus my card and said his son would always be welcome if he came by my home in the Snowy Mountains. Jean-Pierre had a wealth of information, which he happily shared. By profession, Klaus was a performer and magician, although he focused on his own discomfort and did not provide us with any entertainment.

I set off the next morning in fine weather. Klaus had already departed, but Manon was still packing. It wasn't long before I realised I was off track. I should not have been walking on bitumen. I had missed a turn, but after asking a resident and two cyclists, I found the signage and pressed on through the Forêt des Landes. A pleasant surprise was the church at

Bostens. From the porch, you entered a side door and found yourself in a *Halte Pèlerins*. Table and chairs, a refrigerator full of cool drinks, microwave, tea and coffee waited for the tired pilgrim. I lingered in the cool longer than I should have, enjoying a cup of tea and reading the various notices, prayers and poems on the walls. Healthy pot plants and fresh flowers on the table suggested that someone close cared for the place. I left a note in the book thanking that person.

After 12 easy kilometres, I found my refuge for the night about two kilometres beyond Gaillères. The *Gîte d'étape* was in the home of Martine. Entrance was underneath through the garage, now a sitting room for the pilgrims. There were five rooms. I was the only pilgrim, although a family member (a son?) occupied one of the other rooms. The house was on a large block with a vegetable garden, a pool and a large black cat that followed me around. Martine and I had dinner on a patio, a meal of tomatoes, aubergine and courgette. Martine was a pleasant lady but her conversation was negative. She had a few gripes and decided to air them on her pilgrim for the night. In her view, everything was going down the gurgler – youth, the economy, the town of Mont de Marsan. Change was far too rapid. I'd say she was disappointed with and sour on her family and felt neglected by her grandchildren. She brightened up when I asked questions about the Forêt des Landes, which surrounded her house. Once unhealthy marshland, the Forêt des Landes covers 950,000 hectares. I mentioned the threat of fires because summer brings bushfires to Australia. Summer's heatwaves bring the threat of fire, she replied, but after serious and murderous fires in the 1950s when she was a child, a prevention plan was developed, including a corps of firefighters, the construction of watch towers, an alert network, water reserves and the construction of fire trails. Her own children had worked on the watch towers during their summer holidays. When you ask a question or two, it's amazing what you learn.

Monday July 29th was my last day of walking the Voie de Vézelay. My destination was Mont de Marson, about 16 kilometres. I was happy that I would have a couple of days of rest before continuing my pilgrimage on the other side of France. I continued to pass through the forest and stopped at Bougue for a coffee and baguette. I joined a cycle track, which took me almost to the centre of Mont de Marsan. The track was busy. No pilgrims but joggers and cyclists, mostly family groups. Some returned my greeting, but others ignored me, suspicious of this friendly stranger. One cyclist, Gerard, stopped to chat. He lived at Bordeaux and was on holidays. He continued on, not before wishing me *'Bon Courage!'*

I knew Mont de Marsan. I made the railway station my reference point, bought tickets for the coming trips, and made my way to the *Refuge de l'Association des Amis de Saint-Jacques des Landes*. The routine was to collect the keys from the Asian grocery just around the corner. However, the hospitalier Jean-Marie was living-in and in residence. Jean-Luc was the other pilgrim for the evening. Whereas Jean-Marie was quiet, Jean-Luc was friendly, exuberant and didn't stop talking. Jean-Marie had prepared some soup, but we bought take-away from the Asian grocer and together we sat down to enjoy our meals. The conversation was wide ranging, mainly stories and experiences of the Camino led by Jean-Luc. Jean-Luc tried to speak in English, but his vocabulary was limited, and he soon reverted to French. He blamed his school; he was taught English by French teachers. Unlike Mikel, Jean-Marie was happy to accept help with the clean-up. I went to bed content that I had completed the first leg of my walking, but as usual I was anxious about the next phase. I tried to drum into my head the usual slogans:

Don't worry! Stay with the moment! Live today today! Etc, etc.

I missed Jean-Luc in the morning but had breakfast with Jean-Marie. He was expecting six pilgrims that evening and was keen to see me leave so that he could prepare for them. I would have liked to leave my pack for the morning, as the train for Paris departed at midday. I took it and left by 8.00 a.m. I spent the morning watching pigeons in the square outside the post office, entering the cathedral hoping to light a candle (there were candles but no matches), visiting a Salon du Thé (where I learnt from a poster in the toilet headed Analysis of a Murder that a cigarette contains 28 poisons), arriving at the station just in time to miss a sudden shower. It was comforting to hear the rain pounding on the roof and remaining dry. I thought of my brother and sister pilgrims diving into their packs for rain gear. The train arrived on time, and soon we were passing vast pine forests and a huge timber mill, the only conversation was my agreeing to change my seat for a family.

*Mikel and Françoise, hospitaliers at the Refuge Vialotte*

*Jean-Luc (pilgrim) and Jean-Marie (hospitalier)
at Refuge Mont de Marsan*

## Via Gebennensis

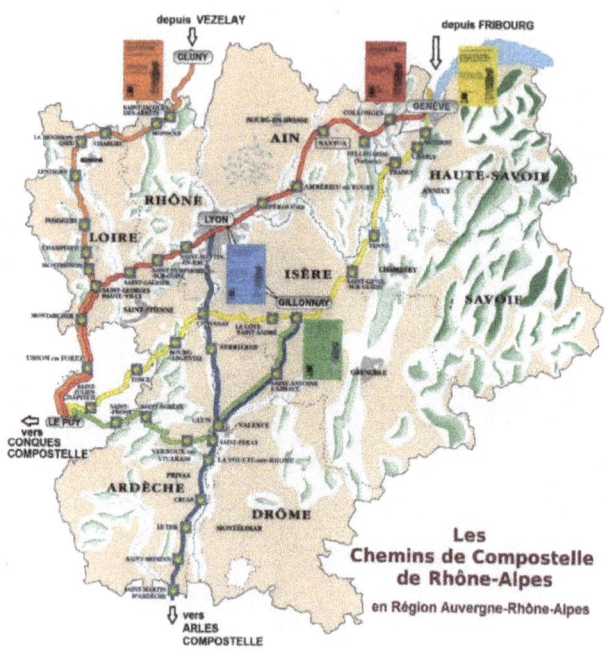

## 15.

*Les difficultés sont faites pour être abattues, non pour nous abattre.*
*(Difficulties are made to be broken down, not to break us down.)*

Seyssel came up by surprise. I was about to walk the Via Gebennensis, the Camino route between Geneva and Le Puy-en-Velay. Not one of the great medieval routes leading to Santiago, it was developed to fill the gap between the Swiss route, signposted between Constance and Geneva, and Le Puy. Le Puy has always been a traditional place of gathering for pilgrims going to Santiago. I commenced my first Camino in this beautiful medieval town back in 2010. The Via Gebennensis avoids the big towns and follows, where practical, ancient routes. Those who use it may enter into the same spirit of pilgrimage as other Camino routes. Listed in the guidebook are a number of 'Accueils Jacquaires', families who open their homes to pilgrims carrying the credential. These 'Accueils Jacquaires' are unique to the Via Gebennensis. They allow pilgrims to discover the spirit of welcome associated with all the chemins leading to Santiago. The route is handy for pilgrims coming from Switzerland, Germany and Central Europe. The guidebook is available in French and German, making the route less accessible to the English-speaking world.

I had taken the train from Paris. The Gare de Lyon fascinates. So many travellers, hundreds of them, waiting for their trains, all encumbered by their luggage. By now, I have learned to take as little as possible, and it continues to surprise how much people take on their travels. Every eye is turned to the screen on high announcing times of arrival and departures. A crowd moves as soon as the platform number appears, dragging their cases like tails behind them. Their number is soon replaced by passengers arriving, anxious to get out of the place as rapidly as possible. Such a swirl of constant movement as if some unknown hand was choreographing the scene. I, too, stirred when the screen announced the platform for Lyon. Movement is more measured to the TGV; seats are reserved, but faces show the strain of pulling heavy loads. Their next challenge is manoeuvring bags onto the train, up a high step over a gap between train and platform and possibly stairs to the upper level. I am pleased that my pack is on my back as I squeeze myself into my seat. At Lyon, I changed trains for Geneva. This time, there was a scramble; the train was full and overflowing. Each carriage had a number of compartments with eight seats, but the corridors were jammed packed, and this time everyone seemed to have a backpack. I found a seat in a compartment midway along the carriage and heaved my pack into the overhead rack. The train stopped several times but no one descended to relieve the pressure. In no time, the train was pulling into Seyssel station. My heart took a jump. Don't panic. I have to get off quickly. I was surprised at my agility, dragging down my pack, and without ceremony, pushing my way out of the compartment, through the crowded corridor and falling out of the train just as the guard was flagging departure.

 The only one to quit the train, I was alone at the Gare Seyssel. Job done, the station attendant was already in his car. No one to ask which way to go! I sat for a moment on a stone wall to recover from my fluster. I looked down the road and saw cars crossing a bridge and other cars parked outside shops, so I started walking. It was after 4 p.m. I had to find Les Côtes, two kilometres from Seyssel and 250 metres higher in altitude; I expected a steep climb. I looked around. I was in beautiful country, surrounded by hills covered with forests and fields and dotted with houses. The road bordered the wide river Rhône. I entered the pharmacy and asked the pharmacist directions. He pointed vaguely across the bridge and said Les Côtes was about five kilometres. I found that no help at all but thanked him and walked across the bridge to begin climbing, not before guessing which one of several roads to take. One challenge after another! The road zigzagged up the hill. As I climbed higher, I realised just how hot the day was. Sweat poured out of me, and I stopped many times for a breather but, at the same time, admired the wonderful view. I climbed for an hour. My pack was heavier with each step. Traffic moved slowly and carefully. Most ignored me, but a few waved. I wished that one car, just one, contained a kind soul concerned for my plight, would stop and offer me a lift. No such being passed until I had almost reached the top. Vivienne pulled over and invited me to jump in. For an instant, I thought I should decline since I had been walking only for an hour. Just as quickly, I dismissed that scruple and accepted. She said she knew where I was heading as her neighbour ran the gîte, the only gîte in Les Côtes. Within a few minutes, we arrived outside *'Gîte d'étape Edelweiss-Les Côtes d'en Haut'*, an ancient stone building with a modern addition in wood. My host Sylvie showed me the dormitory where I was the only occupant. In another room were a couple whom I met later at the evening meal. Dinner was served in the wooden structure, large enough for weddings and conferences. Breathtaking was the view overlooking the town and valley. Here I met the couple. Bea and Forsten were Germans. They had little French, nor English, but I worked out they'd been walking the Camino two weeks at a time for 6 years and would reach Santiago one of these days. Dinner was cooked and served by Sylvie's teenager son, Clément. Sylvie showed up later and asked jokingly for a report on Clément's efforts. The three of us gave top ratings to the son being groomed for the family business.

Next morning, I found the signage for the Chemin and followed the shell of St Jacques all the way down the hill along a rough steep track and across the bridge to Seyssel. I could have saved myself an awful lot of effort by staying the night in the town, except that all accommodation was expensive. At the tourist office, I met two pilgrims, the only ones for the day. Two friendly Germans with broad smiles, one with a backpack both front and back. I joked with them that I had the choice of three languages to greet them – French, German or English.

So began my Via Gebennensis. I should have started at Geneva, but I shaved about 50 kilometres off the journey and avoided the possible hassle of having to cross borders. I walked for 14 level kilometres to Serrières-en-Chautagne, mostly along the banks of the river Rhône, past dam walls and locks and in delightful leafy shade. In a sports and nature reserve, I found a small kiosk getting ready for lunch. An ice cream for morning tea would be nice, I thought, and in French, asked the lady for one. A chap doing some modifications to the shutter asked where I was from, and in English said he was a New Zealander. Ken has lived in France for 18 years. Still a New Zealander, no way was he relinquishing his citizenship. He continued with his job while I focused on my ice cream. I returned to the river track and somehow lost the Chemin until I emerged onto a road that seemed to take forever to lead me to Serrières-en-Chautagne.

I had tried to ring several times the camping place, and left a message, so I pressed on. The *Camping Le Clairet* looked very nice with accommodation and a snack bar for meals, but it was full (*'complet'*). I tried the *Hôtel-Restaurant-Auberge Chautagnard*, a quaint old building with modern add-ons, far more expensive than the Camping, but I wasn't prepared to move on. Fourteen kilometres was enough. I was the only guest. The Hôtel was the local watering hole. I would have loved to join the group of men at the bar and find out a little of their lives. Their French was so natural and spontaneous while mine is so measured.

Serrières-en-Chautagne is an attractive village. It boasts a well-stocked secondhand bookshop. When I find a bookshop, I never fail to browse and often buy. Not this time! The camping was by a small lake and lots was going on. Family groups were swimming while older people played boules with much shouting and laughter. Groups of teenagers roved around. Not a pilgrim among them; everyone was on holidays. The snack bar turned out to be a full-blown restaurant with live music entertainment.

Back at the Hôtel, I realised my glasses were missing. I had them in my trouser pocket, so I retraced my steps. Anxious thoughts had me imagining life without them. No luck! I had almost resigned myself to a semi-blind existence for the rest of my French adventure. I'll try the snack bar, I thought. There they were, sitting on the counter. With immense gratitude, I thanked the girl and was equally thankful to the kind person who handed them in. Lesson learned: be more careful. Life could have been quite a strain without my reading glasses.

Someone was looking after me.

The village hadn't come to life as I left next morning, passed the camping, the lake and a parking lot full of motor homes. The signage directed me to a cycle path that led into a forest '*Forêt Dominale de Chautagne*'. Straight ahead, I could see a vehicle and a man cutting overhanging branches with a saw on a long pole. I stopped for a breather and for a chat. Christian was ready for a chat too. A forester with the Office National des Forêts, he told me that the forest contained the largest poplar grove in Europe. The 850 hectare site was originally part of the Rhône River flood plain known as the Marais de Chautagne and was used for raising cattle and as a source of vegetable fertiliser for the region's vineyards, and eventually became the forest. Christian was proud of his domain, and I left him to his job while I continued on with my job of following the track until it came back to the River Rhône. Most of the day was spent on this shady path with the occasional warning that this was a flood plain and to keep my eye on the river level. Not much chance of a flood with France almost as dry as Australia! A number of seats lined the path, and I took the opportunity to rest, sometimes only a few seconds but long enough for brief relief of the pressure of my backpack on my aching shoulders. On one of these seats someone had scratched:

> La nature n'est pas votre poubelle. Ramenez vos déchets. Merci.
> (Nature is not your rubbish bin. Remove your rubbish. Thanks.)

Two pilgrims passed me without saying a word despite my greeting. Perhaps they were Germans with no French, or were intent on the serious business of covering as much ground as possible in the shortest possible time. Three cyclists stopped. They responded to my *'Bonjour'* and were happy to pass the time of day, being tourists out for the day and by the way they wobbled, not often on bikes. Otherwise, I had this lovely shaded path to myself with the waters of the river on the right sometimes obscured by the foliage. Via Gebennensis was going to be quiet. Around this lovely valley, the mountains towered, with bare white rock cliffs and forest cover. I would have to cross them sometime, but not today.

After 13 kilometres of this lovely walking, I arrived in Chanaz, a picturesque town indeed. My first view was that of a canal lined with outdoor restaurants under white canvas. A few boats were in the water, but the activity was in the street edging the canal. The restaurants were full of diners and waiters were dashing across with orders. Such a concentration of tourists in a small space! All shops were given over to tourism – bars, gift shops, lacework, wine cellars. The village streets ran up the hillside, and along one of these streets I found the *Gîte et Chambre d'Hôtes El Camino*, as picturesque as the rest of the town with its ancient stone-walled building that housed the Chambre d'hôtes. The gîte for pilgrims was in a wooden building at the rear. Gisenal was looking after the place for the day. I shared a cool drink with her and Lily, the only other guest. She was not a pilgrim but here for the weekend to do some leisurely walking. I explored the village and some of the shops before returning for dinner, which was vegetarian and, I have to admit, very ordinary. At breakfast, I met the owner Denise, a very pleasant outgoing lady and wondered if she were a better cook.

I was worried about the next stage of my journey. Yenne was 17 kilometres and involved some climbing. I thought about a taxi but decided to give it a go. The first part involved steep climbing past an ancient mill and a chapel, built in 1845 by the locals for the Virgin Mary to seek her protection and restored in 2005 to its original colours. I read a delightful poem about love, addressed to those whom the passerby met yesterday. They are no longer present, but one wants to discover their qualities, and for one's heart to accept them as they are. At the top, I was rewarded with excellent views of the countryside. I felt encouraged; morale was high that I had met the challenge and handled the climbing. I continued to walk through vineyards that extended across the hills and valleys against the ever-present surrounding mountains, like sentinels guarding the vines grown in this beautiful undulating land for centuries.

I stopped to chat to Christian, a local, who was varnishing a window frame. He was in the process of restoring a farm building bordering the Chemin. A stop for a future refuge, perhaps? Just at the entrance of Yenne, a pilgrim came upon me as I was taking my final rest. A young man with long hair and beard looking like Jesus, Tristan was German. He, too, had stayed at Chanaz. He started walking from Switzerland.

By the time I reached the town I was worn out, but at the same time pleased I'd made it. Longing for a rest and to remove my pack I enquired at the tourist office for direction to the address of my first Accueils Jacquaires, the families that accept pilgrims into their homes. I felt as if I was approaching something sacred and, with just a touch of apprehension, knocked on their door. There was absolutely no need to worry. My reception was excellent. Warm and caring persons, Alain and Marie-Noel had been receiving pilgrims into their lovely home for 10 years. They offered me a beer, and we sat on their balcony and chatted. They made me feel a special guest, and later we enjoyed a delightful meal of four courses. Over dinner, I told them of my plans to stop for a week at La Côte Saint André to be a hospitalier. Marie-Noel was delighted; she had been a hospitalier herself in the same place.

My first experience of staying with Accueils Jacquaires was excellent. Such wonderful hospitality! I looked forward to staying with others.

The next morning, I woke feeling refreshed and raring to go. It always amazes me what a fine meal in good company with a red wine or two plus a sound night's sleep can do. My destination that day was Saint-Genix-sur-Guiers, about 24 kilometres. When I began Camino walking in 2010, such a distance was normal, but now, 9 years later in my 87th year, I did not have the confidence in my own body to last the distance. I tried to ring for a taxi to take me to Saint-Maurice-de-Rotherens without success. Instead, Alain drove me. On the way, he chatted about the Chemin. He led a team of volunteers that was responsible for a section, and he walked it himself every three weeks to ensure everything such as signage and track conditions were in excellent order. I could not be thankful enough for the generosity of such people who cared for the route and tried to ensure the safety of the passing pilgrim.

I was left with about eight kilometres. I had missed some serious climbing, and thankfully the way was mostly downhill and in shade. I paused to visit three churches, all open. The first one was at Saint Maurice, complete with a wooden image of Saint-Jacques. I lit a candle for Maris in the church at Grésin, Notre Dame de l'Assomption. A sensor set off Bach music, which played for the duration of my visit, a delightful touch. Fresh flowers indicated that someone unseen loved the church. On the wall was a wooden statue of the Curé d'Ars and a handwritten notice reminding the visitor that today August 4th was his feast day. In the porch were cut-out figures of pilgrims suggesting this church was a place of welcome. Other signs of welcome greeted me along the way. An open barn invited the passing pilgrim to pause. Against a stack of wood for the winter fires was a table of drinks. A notice invited the passing pilgrim to help themselves to a shell. The writer indicated that they had been gathered by their son Malik off the coast of Bretagne and included his photograph in diving mode. I lit another candle in the Chapelle de Pigneux. This time, a notice that I had seen before in other churches, reminded me that through the lit candle my prayer would continue after I went on my way.

The temperature had reached 35 degrees by the time I reached Saint-Genix-sur-Guiers. I had rung another Accueil Jacquaire who were happy to have me. I eventually found the address, but no one was home, so I left my pack outside the locked gate. The house was in a cul-de-sac, so I hoped it would it be safe; I did not feel like lugging it around on that hot afternoon. I had heard of packs being stolen from outside bars by an opportunistic thief driving past even though the owners were sitting beside them. There was no shade to wait in, so I headed back to town to visit the church, find a boulangerie for the morning and a bar for the present moment. Outside the bar was a signpost indicating the distance to various places such as the Maldives, Mexico and Sao Paulo. Sydney was only 18,816 kilometres.

Back at the address, the gate was open and my bag was by the garage wall. My Accueils Jacquaires were Marie-Pascal and Roland, not as spontaneously open, but nevertheless welcoming and caring. Marie-Pascal was interested in the reason why I was walking the Chemin. I told her about Maris and how she is walking with me. I spent a pleasant evening with them, Marie-Pascal frequently correcting my pronunciation. Roland rang for me two Accueils Jacquaires in Les Abrets. One has stopped taking pilgrims; the other had grandchildren visiting. He was successful with a third, three kilometres after Les Abrets, which he told me was very good. They seemed to have a network and knew each other. After dinner, he showed me his vegetable garden, which he watered, paying special attention to the newly planted lettuce. I felt a complete and uncomplicated acceptance into the family and its routines.

Next morning, walking along a river was easy, but the

hills followed, stiff testing climbs. I was relieved to pause for a breather with two young exuberant walkers. Roland and Maxine were Swiss; they had completed their schooling and were walking in their holidays before going on to university. The undulations continued – great on the downhill incline. I passed a friendly donkey who kept pace with me as I walked by. Tristan, whom I met two days previously, caught up and passed on. I lost count of the number of times I climbed up and down, but the last climb into Les Abrets was the toughest. I had to push myself, repeating the old mantras: 'One step at a time;' 'Each step brings me one pace nearer;' 'Come on Noël, you can do it!' I managed to stagger into Les Abrets, but the traffic intensity and noise were no comfort, and I had three more kilometres to survive. After some lunch I set out again to face more steep climbing. Just as I reckoned I must be close and quickly running out of puff, a car stopped and the driver offered to take me. He was Alain, my host for the evening. I heard later that he often drove out this time of day to pick up pilgrims struggling up his hill. We were not far from his home in Charancieu.

What a wonderful host he turned out to be! I met his wife Florentine, from Madagascar, equally warm and outgoing, as well as her daughter Ophelia, who was on holidays from Paris. Rather than call themselves *Accueils Jacquaires*, they were *Chambre et table pèlerin*; the main difference being that they had a set charge, whereas the other asked for a donation. Their home was a rambling affair of the old and the new. Alain's influence lay in the old part; it looked as if he had never thrown anything away. Pots and pans of various ages hung on the barn wall. Florentine's influence lay in the bright colours, flowery wallpapers, art and objects from Madagascar. Everything had been thrown together. The total result could have been a mess, but the whole was picturesque and charming. Added to this was an extensive orchard and vegetable garden and a magnificent view. Gnomes and dwarfs, a multitude of potted plants filled the corners, leaving an open space between gate and house. Alain believed that his place's greatest charm lay in its tranquillity.

The other guests were Bea and Forsten, the German couple whom I had met five days previously at Les Côtes – Gîte d'étape: l'Edelweiss. They stayed the night before and were finishing this year's walking that day and would return home to Germany. Alain drove them to the station to catch a train to Paris then bus. When Alain returned, he brought out the local aperitifs. The conversation flowed. Alain was due to have a cataract removal from his right eye the following morning and would be off early to hospital. In the meantime, Florentine tried to find a bed for me at Le Pin, but nothing was available. I was concerned because the next place would involve far too much walking, 26 kilometres to Chomat. Alain intervened, *'There is always a solution'* and suggested that I walk to Le Pin, and he would pick me up and bring me back to his place for another night, then take me back to Le Pin the following morning to continue walking. I protested that he had his own health worries. I had had cataracts removed from both eyes and knew what was involved. He insisted his cataract removal was no big deal. I was overwhelmed, in fact tearful at his amazing generosity. Florentine prepared a great meal, and we dined together outside on this balmy evening.

Alain and Florentine had already departed by the time I surfaced. Ophelia prepared breakfast. On holidays from her job as a school teacher, she discussed some of the discipline problems a young teacher can experience. Classroom management, as they call it, is the most difficult part of the job. Unless the young teacher is on top of it, they can't be effective. I was not sure if Ophelia was looking forward to going back to work. She helped me to prepare a sandwich for lunch, then drove me the kilometre or so to the route where I could follow the signage to Santiago. I set off, my heart full of gratitude for this amazing family, to walk the 14 kilometres to Le Pin. Because I would be staying an extra night with Alain and Florentine, I left most of my pack's contents behind.

Lightening my physical load was easy compared with some of the other stuff we carry. Things like self-doubt, shame, guilt, fear of the unknown, false beliefs, unexamined opinions, stuff I believed about who I am, things people did to me, things people said to me, desire for approval are all hard to dislodge. Sometimes we get rid of them, but they have a nasty habit of returning and upsetting the balance.

The lighter pack was delightful, and I had a moment of envy for those who walk with a day pack and have their baggage transported. I had a lighter load, but nevertheless, my body protested at the series of climbs up steep hills, and its various parts took their turn to complain, sometimes all at once. I walked along the ridge line and was rewarded with magnificent views over the valleys. (*Why climb the mountain if you don't stop to look at the view?*) I passed through the villages of Valencogne and Saint-Ondras and arrived at Le Pin. Three walkers passed me as I entered the town. They had lunch at the cafe but apart from a greeting, I didn't talk to them; with their day packs I guess they were not pilgrims but out for the day. I had a Coke, visited the church and lit a candle, then rang Florentine. About half an hour later, both arrived, Alain driving and wearing a patch over his right eye. I was pleased that he was driving on quiet country roads and somehow felt safe in the back seat. Later, he removed the patch, but the light was too intense, and he had to find his sunnies. The pain grew on him as the anaesthetic wore off. Even then, he battled on and set out on his afternoon drive and returned with two pilgrims – Felicitas and Margot from Germany.

The sky darkened and thunder rolled in the distance, so the five of us had dinner inside. Margot had no French but spoke English while Felicitas was fluent in both, so the conversation flowed. Felicitas seemed intrigued by me, an ancient pilgrim all the way from Australia. I told my story. Florentine told us their story. They passed the summer here at Charancieu, and the other half of the year in Madagascar where they worked on raising funds for schools for the disadvantaged. She showed us many photos.

We had breakfast together. I learned that Felicitas and Margot were booked into the same place as me for the night; I was pleased I would see them again. The sky was dark, and rain was threatening. We prepared ourselves for a soggy day, and as we were leaving, Margot turned to me with a sigh and said :'Why are we doing this?' 'I guess many pilgrims ask of themselves the same question,' I replied.

Felicitas and Margot set off to walk the 26 kilometres to Le Grand-Lemps; Alain and Florentine drove me to Le Pin to walk 12. Rain on steep slopes created mini-streams running down among the rocks and created further challenges, but I managed to keep my foothold. On the hill above Le Grand-Lemps, the pilgrim faced a choice. Taking the road involved three kilometres, but descending down a steep slope meant only two. My better judgement told me to take the road, but the other side of my brain only heard the shorter distance. Besides, by now, the rain had stopped, and the sun was shining. So down the steep slippery slope I went. Sometimes, the slippery slide leads to ruin, and it did not take long for me to realise I had made a mistake. The slope was indeed slippery and wet. Little rivers were still running; the overgrown foliage was damp and brushed against me. The rocks large and small made finding a foothold hazardous. Several times, I almost went over but for my walking poles. The track went on and on, and I took much longer than if I'd walked the road. Eventually, all bad things come to an end.

At Le Grand-Lemps, I enquired at the post office for the address of my Accueil Jacquaire. Paul and Line were preparing gooseberries for jam when I arrived, but they knocked off to welcome me and offer a beer, a great way to quieten my nerves, still jangly after the hazardous descent. Their house was well lived in and had all the signs of raising a family. From the many books, most of them religious, I guessed Paul and Line were committed church people. Felicitas and Margot arrived. We greeted each other with enthusiasm. Felicitas was worried she would find me on the slippery slide. They, too, had decided to take the short cut. Even though I had only met them the night before, they were like old friends. Actually, they were; they were part of my Camino family, the many pilgrims I had met during my six Caminos. Although the individuals are changing constantly, the same spirit of bonding and love remain. Each of those individual pilgrims have left a trace in my memory, but I think of them as a collective that exists beyond my mind.

The five of us sat down to a meal. The conversation flowed, and it became obvious that our hosts were well involved in the parish. Next morning, Paul left early to cycle to church for Mass, so the three pilgrims ate with Line. I left just after the two girls. I had trouble finding my way out of town. I saw the signage the day before, but couldn't remember where. After wandering around in circles for about half an hour, Line drove by, probably on the way home after Mass. She pointed me in the right direction, further back than I had expected, so away I went. Someone will always turn up to help you; that's the magic of the Camino.

The walking was mostly level with a few climbs, but the day was hot, and I was pleased I would be stopping for a week. The thought of not wearing my backpack was delicious. I stopped at Saint-Hilaire-de-la-Côte and took advantage of a pilgrim shelter. A large panel welcomed the pilgrim and provided a map and other information on the Via Gebennensis. The Association Rhône-Alpes des Amis de Saint-Jacques has done a fine job in managing this part of the Chemin. I stopped, too, at the Stèle de Stéphane Gantelet, a small monument marking the crossroads of two chemins, the other being the way from Le Puy to Arles in the south. Further on, I visited the church at Gillonnay-Rondet before the final run into La Côte-Saint-André.

*First view of Chanaz*

15.

*Alain and Florentine — Chambre et Table Pèlerin at Charancieu*

*Margot and Felicitas*

## 16.

*Il ne suffit pas de donner des années á la vie.*
*Encore faut-il donner de la vie aux années.*
*(It is not enough to give the years to life.*
*One must give life to the years.)*

The *Patrimoine* is well preserved in La Côte-Saint-André. At the entrance to the town is a series of older buildings including the Maire, which is an 18th century chateau. Then you go down a series of steps, some enclosed, until you arrive at the Halle, an ancient building where markets are still held. As I walked across the large covered space, I heard my name. 'Noël!' Felicitas and Margot were waving from a bar (*Le Berlioz*) on the other side. I came across and joined them. The day was hot, I was near the end of my walking and, knowing I should not have far, I joined them for a beer. They had made good time and were relaxing after a lunch. They had not decided on their destination for the evening. I told them I was making for the *Apprentis d'Auteuil* where I would be the hospitalier for the coming week. After some discussion, they decided to stay in La Côte-Saint-André, too. Armed with directions from the bar owner, we walked downhill, along a tree-lined avenue, past the swimming pool, crowded that hot afternoon, about a kilometre until we arrived at the security gate of *Apprentis d'Auteuil*. I pressed the button, spoke to a voice and the gates opened. We had another 400 metres to the building, an imposing old affair built in the early 1900s with thick walls that were meant to last.

The entrance was in front but a shell sign directed us to the pilgrim refuge on the left. Up a grand staircase to the first floor where we were welcomed by Marie-Rose, the hospitalière whom I was to replace. Marie-Rose also organised the roster. We had exchanged a series of emails, so I was keen to meet her in person, a quiet but friendly lady, warm and welcoming and able to put the anxious pilgrim at ease. We were also greeted by Alfred, a Swiss pilgrim who had arrived by bicycle. The girls decided to go back to the town for dinner, but Alfred and I sat down to a meal prepared by Rose-Marie. Her meal was potato-based and included ravioli, a dish from the north of France. I questioned her about the recipe, for I was keen to get as many tips as possible. Alfred, a solid, well-built exuberant man in his sixties, had none of the litheness of the younger cyclists. No doubt he was slimly built one day. He had recently retired and was cycling to Santiago, covering about 80 kilometres a day.

Margo and Felicitas left early with the promise they would send me emails of the places they stayed at, so I had breakfast with Alfred and Rose-Marie. We talked about the various health problems each of us had to manage to continue our normal day-to-day living. After we farewelled Alfred, I shadowed Rose-Marie to learn the ropes of being a hospitalier Rhône-Alpes style. I had already been a hospitalero for 2 weeks at Rabanal del Camino in Spain. Each refuge has its own routine. At Rabanal del Camino, for example, there were three separate mops and buckets, each with its own colour code – one for the kitchen, one for the bathrooms and the third for the dormitories. If they were mixed up, they had to be sterilised before re-using. Here they were not so fussy, but I knew the rigorous training in industrial cleaning I received at Rabanal del Camino would hold me in good stead. The major chore was washing the sheets. The laundry was on the other side of the building, a good 5 minutes' walk down the stairs along a long corridor, through three sets of doors and a toilet. You had to make sure you brought the correct tokens for the machines. Back to retrieve the sheets, etc, and put them in the dryer. Back again to bring the clean sheets home! At least, the doors weren't locked but the toilet was sometimes.

All the morning we chatted pleasantly. Rose-Marie had little English. I had trouble getting the pronunciation of *'Apprentis d'Auteuil'* correct. I'm murdering the language, I said to Rose-Marie. *'Je suis assassin de la langue française.'* I used that joke many times. The French seemed to love it.

We had lunch together, then Rose-Marie departed, leaving a clued-up Noël to await his first pilgrims. I had a booking for two. I waited and waited, and eventually received a call about 6.30 p.m. My pilgrims were at the gate and couldn't get in. I grabbed the device for opening them, locked and left the refuge to walk down to the gate and I met them halfway. They entered as a car went out. Michael and Angela were Swiss with very good English. They were a weather-beaten pair, with wide smiles and intensely blue eyes. They lived their lives outdoors. I brought them back to the refuge, went through the welcome routine and showed them their rooms. Being a pilgrim myself, I knew what pilgrims appreciate and I was keen to provide it. I prepared their meal, and we sat down together. They were vegetarians and environmentally conscious. Global warming was an immense problem. I found it encouraging that ordinary people throughout the globe have the same concern. They want to leave a healthy planet for their children and grandchildren. Their daughter was with them until today. She had returned home for work, and they were continuing on to Santiago.

They left about 8.30, and I went through the routine of cleaning, washing and getting rid of the rubbish. I walked to the supermarket and boulangerie, over a kilometre. I was asked directions twice. I looked like a local, I suppose, with my bag, an old bloke doing his Saturday morning shopping. I recalled the advice my daughter Angela gave me before my first trip to France. *'Look like a local, Dad. Blend in!'* I returned to the Apprentis d'Auteuil and waited for the telephone to ring. I carried the phone in a pocket all the time. Work was done. I had only to wait, so a good time to explore the building.

The Apprentis d'Auteuil is a Catholic foundation founded in 1866 when a French priest Abbé Roussel took in abandoned orphan children wandering the streets of Paris. He decided that all children should be helped, whatever their background or belief. He wanted each child to be welcomed, cared for, taught to read and write, receive a Christian education and have a job. From these small beginnings, the organisation has grown with 240 establishments in France and is present in 32 countries. Its main goal is to help youth in difficulty by conducting educational projects and boosting their ability to participate in society as full-fledged citizens through training and insertion programs. In addition to helping vulnerable children, Apprentis d'Auteuil assists struggling parents in their family obligations in a partnership to bring up their children as free and responsible adults.

The Apprentis d'Auteuil arrived in this building, Le Maison de la Côte St. André, in 1987. It's a grand old lady, built when buildings were solid. Its construction began in 1899 as a *'Petit Seminaire'* and welcomed its first young people in 1902. Its use has varied over the years. It had periods when it was closed and was a military hospital during the World Wars. Today its use includes college classes, training classes for apprenticeship, a home for young workers. I saw a few in the grounds.

The *Association Rhône-Alpes etc* has leased a wing of the building for use as a refuge for pilgrims. It's out of town and as there are other places for pilgrims, I wasn't expecting to be inundated. Not only it is out of town, the pilgrim also has to run the gauntlet of getting through the gate and walking uphill about 400 metres and then finding the refuge in the large rambling building. Once they arrive, they find an excellent facility.

I had no one Saturday night, but three pilgrims arrived Sunday. A German lady Anke arrived about 3.30 pm. Outgoing, she spoke excellent English and had a broad warm smile. Catherine, a Swiss lady, arrived a little later. She was quieter and asked if there was a quiet place for prayer. The weather deteriorated and soon driving rain drenched the afternoon. Anke and Catherine had arrived in the nick of time. Not so for poor Florian. I had to wait for him. It's like waiting for a family member to return home; once a pilgrim has rung to make a reservation, they are part of the family. Eventually he arrived, delayed by the storm, thoroughly soaked. Fortunately, the refuge had a large room where pilgrims could leave their wet weather gear to dry and where they could stuff paper into their boots. Florian, a younger man, was French but lived in Spain near Santiago. We sat down to my meal, and as always, a meal bonds pilgrims. They arrive as individuals and leave as a family. They were interested in me; they wanted to know what was an elderly Australian hospitalier doing here in a place like La Côte-Saint-André. I told them I ask the same question of myself.

In the morning, Anke thought my coffee was weak. I replied that I had come to France not only to butcher the French's language but to weaken their coffee. The three left about 8.30 after much deliberation on destination for the day and what to wear. It was not raining, but the skies were threatening. I was left to myself, for once again, I had no reservations. The highlight of the day was meeting one of the residents of the Apprentis d'Auteuil. I met him at the gate as I walked to the supermarket. We walked together. He looked about 14. Very polite, he told me his name and where his family lived. I did not ask him why he was living away from his family. Having no idea of his background, I was just a little wary. However, he chatted and then asked me for 5 euros. I was not sure of the protocol. He offered me a book in exchange. That seemed okay, so I accepted. The book *Des Ombres sur le Rocher*, a translation of Willa Cather's *Shadow on the Rock* about French colonial exploration and life in early Quebec. Later, I met him in the supermarket. He asked for more money, but I declined. I enjoyed reading his book.

I received a phone call from Marie-Noël who was my host at Yenne. She had been a hospitalier here. She wished me well. I received a booking from Line from Chomat. She wished me well, too. I had told both that I would a hospitalier here. In bed that night I read a booklet by Esther Ostrach on how to get your pack down to 3.5 kg. I wish!

Next day, Tuesday August 13th, I was confused about how many pilgrims I would welcome, for the same people rang twice. My pilgrims turned out to be a family of three, Marie, Jorge and Naia, their 22-month-old baby. They arrived tired and flustered, complete with a large pram. Marie carried Naia in a bag at the front, while the pram was used for conveying all their stuff, including a little scooter and lots of toys. They left almost immediately for a doctor's appointment. They had arranged for someone to pick them up. At first, they said they would find an evening meal elsewhere but later rang to ask if it was possible. Back they came about 6.30. They had done some shopping, but realised they had a potential crisis on their hands; they had forgotten baby napkins. I would have loved to have said that the refuge kept a few on hand for such emergencies, but seldom did it have babies as guests. I told Marie that the supermarket closed at 7 p.m., so she did a sprint and arrived in the nick of time. I sighed in relief when she returned triumphantly waving the package.

## 16.

Naia was a handful. She kept snatching the phone, etc. and had to be coaxed to give them back. I admired her parent's patience, gently guiding and encouraging her. There are enough challenges on the Camino, I thought, without having to manage a two-year-old. I was inclined to think that walking the Camino was Jorge's rather than Marie's idea. She seemed worn out. Jorge struck me as a determined person with strong views, which he was prepared to express forthrightly. He was Spanish while Marie was French, but they both spoke good English. They were walking towards Geneva against the stream. They had just passed through regions I would be walking, and I had covered what would be their chemin. Over dinner, Jorge and I swapped information on places with a *'big heart'*, places where the welcome and hospitality were exceptional.

The next morning was a late start, waiting for Naia to wake up. She was out-of-sorts and grizzly; her parents were sluggish and slow to get going. Perhaps, I should have suggested they stay another day. I rang and reserved a place for them at Line and Alain's at Le Grand-Lemps. That was certainly a place with a big heart. I knew that they would be warmly welcomed and cared for. With their large family, they would be very used to small children. It was a procession, the departure of my little Camino family. Naia, still crying, decided to ride her scooter, Marie close behind, ready to pick up both Naia and the scooter, and Jorge, burdened with a large backpack, bounced the loaded pram down the stairway, the clack-clack echoing up the stairwell, following them out the door into a grey morning.

My week as a hospitalier was drawing to a close. I had two more nights and a guest on each. On Wednesday, Laurence arrived about 3:30 p.m. In her 30s, Laurence had been a hospitalière at this gîte. She was attending a meeting that evening, so she would find something to eat in town. She was not late coming back, so we had an opportunity for a chat. She was in La Côte-Saint-André for the Hector Berlioz festival of 2 weeks, due to commence on Saturday. La Côte-Saint-André was the birthplace of the renowned composer and this was his 150th anniversary, so a special program had been organised. Laurence would be a volunteer in the second week and would stay in the gîte. Several rooms had been reserved for the musicians, so there would be little room for pilgrims. Indeed, the guide books included a warning that accommodation in the town would be scarce during the festival.

Thursday August 15th was a public holiday. Not that it made any difference as I went about my chores and shopping. However, I visited the market in the Halle and bought some trout. I was confused when Alain rang twice. I thought I would be hosting two pilgrims both with the name of Alain. He turned up late afternoon on a motorised bicycle. He was a quiet man, and I found it hard work keeping the conversation going, a good test of my French. However, he lived in Chambéry where I studied French in 2006, so I had my memories of the town to discuss. He was recently retired and had been a dairy farmer. I thought about serving him the fish but decided to keep the trout for lunch with Bernadette, the new hospitalière.

Alain asked for an early breakfast and left by 7 a.m., so I had an early start on my chores. I worked hard and thoroughly, as I wanted to leave the gîte sparkling clean for my replacement, even scrubbing the bird shit off the balcony. Quiet during the week, the building sprang alive; people were arriving, and I thought Bernadette was among them, but they were visitors for the festival, who were staying in the Apprentis d'Auteuil. She arrived late morning. A quiet and pleasant lady, she asked many questions, and I did my best to take her through the routines. I left about 2 pm to continue my adventure.

*My first pilgrims at Apprentis d'Auteuil at La Côte-Saint-André Bright-eyed, blue-eyed Michael and Angela from Switzerland.*

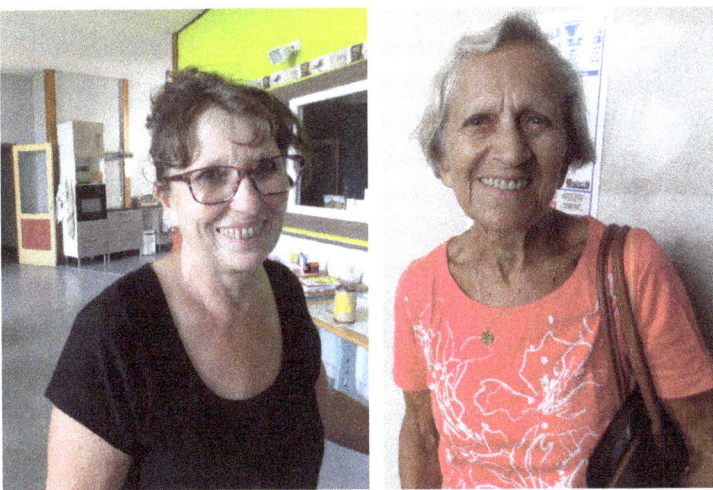

*Rose-Marie and Bernadette, hospitalières at Apprentis d'Auteuil*

## 17.

*Qui veut voyager loin ménage sa monture. (He who wishes to travel far spares his mount.)* – French proverb

I walked along Avenue Hector Berlioz back into the town, past his statue and by many posters advertising the festival. The afternoon was warm, but I wasn't concerned as I would be walking 5 kilometres to Ornacieux-Balbins. I was happy with myself. I had completed my week as a hospitalier and thought I had done a good job. Pity the gîte was out of town and off the route because the facilities were excellent and, from the reactions of my pilgrims, exceeded expectations. There were few pilgrims in the first place on this Via Gebennensis. Tomorrow, I would walk about 20 kilometres, but for this afternoon, I was content with five. I enjoyed leaving the town and finding myself back in the country amid farmland and forest.

I paused for a rest outside Ornacieux-Balbins. Along came a pilgrim. Udo was Dutch and spoke excellent English. He was a big man, spoke in a loud voice and had plenty to say. He left me to continue on; he said he still had plenty of walking to do that afternoon. Before following, I felt in my pocket for my handkerchief and, to my horror, pulled out the gîte's phone. The hospitalier was supposed to answer the phone at any time so it was natural that I carried it. This morning, I had automatically put it in my pocket. There was only one way to give it to Bernadette and that was to return. So back I dashed, my usual leisurely pace abandoned. By the time I'd arrived I was soaked with sweat from the day's heat, my hurried exertion, annoyance and anxiety. Bernadette had been looking for the phone. I'm sure she would have driven me back, but it was 4 p.m. and she was waiting for three pilgrims. I felt exhausted, rested for about 15 minutes, drank a litre of water and rang Marie-Christine at Ornacieux-Balbins to say I would arrive later than expected.

I arrived at Ornacieux-Balbins about 6:30 p.m. The next challenge was to find Marie-Christine's Accueil Jacquaire, but she was standing in the middle of the road waiting for me. She spoke good English, led me up the hill to her place, a solid ancient house covered with ivy. A more or less wild garden with vegetables growing randomly rather than in neat plots added to its charm. I was surprised to find Udo; I thought he had moved on. I felt as if I had walked far more than 11 kilometres and was grateful for a shower. Refreshed but tired, I joined Udo in the garden for a meal that Marie-Christine cooked in a garden oven, heated by the sun. I was intrigued. She was into natural ways and organic foods. Over dinner, Udo expressed his views on many subjects. He was strong on conspiracy theories, including what was 'really' behind the 9/11 twin towers tragedy. Despite his authoritative ways, he was a pleasant man, and I enjoyed the opportunity to challenge his views. People passed by and chatted over the fence. They were Marie-Christine's friends, some were Accueils Jacquaires themselves. There were six in the village, and through their network, passed pilgrims from one to the other. I had good vibes; it seemed a close-knit community.

As night fell, I was happy to retire with the birds. I shared the room with Udo, and although loud enough when awake, he was quiet in sleep; I expected him to snore. In the morning, he posed the question: 'What is the definition of sin?' His point, I think, was that what was once a sin is not one now, and vice versa. I proposed it was a weighty subject to discuss over breakfast and could give us indigestion. A pity he didn't raise the issue the night before. I left before him, as he needed time to collect his belongings and his thoughts, but he caught up with me and, with his long strides, forged ahead. I had given myself a target of 20 kilometres. The walking was reasonably level with a steep climb into Pommier-de-Beaurepaire. I met no other pilgrims although a profusion of grasshoppers accompanied me every time I passed through open fields. My destination was Revel-Tourdan, or rather, a gîte 1.5 km beyond. The *Gîte d'étape La Ferme des Bruyères* was a long 1.5 km. With no signage since the village, I thought I had missed a turn, but a large tractor tyre filled with shell and name of the gîte reassured, and I made my way up the track to a restored farm house.

Margot and Felicitas had recommended the gîte in their email. So did Jorge, one of my pilgrims at La Côte Saint André, as a place with a 'big heart'. I was greeted by an Indian lady in sarong and red spot in the middle of her forehead. The dormitory for pilgrims, she said, was upstairs, but she would put me in a room on ground level. I guess that, although I had just walked 20 kilometres, she thought I was old and doddery and not up to the narrow stairway. I did not mind. I had a comfortable room with queen-size bed and my own bathroom. The Indian influence was strong. The room was very bright with multi-coloured sheets on the bed and pictures of Hindu gods on the walls.

After my shower, I wandered outside to an extensive, orderly vegetable garden, complete with hot house. I found Udo by the clothes line. He had arrived early in the afternoon and was in the dormitory. I guess our host had thought he was up to the stairs. A car arrived and out climbed Anke who had stayed with me at La Côte Saint-André 6 days previously. She could not find the gîte, and our host, Yvan, went out to find her. Yvan was French, extrovert, exuberant and outgoing; such a contrast to his wife, Laksmmi, who was quiet, gentle and shy.

Later, Anke, Udo and I sat down to dinner with Yvan and Laksmmi. What a multinational bunch we were! German, Dutch, Australian, French and Indian, eating Indian food in the middle of the French countryside. Yvan reminded me of a comedian in search of an audience. He was a delightful host, attentive to the three of us, Laksmmi quietly supporting him in the background. He certainly made his gîte a place with a 'big heart'. To this couple, hospitality was not a serious affair; theirs was full of fun and laughter.

Anke spoke to me quietly. The day she left me at La Côte Saint-André, she received news that her sister had died unexpectedly. She returned immediately to Germany to meet with her family. The funeral would not be until September, so she thought in the meantime she might as well grieve on the Camino, so back she came. I did my best to support her as she shed a few tears.

I learned that Udo was a teacher. Perhaps that explained his dogmatic attitudes, used to laying down the law to adolescents. He told some good stories about finding a bed for the night. The one I remember was his sleeping in a church. He had arrived late in a town and could find no accommodation. Eventually, he found the church was open and a lady was busy cleaning. He asked her if she knew of any accommodation. The lady replied there was a room in the church that he could use. It had a bed and toilet but no shower, but it did him for the night. Another example of the way the Camino (or God) looks after its pilgrims.

The next morning was Sunday. Yvan was just as playful, emphasising his role of servant to his pilgrims. His gîte was open anytime of the day, and he would go out of his way to ensure that they felt at home. He also home schooled his two sons, Adhavan and Mayilan. They were away with their French grandfather at that time, but they were usually part of the welcoming team. In an old stable next to the house he had built with his own hands a dormitory on the first floor and, on the ground floor, a school room, which he took pleasure in showing me. I was impressed. Wall maps and books created a learning and creative ambience. Yvan was also aware that his sons' learning needs would outstrip his competence, and they would need to attend school.

It was hard to leave this welcoming world, which Yvan and Laksmmi had created. In the face of a strong wind, the three of us departed together, but Udo and Anke soon moved ahead. I was faced with a steep climb out of the valley, but soon I was walking along level ground through woodlands, buffeted by the strong and noisy wind, sometimes sounding like a train charging through the forest. I came across Anke and Udo resting in a hunter's lodge. They were on their telephones trying to find a bed for the night. They were not having much luck. I had already found weekends difficult.

During the afternoon, the wind abated and the walking was mostly level. I found myself on the outskirts of Saint-Romain-de-Surieu. I had met no one on the route, but a number of young cyclists arrived, all wearing the same red T-shirt. An adult was leading them and shouting directions. They greeted me enthusiastically. They didn't go far and soon they were back, passing me with the same greeting. *'Bon Chemin!'* Shortly, I came across their camp site, a series of tents and a building like a gîte. They were having a meal, a late lunch or an early dinner. I thought I had arrived at Saint-Romain-de-Surieu, but it was an abbey, Carmel Notre Dame de Surieu. I asked people directions, at first without success because they were visitors. I struck it lucky with a strolling couple. They told me the village was three kilometres further on. They asked me where I was staying; the lady became excited because she was a close friend.

The good news was that the three kilometres were downhill through forest along a steeply winding road. My Accueil Jacquaire was easy to find from the shell and staff attached to a tree. Françoise greeted me warmly; hers was a place with a 'big heart'. Everything that happened that evening confirmed my first impression. She invited me into her home and offered me a beer. I met her husband, Michele, who was as quiet as Françoise was talkative. She had walked the Camino and had plans for more. Being Sunday, I had thought about attending Mass if possible. Françoise mentioned that Mass would be celebrated that evening at 6 p.m. at the chapel. She pointed to the building on the top of the hill. My enthusiasm faded at the thought of climbing the three kilometres back up to the abbey, but when she said she was going herself and offered to take me, I promptly accepted.

The church was packed with young people and three priests concelebrated, all from the camp, quite a gathering of Catholic youth. It's so unusual to see so much youth in church; it's reserved for the older generation these days. I was moved by their reverence and devotion. I admired the priests, all young, and they read the prayers in clear and well-enunciated French. My prayers were about gratitude, thankful that I was here and participating, thankful that I had arrived and meeting the challenges of each day. I hoped Anke and Udo found a bed.

Back home, Michele had prepared a great meal, which we ate on the balcony. We overlooked the village and the hills, arranged all around us, slowly fading into the night. I told

## 17.

them I was aiming for Chavanay the following evening. Françoise knew the town well, as she worked in its pharmacy for many years.

Next morning Françoise prepared me a sandwich with egg, cheese and tomato. I left in light rain, my heart full of thanks for this generous couple. When a host has been a pilgrim themselves, they seem to reach a deeper level of hospitality. The rain ceased, and although overcast all day, it held off. I was pleased with the steady, even walking with a few manageable climbs. I stopped for lunch at Clonas-sur-Varèze. Everything was closed and silent, being Monday when France generally closes down. I had thought about staying in this village, but I was pleased I didn't. In some villages you feel that someone loves the place and takes pride in caring for it. Not Clonas! The squat public dunny was filthy, the worst shithouse that I'd seen in my many kilometres of walking. I had already received the promised email from Margot and Felicitas, and they had recommended giving the grotty auberge a miss. The overcast day and impending rain did nothing to relieve the morose gloom. I was happy to shake the mud of Clonas-sur-Varèze off my boots.

Onwards to Chavanay. I had met no one on route and was pleased to cross the River Rhône and enter this small town, which was in the middle of a carnival. A tent had been set up and a band was playing. Harlequin-suited men were strolling around, and by the number of plastic glasses in the gutters, serious drinking had taken place. I enquired at the bar that served the beer the whereabouts of Rue des Pèlerins. Everyone was well oiled including the bar servers. What a contrast I was! A tired pilgrim, shell on backpack just wanting a quiet spot to rest, seeking help from a half-tanked mob. They discussed my request with loud gusto, directing me up the mountain, pointing to a chapel way on high. That did not seem right. I sensed they were a pack of galahs having a bit of fun at my expense, so I propped outside the church and rang my host. She arrived in less than a minute; Rue des Pèlerins was just behind the church. Ghislaine greeted me warmly and led me up the narrow, cobbled street to her home, squashed between the other buildings part of the ancient fortified town.

Inside, I was offered a drink and I met the family, Ghislaine's daughter, Maud and her granddaughter, Lybo, eight cats and two dogs. Ghislaine explained that the cats were not all hers; she was minding three for friends. Maud, in her early 20s spent her time feeding her baby. Lybo spend her time in her high chair, a placid baby full of smiles. The house revolved around her care, looked well lived in, but love reigned supreme. The four of us shared a meal. The cats did not take much notice of me, but one of the dogs, large and black, took a liking to me and rested her head on my lap. I relished my meal and being part of the family. Ghislaine said she enjoyed having pilgrims. Most were lovely people, but some did not have the *'mentalité'*. Any pilgrim wanting a neat, tidy household with everything in its place would not find it at chez Ghislaine. Those who sensed, under the chaos of the stuff needed to rear a baby, warm hospitality and love would feel at home. It was a privilege to share their house, to find my way through their stuff. I had my own room, up narrow, steep, squeaky stairs, cosy, comfortable, well-worn furnishing as ancient as the house. Outside, the music from the Carnival continued well into the night, but I was tired, and my sleep was not disturbed. Something was stirring in the roof, but I never worked out the cause. If this ancient house had ghosts, it would be no surprise.

In the morning, we sat down together to breakfast, but a crisis intervened. Ghislaine did a roll call of the cats, and one was missing. Ghislaine asked me to stay and mind the baby while Maud and she went out into the rain searching. Maud took Lybo out of her highchair and placed her in a bed in a play pen (to protect her from the dogs). I felt genuine acceptance that they should trust me, a stranger, with their baby. About 20 minutes later, they returned with a frightened cat. On departing, Ghislaine gave me a postcard; on one side were photos of the newly born Lybo, on the other she had written a message. A rough translation follows:

> Noël. A big thank you for your visit, a very pleasant occasion. Maud, Lybo and I wish you the best for the rest of your Chemin. Despite the rain, our little ray of sunshine offers you the best smile. Bonne Continuation on your Chemin, with some lovely days and meetings to come.

I shall treasure that postcard among my best souvenirs. Although a very ordinary spot, Chez Ghislaine was a sacred place for me. My words carry none of the life of the experience.

Rain fell all day. At first, the climb was steep to the Chapelle du Calvaire, the place that the drinkers tried to direct me to the previous afternoon. Ghislaine insisted that I should pause, as the chapel was dedicated to the pilgrims. The chapel was built in the 16th century, but fell into ruin. In 2000, a move was made to restore it to its original condition. In the rain, I read a board outside outlining the history of the chapel and the project, complete with photos and newspaper articles of the day. Before entering, I stopped to look back over the town and the Rhône beyond. Even in the gloom of the rain, the view was magnificent. I'm sure I would not be the first to say this was picture postcard material on a sunny day.

At the front were three large wooden doors each with a cross as large as each door. The entrance was at the side. The furnishings were simple. A wooden statue of Saint James as a pilgrim, a fresco of medieval pilgrims, an altar and two wooden benches. Two stained-glass windows added to the ambience, a place for meditation and peace. Another pilgrim was inside. I greeted him, but he was a man of few words, in fact, none. He sort of acknowledged me and continued to study the walls and take photos. Was he doing a silent pilgrimage, was he absorbed in the atmosphere or didn't feel we had a common language? I left my mystery pilgrim and emerged into the rain to continue on my way.

I left Chavanay with many pleasant memories, another place with a 'big heart', not only for its warm welcome but also for the beauty of its medieval restoration. The people of Chavanay love their town.

My silent friend passed me with a nod, and for a while I could see him in front, the only other pilgrim I saw to that point. After the initial steep climb to the chapel, the route was level through open ground, through one apple orchard after another. I followed the signage until I came to a fork. Ahead of me, my mystery pilgrim took the left turn. The signage was ambiguous, but I followed him. The signage disappeared. I was fearful I had taken the wrong turn and hoped that it would eventually reappear. No one to ask! I had been walking along rough tracks and was now on a road. A car stopped. I was on the wrong route to Compostelle. As I was walking back to the fork, another car stopped with the same message. The driver asked me my destination. I mentioned I was planning to stop for lunch at Bessey, and he offered to take me. I declined. I wondered about my mystery pilgrim, but we arrived back at the fork at the same time. I thought we might have something to talk about, but no. He continued on in front and disappeared.

## 17.

I was annoyed with myself for refusing the lift as the rain fell more heavily, and I was keen to find shelter. Eventually, I arrived in Bessey, a tiny town, where I found the *'abri pèlerins'*. What a delight to remove my poncho and access my water bottle and lunch! The rain continued to fall, but I felt dry and comfortable in my shelter. Two young walkers passed but they did not notice the wooden structure with bench, seat and noticeboard with a map for the way ahead – a sanctuary for the moment.

I would have happily stayed for the afternoon. I redonned my wet-weather gear and pressed on to Le Buisson where I was to stay at the *Gîte d'étape: La Maison du Tao*. The building was impressive. Old farm buildings had been restored with remarkable attention to detail. After passing through a heavy gate, I found myself in a courtyard with a stairway to an upper level. Accommodation was on one side, kitchen and dining on the other. Primarily built for a tourist trade, which enjoyed farm-like accommodation and peasant-type farming, it offered places for pilgrims because, I guess, the way to Compostelle passed by the front gate. My first impression was one of neglect. Weeds were growing through the cobblestones and on the steps, as if no one had stayed for a while. It needed a decent tidy. A good day's work would clean the place and show it off at its finest because it was a beautiful and stylish building. I wondered if its owners were flat out in other jobs and had no time for routine maintenance.

The owner, Pascal, arrived and showed me to my room. Careful attention to detail was evident all around from the bed to the window frames while the bathroom had the best modern fittings exuding an air of luxury. This close attention to detail continued in the dining room. The tables and chairs matched in their inlays, while I had to admire the door into the toilet with hinges that disappeared into the wood. I was not surprised when, after my comments, Pascal told me his wife was an architect. She had made their home a project. It took two years to build, and in the meantime, they lived in a yurt which was still at the rear of the property. Pascal was a practitioner in Qi Gong and saw patients at home and in Le Puy. He was very busy, he said, which explained why he seemed to be in a rush all the time. However, he was obliging, asked me many times how things were as he dashed back and forth from the kitchen. Qi Gong, I discovered, is a diverse set of practices that coordinate body, breath and mind through movements and still meditation and used for the purposes of health, spirituality and martial arts training.

I mentioned that I hoped to stay in Saint-Sauveur-en-Rue in two days. Pascal knew the Accueil Jacquaire. He rang, chatted to his friend and ask for accommodation for a pilgrim. He told me that was okay, and I was happy that I had a bed for the next two nights. I left the *Gîte d'étape: La Maison du Tao* with mixed feelings. I had a comfortable night and could not fault Pascal's attentiveness. Yet he was in a rush and seemed keen to attend to other matters. He told me he had clients at his home that day and needed time to prepare. He was keen to see me go. I did not rate the gîte high on the 'big heart' scale. I have to admit I had been spoilt by the many places I stayed at with 'big hearts', full of a sacred energy. What a contrast to the night before! Ghislaine's heart was as big as they come. Her place was messy in contrast to Pascal's, yet love exuded from every corner.

The morning was cooler, but the sky was cloudless. I passed a monument that told me that Santiago was 1600 km, but Le Puy-en-Velay was only 100 km. Only 100 km to finish my walking! Along the way, I had many doubts that I would cover the distance still sound in body and mind, but with only 100 km to go, it looked as if my eighty-six-year-old self might just about make it. I passed more apple orchards. I tasted an apple, and although it had a nice colour, it needed more ripening, which I guess is why the trees were still laden.

Apart from the grasshoppers, I had no company until I reached Bourg-Argental. It looked grubby and nothing to get excited about. There was nothing on the street to indicate the presence of the *Gîte La Bulgarana*, but I found the owner Nadia around the back through an alleyway. The gîte offered nothing but a bed, not even sheets; it scored next to zero on the big heart scale. I visited the local supermarket and cooked my own meal. There was a microwave in the dormitory, and I felt as if I was trespassing when I crept into the family's kitchen for some extra utensils. My attitude softened when the husband arrived home late from work. He introduced himself and, more or less, apologised for not being present to greet me. Another occupant of the dormitory arrived. A young man, he seemed to consume innumerable bottles of beer before he retired. He had nothing to say, but was chatty in the morning. Patrick was a salesman and was travelling for his work. He had never heard of the Camino and was bemused at the thought of long-distance walking. He made me realise another world was still out there.

I was on the fringe of Bourg-Argental. I left in the morning and had a short steep climb to a track, which led me into the town centre. I had been on the dingy edge, but I found the town itself charming and attractive. A market was in full swing, and people were carting off trays of mangos. I visited the church and found a candle to light my Maris on her way. I hadn't lit a candle for some days, so I paused to think about her. The fifteenth anniversary of her death would be coming up soon. She continues to walk with me. Even when I'm not thinking of her, she is there silently by my side.

I expected stiff climbing and I was not disappointed. As I paused for a breather, another pilgrim arrived. Barbara was German and chose to speak English. She had walked from Switzerland and wanted to talk. Climbing up a hill was hard enough, but combine that with conversation and attempts to be polite was tough. I invited her to go ahead, as I was a slow walker, but she said she would stay with me, as she found me interesting. Yes, she really did say that! I only half heard what she was saying; I just wanted to focus on one step after another. Eventually, however, she did decide to press on, not before a round of photos. I felt a touch of guilt. If we had shared the same gîte one evening, we could have had an excellent chat. I never saw her again.

After the steep climb, I arrived at a plateau and walked along an old railway track converted into a roadway. The view was breathtaking, a patchwork of villages and open farm land under a clear blue sky. A herd of cows walked beside for a time until I came to the outskirts of Saint-Sauveur-en-Rue. The old railway station had been preserved and now served as a book exchange, although it had not escaped the attention of graffiti artists. The trains ran from 1883 and closed in 1953. Then began the descent into the town along a winding road, past factories, buildings and timber mills to the church where I stopped to get my bearings. The village was built in the valley. I had descended one side and I looked to the other hillside to see houses and roads winding their way up to the top. I hoped I did not have to walk up there. I rang my accommodation for the night. No answer, but I left a message. I was always uncomfortable leaving a message because I never knew if it would be heard. There were few people around. Those from whom

## 17.

I asked directions were themselves tourists, but eventually I found a local who used his phone. Sure enough, my street was at the top of the hill. I began to have doubts and wondered if I should look around for other accommodation. The camping seemed to be the only alternative. Pascal had rung for me two nights previously, so I assumed I should be fine. My hosts were out and would be home later. Under the hot sun, I began the slow ascent up the windy road until I reached a new estate. The only person I met was an old chap sitting in a bus shelter at the entrance to my street. He was chatty, but the conversation was one way, and he did not seem to understand my questions. I wondered if he had escaped his carer's attention. My street was long and the house of my host was the last, next to a wheat field. I found some shade under the balcony and rang. I could hear the phone ring inside. I rang the mobile number and left a message that I was waiting outside his home. I waited for about 2 hours. My anxieties rose. I should have sought other accommodation while I was down in the village. I should trust in God. Things will turn out okay, like they always do. A fountain was running in the garden; I argued with myself, 'They would have turned off the pump if they were away.' A vehicle with trailer attached was sitting in the open garage under the house. Did that indicate the owners were not far away?

By 6.30 my anxiety was nearing the top of the scale. If they were a working couple, they should be home by now. Did Pascal get the day wrong? A man came walking up the road speaking on a mobile. He was a neighbour, he said, of Pierrot, and Pierrot was on the phone. I spoke to him. The place was closed for this week, he explained. Try the camping. I thanked him and handed back the phone to the neighbour, Jean-Marie. Jean-Marie apologised. If he had the room, he would put me up. If he owned a vehicle, he would drive me. He explained how to get to the

*Camping des Regnières*, on the other side of town. After thanking him, I walked back into town, past the bus shelter (the old bloke was gone) and down the windy road, then out along another road along another valley, all the time wondering if I would get a bed or a meal and annoyed that Pascal had got it wrong.

I arrived at the *Camping des Regnières* after 7:00 p.m. The first sight was that of a pond and a young man urinating strongly, suggesting he may have spent the afternoon filling his bladder, his drinking mates egging him on. I pressed on. I found the person in charge, a young lady with a baby. Yes, they had a bed, and a meal was available. A sigh of relief! She led me to a chalet reserved for pilgrims. Another pilgrim was already in residence. He was probably expecting to be on his own and was already ensconced in the bottom bunk, but he saw me, an old bloke showing his fatigue, and moved to the top bunk. Just another example of the way that pilgrims look after each other. Joseph was Austrian. He had started walking from Interlaken in Switzerland and was hoping to reach Santiago in November. We had dinner together in another chalet by the pond, a simple meal of hamburgers.

That night, I expressed thanks. Another day had turned out well, although not in the way I expected. The Camino looks after you. What a slow learner I am!

The next morning involved walking back into Saint-Sauveur-en-Rue and out again up past the old factories to the restored railway station and along the railway line, now a shared road – vehicles, cyclists, walkers. The view of the village below in the warm sunshine followed me, a beauty that fostered a sense of peace and tranquillity. I felt a joy to be alive in these surrounds, the frustrations and fatigue of the previous day forgotten. Then came the hard work, a steady climb from 760 to 1200 metres through a fir (*sapin*) forest – la forêt de Taillard. The track was narrow; the communities of trees were dense, and my footsteps were silent on ground covered in delicate moss. The sunshine had a job filtering through the foliage. As I emerged from the trees onto an open plateau of farmlands, a pony ran to the fence as if to greet me; an eagle soared above and seemed to follow me. I had good vibes about the next village, Les Sétoux Riotord, where I was planning to stop. I found a neat and tidy village, well loved by its inhabitants. Two residents shouted greetings. Pilgrims are welcome here. The stone church is comparatively new, built in 1958 on the site of an ancient structure; records of the village go back to 1273 as a place where pilgrims on the way to Compostelle are welcomed. Outside the church is a statue of St Jacques blessed in 2012 and a fountain with an image of St Jacques the Pilgrim erected in 2013. Equally impressive is a memorial plaque dedicated to the US Air Force for a raid in 1944. The story is told of 'Patsy Jack' and its crew is listed. Inside, I found the candles and lit one inscribed with *'Sur le Chemin de Saint-Jacques'*, but I dedicated the flame to Maris.

    Outside I met Emmeline. She had arrived by car and was looking for accommodation. I told her I was staying at the *Gîte d'étape Le Combalou*. Together, we found it easily. The notice on the door invited us to make ourselves at home. The building could sleep up to 39 people in four dormitories. It had a large well-equipped kitchen and dining area, catering for large groups. It accepted everyone, not just pilgrims on foot or cycle, and was a ski lodge in winter. We had plenty of room to spread ourselves. Soon after, another pilgrim arrived, a tall slim Frenchman named Frederic. Then our Monique turned up not only to collect the fee but to yak. She rattled off her French and managed to cover a wide range of topics in a short space of time. She was intrigued by my presence, all the way from Australia, a good French speaker (sic) and aged 86. I mentioned that I had enrolled at French language schools in Chambéry and Amboise. My fellow guests chimed in; Frederic came from Chambéry and Emmeline from Amboise. That stirred my memories of these two towns. Our meals were in the refrigerator and only needed heating.

Monique departed, and the three of us sat down to our meal and wine. At first, I felt Frederic was distant, as if he was giving me the once-over, but he must have decided I was okay. If he were an Aussie, he probably would have said, '*You'll do me, mate!*' a great Aussie compliment. We were mates (*copains*), and he used familiar French. He, too, was intrigued at my age. I said I took care of myself. He quoted a French saying:

*Qui veut voyager loin ménage sa monture*
(He who wishes to travel far spares his mount).

He quoted La Fontaine's fable; *Rein se serve á courir, il suffit partir á point* – the French version of *Slow and steady wins the race*. He was a wise chap, Frederic. He'd been a truck driver, only recently retired and hoping to reach Santiago. He spoke slowly as he was considering his thoughts and took his time to roll his own. Emmeline was staying the weekend. She was planning to walk locally.

Another pilgrim arrived just on sunset. Johanne was German but had communication problems because he spoke neither English nor French, and none of us were fluent in German. That was unusual; most Germans had some English. He had a tough road, I thought and felt sorry for him. I sensed that Frederic was a little intolerant and made no attempt to communicate. I had a go, however, with my limited German, and he seemed grateful that I was trying. I helped him find something to eat. I felt for Johanne because I know something of the sense of isolation that not knowing the lingo creates. I worked out that he started walking from home and was hoping to reach Santiago. His wife at home was sympathetic, and he always rang her when he had problems. He seemed timid and anxious and, with his short moustache, reminded me of Charlie Chaplin's Little Tramp. I wished I had more German to ask him why. In the morning he was first cab off the rank, but I was up, and he made a point of saying goodbye. I hope the poor guy made it to Santiago.

The 19 kilometres to Montfaucon-en-Velay were gently downhill with three solidly steep humps over rocky tracks. I left before Frederic, but he caught up with me on one of my rests. He was having trouble, he said, problems with his body and, to compensate, he walked with a slow shuffle, which made him one of those rare pilgrims who was slower than me. He was hoping his body would see him through to Santiago, an almost universal hope among pilgrims. We stopped later in the forest and sat on a pile of logs for lunch, which had been supplied by Monique. I saw him again in the afternoon. We had passed over the third hump, and I assured him there were no more that day. I missed saying good bye, as he entered the town before me. I assumed he was making for the *Municipal Gîte d'étape*, which permitted one night stays only. After walking nine difficult days and climbing from 150 to 1200 metres over rough tracks, I decided on a rest day and a private room for the Sunday. I passed three people on the edge of town, and all three ignored me. What sort of welcoming place is this? I booked into the *Hôtel-Restaurant: L'Avenue*. Bernadette's warm and supportive welcome cancelled out the bad vibes, and I asked for two nights. The hotel room was comfortable; the restaurant was classy, and the staff were friendly. What more could I want?

*Chez Ghislaine at Chavanay, a sacred place!*

*Yvan and Laksmmi, Gîte d'étape La Ferme des Bruyères, Revel-Tourdan*

17.

*Pascal, Gîte d'étape La Maison du Tao, Le Buisson*

## 18.

*I am leaving not only on a journey... I will be walking, I will be walking under the burning burden of the sun Through pelting rain and in the wild winds But as I walk the sun will warm my stone heart And in the rain the garden of my hopes will flourish. As I wear out my shoes so my old ways will be worn out. My walk will be a new departure And I shall be walking not so much to the end of the road as to the end of myself. The pilgrim treads the path of innocence, in order to meet himself, others and his Lord. I will be that pilgrim, for I am leaving not only on a journey I will myself become a journey, a pilgrimage. – Jean Debruynne*

I had given myself five days to cover the remaining 56 kilometres to Le Puy-en-Velay. As I set out from Montfaucon-en-Velay after my rest day, I was feeling fresh and eager. On Sunday I had donned my tourist cap, attended Mass in the morning and visited the sites including the chapel Notre Dame de Montfaucon, which housed a collection of 12 paintings by Flemish painter Abel Grimmer. At the same time, I lit a candle for Maris and thanked her. The thought of her being constantly by my side encouraged and supported me. Her death has led me where I would never have otherwise ventured.

I was sure it would be no cinch, but I expected reasonable walking for most of the day. The track was through forest and open land with a few short climbs, nothing lethal. I had two encounters. On a narrow forest I met a chap on a tractor pulling a trailer loaded with wood. Above his popping engine noise, he yelled '*Bonne Continuation*' and something that I could not understand. As I was passing through a collection of farm buildings, a pilgrim caught up with me. We spoke to each other in French, asked a few questions, then realised we were both addressing an Australian. Tim was from Melbourne and he was fluent in French because his wife was French. What a delight to hear an Aussie accent! A touch of home!

On entering Tence, the Hôtel-Restaurant: La Chatiague was easy to find, directly on the route. My hosts were warm and obliging, and I felt as if they were prepared to go out of their way to make their guests welcome. The building was old and its furnishing dated, but it worked well and with just a little work could be regarded as a 'boutique hotel'. After a rest, I explored the town, quite a charming blend of ancient buildings and modern boutiques directed at the tourists. I had good feelings that this was a town its residents cared for. I returned to the hotel and found two pilgrims at the bar. Alvin and Klaus were Austrians. Neither spoke French, but their English was excellent. We spent the evening together. They were intrigued at my age. Alvin was 71 and Klaus 61. They thought that was old enough, but meeting an eighty-six-year old pilgrim had been beyond their expectations. I was surprised at how much they knew about Australia, its geography and its politics. In particular, they saw its immigration policies as harsh. This allowed me to sound off some of my thoughts about our treatment of asylum seekers. I could not distance myself from such policies because they were my government's and I, with the rest of Australia, have to share the collective shame. Alvin and Klaus met three weeks ago and had walked together since. They were aiming for Santiago. It looked to me that their Camino walk would make them lifelong friends. That's what the Camino does.

Other people were dining, also staying in the hotel. I noticed a couple in their sixties. They could have been pilgrims. I guessed they were French. Six Germans shared another table. They wore the same company T-shirt and outside three vehicles bore the same logo. Alvin spoke to them. They were from a well-known engineering firm working on a local installation job.

My first thought on waking next morning was: 44 kilometres to go. I heard cheerful conversation, and when I looked out the window, people were setting up a market. I had breakfast with Alvin and Klaus, both elegant gentlemen whose company I enjoyed. I said good bye and walked through the market, which extended through many streets. Everything was on sale from food to homewares. One stall had a stack (literally) of mattresses. My contribution to the economy was the purchase of a peach and a banana. I found my way out of town without any difficulty for a change. I like Tence, a good town for tourists as well as a stopping place for pilgrims on the way to Compostelle.

Alvin and Klaus passed me with words of encouragement on the first hill, which I was tackling in my usual slow and lumbering fashion. I was gradually ascending to the highest point on the Via Gebennensis through a mixture of forest and open fields. At Saint-Jeures I visited the church (Eglise Saint-Georges) and found Alvin's and Klaus's signature in the book.

On the Camino candles are the first thing I look for on finding a church open. I found them today and lit one for my Maris. How often have I carried out that ritual in the years since her death? It's one of my ways of connecting with her, slowly chipping away at my grief and allowing its power to gradually soften. It's like taking a tiny piece at a time and to process that bit in my own time. I know that my ritual will never stop the grief from returning unpredictably, but it allows me to connect with the pain of losing Maris and to renew my relationship with her. Sometimes I just watch the flame, say hello silently or out loud. Other times, I talk and tell her what's been happening. Sometimes, I just sit and meditate, but the silence brings a sense of peace. Sometimes, I leave the church with a sense of regret, but more often I feel empowered to face the day's challenges and to press on.

A sense of inner peace accompanied me, and opposite the church was a small park where I ate my lunch and watched the pigeons flying back and forth from the church roof to the park, an exercise in precision flying.

Apart from Alvin and Klaus, I met no one for the day. Araules came up quickly. I was content with my 13 kilometres and was happy to stop. My hosts were Accueils Jacquaires, Gilbert and Ninou. They had big hearts and welcomed me warmly. I was hoping that Alvin and Klaus might stay, but my distance would have been short for them. After a rest, I toured the village, which took about two minutes, but I visited the church of Saint Marcellin, lit a candle and read about the miraculous picture of Notre Dame d'Araules. Not much was going on in the village apart from some children on their bikes. Back at my hosts, another couple had arrived. I recognised them as the couple having dinner at the *Hôtel-restaurant La Chatiague* at Tence. Laurent and Margot were French. They had walked to Araules, but had their bags transported, and soon after the lady from the *Hôtel La Chatiague* arrived with them. She recognised me and told me I could have had my backpack transported too.

Over dinner, Ninou did the talking. They were very involved in the church and for 16 years had been welcoming pilgrims coming from many nations, including Australia. Their flags were displayed over the enormous open fire place.

Over breakfast, I heard Laurent arranging with Gilbert to transport their bags to the next place. I left at about 9 and had the usual problems of finding the route out of the village. At first, I found myself walking back along the way I had arrived and had to retrace my steps until I found the signage. I passed the church and saw Gilbert with a wheel barrow. It should have been downhill all the way to Le Puy as I had reached the highest point, but the day saw a surprising amount of climbing. On one of these slopes, a pilgrim passed me. Susanna spoke good English. She was Swiss and had started walking at Berne. I am always interested in the Swiss because that is my heritage. My grandfather Josef Braun was born Swiss in 1864 and came to Australia in 1882, never to see his family again.

Susanna did not stop for long, as she was hoping to reach Le Puy that day. I had given myself two more days. What time do you have, I thought, to look around when you are in such a rush? I was fortunate that I was walking in such wonderful country. Each day had its beauty – forests, farmland, and from the heights wonderful views of small villages scattered across the landscape. I was in the region of the Haute-Loire, the department of the Auvergne, an area with dramatic landscapes and history. The people take care of their heritage, and villages have been carefully restored. Such a village was Queyrières where I stopped for lunch. Instead of keeping company with pigeons, I had an old black dog for company. He was sitting by the picnic table and didn't budge when I sat down. He didn't challenge, he didn't bark; he just accepted me. I admired the surrounds – extensive green fields leading to some ruins, but most buildings were restored. The village nestled around an enormous piece of basalt, shaped like organ pipes, evidence of volcanic origins, a perfect picture postcard. I said goodbye to my canine friend and pressed on, taking several photos of the village from different views. One of these will be a favourite.

I passed through the tiny village of Monedeyres, another faithfully restored village. No other pilgrims yet, just a boy riding his bike, a chap pruning a tree with a long knife and an elderly lady with walking stick picking blackberries. I continued on through forest and followed the signs directing me to the Moulin de Guérin, one of many mills that used to operate along the stream. It was built in 1820 and was active until 1982. A panel told the story of this decayed old lady. A nearby picnic table was rotting away, unsafe to sit on. Besides, so damp and green was this little valley that I'm sure a leech or two would find you if you paused for too long. While reading the panel, a young couple arrived. Christophe and Teresa were students from Austria, walking for a few days. A steep climb brought me back into open country with magnificent views of volcanic landscapes.

I met Laurent and Margot resting by the track. Margot was having problems with her feet. I met them again on the outskirts of Saint-Julien-Chapteuil as we were heading for the same accommodation. André and Suzanne offered 'Chambres et table pèlerins.' They welcomed pilgrims and provided comfortable accommodation and a meal. The six of us dined together. André did all the talking while Suzanne stayed in the background. I learned that two other pilgrims that I had met in the last few days stayed there too – Frederick the Frenchman from Chambéry, and Tim, the Australian with a French wife.

The next morning, the two grandchildren arrived, two boys ages five and ten. Delightful in their trust and innocence, the two kissed me when introduced. I felt highly privileged and was reminded of my own grandchildren. Suzanne attended to their entertainment while André saw me off. The two boys stopped their play to say good bye, and I have a beautiful photo of their farewell wave. Sadly, I didn't record their names.

## 18.

I took time to tour Saint-Julien-Chapteuil, climbed the hill and the steps to the church, a large impressive building that seems to soar into the clouds. The interior was equally impressive. Its tranquil ambience invited the visitor to pause, pray and to give thanks. I was in no hurry, so I lingered to light a candle for Maris and to reflect. I could have made Le Puy-en-Velay that day, but I decided to spend one more day on the Camino as if I didn't want to finish. This year, I had walked over 38 days and covered 500 kilometres. I've lost count of the number of kilometres since my first Camino 9 years previously. Just three months from my eighty-seventh birthday, it's possible I could be walking my last. My body was happy that I had only two more days to walk. My back was extremely happy that it didn't have to carry that pack. Yet my heart was sad. The Camino had opened my eyes to marvels, and I looked back at moments that took my breath away; like dawn in the mountains with the rising sun lifting the colour in the valleys as they emerged from the darkness; like walking on a misty morning when the mist clears, suddenly revealing the brilliant landscape, crystal clear for a moment before it disappears again in the mist. In such moments, I felt an overwhelming sense of being in the presence of the Sacred that flickered sharply then vanished. May the gift of awe and wonder stay with me when I get home.

Eventually, I had to depart and continue on my way. I descended the steps of the church, back through the town and out on the open road. Three pilgrims left the town just before me, and later I met Danielle and Olaf, both aiming for Le Puy-en-Velay that day. My walk was short, only eight kilometres but hard enough through forest and fields of maize. It was shorter than intended. I was aiming to stay in Saint-Germain-Laprade, but my bed for the night was at *Gîte La Glycine*, three kilometres short of the town, a little off the route but easy to spot because the front gate was decorated with shells. I arrived about 1.00 pm which meant I had a whole afternoon for rest and recuperation. My hosts were Marie-Andrée and Patrick, but Patrick was away at the time on the Camino riding a bicycle to Santiago. Marie-Andrée, however, greeted me warmly and was ready for a chat as if she were missing company. We sat in the shade of a delightful creeper that covered the portico at the front of the house. I asked the meaning of the name *'La Glycine'*. It was the name of the creeper. It looked like a wisteria.

Marie-Andrée explained they had been welcoming pilgrims for 12 months. They had walked the Camino and were keen to offer hospitality in thanks for the hospitality they had received. Although Patrick was absent, I sensed his presence as Marie-Andrée referred to him so often. She missed him, I'm sure. He sounded like the driving force, a very active man and retired from the French Army.

My bedroom looked as if it had been purposely built for pilgrims, a new addition in wood attached to the older building, containing two bedrooms, a bathroom and kitchen. I spent the afternoon resting and reading. They had collected a number of books and magazines about the Camino, and I read an article by Alain Lequien, a French author and adventurer who has walked many Caminos and written a number of books. He described himself as being infected by '*"Compostellitis", maladie incurable attrapée par ceux qui cheminent souvent vers Saint-Jacques de Compostelle*' (*an incurable disease caught by those who travel often towards Santiago de Compostela*). I could relate to that. I, too, am a sufferer of that incurable disease *'Santiagoitis!'* within a day of finishing my sixth Camino. The good news is that the disease is not fatal; in fact, it reinvigorates the soul, renews life and changes the sufferer in so many positive ways.

That evening we shared dinner, a lovely meal with much

attention to detail. In fact, Marie-Andrée worked hard at being the host and had written the menu on a blackboard. We talked at length about many subjects related to attitudes towards life and motivations for walking the Camino. I mentioned that I was a brother to all pilgrims that walked the Camino – at the present time, in the medieval past and in the future. Everyone who walks leave something of their essence behind, and collectively forms a mystical entity that is hard to describe. While there is so much in the world that separates, the Camino unites and fosters understanding, respect and tolerance. The Camino is a gift to the whole of humanity for the values it espouses.

We spoke in French the whole evening and, although they advertised that English was spoken, it must have been Patrick who was the fluent one. No matter! We continued our discussions over breakfast, and I lingered because I enjoyed our connection, my last night on the Camino where I had received hospitality comparable with the best I had received in other places with hearts just as big and warm as Marie-Andrée's. She must have appreciated our conversation, too, for she sent me an email that evening. My rough translation follows:

*Good Evening Noël. Your Chemin on the Way of Saint James brought you to our home at the gîte La Glycine last night. I will always remember our meeting and the exchanges, warm and full of hope, which ran through our evening and the morning. Thank you from the bottom of my heart for the message of love of mankind which you carry and transmit.*

My last morning, Friday, was shrouded in fog as I descended the three kilometres into Saint-Germain-Laprade. I visited the church and continued on mainly downhill. I reached Mont Joie, marked with a rough cross set in stones. This is the point that one discovers Le Puy-en-Velay for the first time. It compares with the Monte del Gozo (Mountain of Joy), which precedes the town of Santiago de Compostela where the pilgrim giving thanks to God recognises that at last the goal of their pilgrimage – Santiago – is in sight. ULTREIA!

After a quiet morning when I met no one, things turned hectic when I reached Brives-Charensac. Traffic and people were everywhere. I crossed a picturesque bridge across the River Loire. I was almost on the outskirts of Le Puy. It should have been easy to pass through the town and continue on, but somehow, I became confused and could not quite find my way through. Annoyed with myself, I eventually found the river and followed a path along its banks until I arrived on the outskirts of Le Puy. Once again, I had to pause. The signage had disappeared (or else I couldn't find it), but eventually I worked out where I was and continued to find my refuge for the night.

In their email, Felicitas and Margot mentioned that when they arrived at Le Puy, they stayed at *Chambre pèlerin; Evelyne et Gilbert Bigot,* where they were looked after by a lady as old as me. I wasn't sure whether that was a recommendation or not, but they were quite comfortable. Rather than sort through the available accommodation of which there is plenty, I had booked in. Rue Sous-Sainte-Claire, definitely in the older part of town, was easy enough to find. The three-level house looked ancient. I wasn't surprised to see a date (1745) above the window. Entrance was through the second level where I was greeted by Evelyne, a lady of the old school, polite, respectful and courteous. An old chap was sitting in a large chair, and when I entered, he left. I wondered if he was Gilbert. Age had not been kind to him. Perhaps he was not up to running a gîte and left the job to his wife. Everything looked ancient. The room was furnished with the memorabilia of a lifetime, perhaps more than one. Crockery filled sideboards, and tables were draped in lace. Perhaps every generation that had lived in the house left something behind. After checking what I wanted for breakfast, Evelyne showed me down the narrow staircase to my room on the ground floor. Comfortably furnished, it had a bathroom with old-style fittings and a kitchenette. Double doors opened on to a small courtyard with its own fountain in the corner. I walked out and inspected the three storeys of the building. Every stone savoured a heritage that had been carefully preserved down the ages. I tried to imagine what kind of lives the people who resided here over the last 274 years had lived. What had happened in the surrounding narrow cobbled-stoned streets lined with houses of similar vintage?

Later, I left the old town for the modern bustling city full of shops and tourists arriving for the weekend. I had a haircut, bought a pair of shoes and visited the supermarket. Although I passed many restaurants and takeaways, I decided I would cook my own dinner and enjoy the comfort of my room and watch some television.

Next morning, I climbed up the stairs for breakfast. Evelyne had everything laid out. She pointed out the jam, bread, butter, coffee, etc, hovered around, wandered in and out of the room, asking frequently if everything was okay. She was pleasant enough but not ready for conversation. I wondered if she was house-bound but decided not to play the curious guest asking questions about lifestyle. Back downstairs, I emerged from my room into the courtyard and admired my fountain. I surveyed the cloudless sky. It was going to be hot. I was ready for my day in Le Puy-en-Velay.

There was much to visit, but I needed to focus on the cathedral where my Camino pilgrimages began 9 years previously. I remember clearly the terror I felt, standing in the porch of the cathedral, looking down the long flight of steps. I was shit-scared, about to venture into the unknown, worried whether my body would cope, whether my preparation was enough. I had to return to that spot. Up a series of narrow cobbled streets I climbed, catching occasional glimpses of the cathedral between the ancient buildings. I zig-zagged and came upon the *Cathèdrale Notre Dame du Puy*, constructed on many levels up the side of a hill. I entered at the porch level and looked down. The steps descended just as I remembered, and the way continued down a narrow alley. I looked back up into the church. There were just as many steps leading up to the nave and altar.

I had arrived where I had started, significant for a pilgrim because the inner pilgrimage, the journey of the spirit, is circular; it finishes where it began, namely with one's self, except that the self to which I returned was not the same, but a new transformed self. The changes began from the time of Maris's death and continued as I walked the Camino. When I first planned to finish at Le Puy, it was more for convenience than for any spiritual reason, but I began to realise as I neared the town, this would be a sacred moment of great significance.

I climbed the stairs to the main level and paused before a statue of Saint James, dressed as a pilgrim. A notice in French and English read:

> "Each morning in front of this statue of Saint James, pilgrims are blessed before their leaving to Compostela. You can write a personal prayer and leave it here. It will be entrusted to a pilgrim who will pray with you on the way."

I remember my pilgrim blessing 9 years previously. I remember, too, receiving a prayer petition and carrying it with me all the way to Santiago. I experienced a strong sense of gratitude. I had just completed my sixth Camino intact. Before I left Australia, I thought to myself:

'There's only one way to find out if at 86 I have the health and fitness to walk 500 kilometres, and that is to do it.'

The fact that I was standing in front of Saint James in the Notre Dame du Puy Cathedral meant that I had achieved what others might regard as not being quite possible.

Out of a deep crevasse in my mind emerged the year 1944 and the end-of-year school concert. At the age of 11, I recited a poem *'It Couldn't Be Done'* by Edgar Albert Guest:

*Somebody said that it couldn't be done*
*But he with a chuckle replied*
*That maybe it couldn't,' but he would be one*
*Who wouldn't say so till he tried.*
*So he buckled right in with a trace of a grin*
*On the face. If he worried he hid it.*
*He started to sing as he tackled the thing*
*That couldn't be done, and he did it.*
*There are thousands to tell it cannot be done,*
*There are thousands to prophesy failure,*
*There are thousands to point out to you one by one,*
*The dangers that wait to assail you.*
*But just buckle in with a bit of a grin,*
*Just take off your coat and go to it;*
*Just start to sing as you tackle the thing*
*That 'cannot be done,' and you'll do it.*

Those verses burst forth like a flower in blossom. I was

amazed I remembered so clearly. They didn't mean much to me back in 1944, but what a valuable life lesson! It's repeated in many forms. For example, a bookmark issued by the Australian Friends of the Camino quotes St Francis of Assisi.

> *'Start by doing what is necessary: then do what is possible: and suddenly you are doing the impossible.'*

Before I set out in 2017 at the age of 84, a lady told me I was tempting fate. What would she say now? I heard the voice of others who said: *'Have a go, mate!'*

I felt a sense of achievement, but I was saddened. I had images of many things on the Camino I had grown to love: the shade of a solitary tree and the light breeze that refreshed on a hot afternoon; the song of the birds, the dance of butterflies, the curiosity of a horse or donkey coming to the fence to greet me; the taste of an apple raised in an orchard or the sweet wild blackberries growing in the brambles; the softness of the evening and the freshness of the morning; the hosts with big hearts; the many 'angels' who came to my aid; the hot shower after an exhausting day; the comfort of a mattress no matter how thin and the deep sleep that followed; such simple things but nevertheless marvels of the universe, and in each, a glimpse of the sacred and the love of God.

A wonderful example of love unfolded in front of me. A Christening party arrived at the main altar, an extended family and friends dressed in their finest. The ladies in high heels that clattered on the stone floor, the men uncomfortable in their suits, the children in brand new outfits, the baby in long white gown, everyone talking and laughing, not showing the slightest sign of respect for God's house, but responding to the joy of a family occasion. Everyone settled down for the ceremony, not a solemn face among them. This was a happy occasion but instead of racing off for the party, the party turned to a side chapel for the regular 11:00 a.m. Mass. I joined the group of tourists who followed. The crowded chapel was respectful and silent. The baby was asleep in either the mother's or godmother's arm, looking such an innocent delicate treasure that no one could not help but love her. The noise returned when Mass was over. The party resumed their exuberant chatter; the children ran, and all went to a room somewhere behind the altar, and no doubt, the celebrations would begin in earnest.

I took one long slow lingering meander around the cathedral and walked down the steps through the building, paused at the porch where my pilgrimage began and ended, looked out over the rooftops at the surrounding hills and Santiago beckoning beyond, just as I did nine years before, and then outside down further steps to the alleyway to the centre of town. My emotions were in sharp contrast. Anxiety, trepidation and a strong urge to chicken out were replaced by gratitude that I had been given the gifts of passion, good health and fitness to press on and undertake the arduous task of walking day after day, laden with backpack, a task that many younger people would find daunting. At the same time, I'm saddened that, while I have been walking across countries, some of my age can't walk across the room. I'm sad too that many older people lose their confidence and close the doors of opportunity on themselves. I left a prayer in the basket that such people might find the courage to press on. Behind me, my old Camino had reached an end, but a new one was just beginning.

*The steps of the cathedral at Le Puy-en Velay The start and finish of my Camino.*

# 19.
# Let us not forget hospitality

Twice before, I had visited the Taizé community. Following the Camino, Taizé is a wonderful place to visit. Instead of returning immediately to the 'real world', I was offered a chance to reflect and to work on my inner Camino. How will I keep the spirit of the Camino active in my daily life? How will I integrate the lessons learnt?

Taizé was not far from Le Puy, two to three hours by train and bus. Taizé is a small village in Burgundy, about 230 kilometres north of Le Puy-en-Velay and close to Cluny. It's home to a community of men committed to following Christ. There's almost a hundred of them, coming from more than 30 countries and various churches. They seek to be a sign of reconciliation between churches and those separated from any church. Their welcome is extended to young people who've been coming from every continent since the late 1950s, but they accept older people, too, which is why they welcomed me, an eighty-six-year-old man.

Taizé draws me back in the same way as the Camino. They both get into the blood. They're like an incurable disease. Fortunately, this disease, like *'Santiagoitis'* or *'Compostellitis'* is not mortal; on the contrary, it invigorates the spirit, renews life and helps us to return home as bearers of peace, love and trust. The same atmosphere of trust and sharing exists in both. On the Camino and definitely at Taizé I've felt the Presence, like a tiny brief glimpse of the Divine.

Its magic is simple. Three times a day, the bells ring and

everyone gathers in the church for prayer with songs sung in many different languages, a bible text read in several languages and a period of silence. The brothers regard singing as an essential expression of the search for God. They're short, those songs, repeated again and again, expressing a basic reality in a few words. They're easy to remember and stick in the mind. In fact, almost every day I find myself quietly singing or humming one of them. These songs, in about 50 languages, are one of the community's gifts to the world and are sung in many places throughout the globe. Never, never, never in my life have I gone to church three times a day, looked forward to going, got there early and left as late as I could. Exactly the same this time, as if I'd never left. Last visit was 6 years ago, and nothing has changed. As soon as I entered the church, I felt a sense of inner peace. I know of no other place quite like Taizé. It's a sacred place where the spirit soars. I felt a sense of sharing, of brotherhood with the 1500 or so people around me of all ages and from all countries. We were on the path of reconciliation among divided Christians, highlighting what unites us rather than what separates. Among those 1500 were people who never go to church or describe themselves as agnostic or even atheist, but are drawn to Taizé in the same way as the committed Christian. I admired these people for their courage, for the risk they had taken. Perhaps everyone hungers to find deep meaning in their lives.

Although everyone attended church together, the adults, about 300, were separated from the young people for meals and instruction. Each morning one of the brothers gave a talk followed by small group discussion. Our instructor, Bro. Richard, of German origin with perfect English, spoke in English and German. He was also fluent in French. In a corner was a Swiss lady translating to the French speakers, and in another corner, a Spanish lady was doing the same with her people. I marvelled at the multilingual environment and the ease with which people could slip from one language into another, truly a remarkable skill that could cut through barriers and draw divided people together. Briefing notes were presented in the languages present – German, French, English, Portuguese, Spanish, Polish.

What was equally surprising was the theme of the week's talk, *Let Us Not Forget Hospitality*. Such a coincidence, as I had been receiving wonderful hospitality throughout my Camino. By now I have accepted that coincidence is more than synchronicity. Sometimes, it is described as 'divine intelligence' or 'God's way of remaining anonymous'. Taizé was about to deepen the significance of hospitality in my life.

Brother Richard told us that we were guests of God. God welcomes us. Several proposals were presented, the first of which was: *Discover the source of hospitality in God*. One of the most memorable experiences of the Camino is hospitality, both for the pilgrims such as myself and the people who opened their doors to them. At Taizé the brothers welcome not only Christians from different churches, but believers of other religions and non-believers as well. All are welcome. God welcomes us all, with no preconditions, and desires our happiness. The brothers seek to erase borders and establish bonds of brotherhood for all comers. Such values are identical with those of the Camino. This hospitality of God towards us touches the depths, overflows and transcends human frontiers. In a world where so many forces are trying to divide us, both Taizé and the Camino are working towards bringing us together. As such, both are a gift to humanity.

Another proposal was: *Welcome our gifts and our limitations too*. The brothers believe that God welcomes everything in us; in our turn, we can accept ourselves just as we are. Let's be thankful for our gifts and our frailties, too, for they are the door to seeking change in our lives. Like the Camino, we may embark on a path of self-discovery and from there seek to become a better person. Sometimes, the old self has to die so that a new self may emerge. Sometimes, I may have to accept that I am lost; I don't know where I am, or who I am. Like the Camino, we are on a path of inquiry and awakening. Who am I? Where am I going? Where did I come from? What does it all mean?

The final proposal was: *Practice a generous hospitality.* Can we receive others not as we would like them to be, but as they are? Can we ourselves be welcomed by them in their own way, not in ours? Can we become women and men of welcome, taking the time to listen to someone, inviting them to a meal, approaching a destitute person, having kind words for those we meet? Can we look for ways in which hospitality becomes an opportunity, not just for those who are welcomed but for those who welcome as well. Person to person encounters are indispensable. Meeting those who come from other places will help us too to understand our own roots better and to deepen our identity.

These proposals on hospitality were fascinating and so relevant to the Camino. I had received welcome and hospitality from generous people. In turn, I worked as a hospitalier at La Côte Saint André and was about to work in another. I was both blessed and the one who gave the blessing. I felt privileged to offer welcome and hospitality to many weary pilgrims.

After each session we were broken up into small discussion groups and were presented with a series of questions. My small group was a lively mob, and we had robust discussions. Such a diverse range of backgrounds, languages and experience, yet united by the thought that Christians are meant to live for each other. Most were German, but we came from France, Portugal, Holland, Ireland and Australia. Conversation was mostly in English, but sometimes people spoke in their own language. We had to pause to allow translation for some of the Germans. I wasn't sure how a multi-language discussion group would work, but it was a lesson in respect, tolerance and patience. The differences soon fell away and were no barrier to our bonding. I felt close to these people. It was sad to say goodbye.

I left Taizé with a sense of renewal. As I mounted the same bus which brought me here a week ago, I felt reinvigorated. In these present times, mistrust seems to be on the rise and gaining ground. I hoped all of us departing would have the courage to live lives of hospitality and allow trust to blossom.

*The bells of Taizé*

## 20.

*Wasn't friendship its own miracle, the finding of another person who made the entire lonely world seem somehow less lonely?*
   Hanya Yanagihara, *A Little Life*

I could not leave Europe without visiting my dear Camino friends Mat, Laura and Maggie Rose. I met Mat and Laura in 2013 at the gîte d'étape communal at Annoye on the Chemin d'Arles (or Camino Aragonés). Mat was English and Laura was Spanish. They had been married 8 years and, in that time, had been teaching English in India and Malaysia. They finished their contract with the British Council and were walking the Camino to help them decide the next phase of their lives. We had a great evening together, along with others, and formed a Camino family that remained until I completed my walk at Puente la Reina. Over those few weeks we formed a deep friendship. I grew to love the couple and was thankful for their support and gentle encouragement at a time when I was getting tired and inclined to chuck in the towel. We missed each other on my last night on the road. I was saddened to miss saying goodbye. They missed me, too, and went out of their way to catch me just as I was about to take the bus.

Mat and Laura continued on to Santiago and then to her parent's home at A Rúa, not far from Santiago. We kept contact through emails. I discovered that the next phase of their lives was a family. Laura was pregnant during her Camino, but they told no one. When I heard that Maggie Rose had arrived, I sent a little gift and have sent a gift each birthday. They stayed with Laura's family for a year and moved to Lisbon where Mat obtained a job teaching English. In 2015, I walked the Camino Portuguese from Lisbon where I stopped for two weeks to enrol in a Portuguese language school. Mat and Laura insisted that I stay with them. I had a wonderful two weeks with this little family who made me feel so welcome. Maggie Rose was a little over one year. She was standing and hanging onto the furniture when I arrived, and by the time I left, she was running across the room.

Through social media, I learned of Maggie Rose's development. The news in Mat's emails was 90% about Maggie Rose. She was brilliant. He admitted he was biased, but nevertheless, she was an extraordinary child. I learned too that Mat had resigned from his job (I knew he was not happy – lack of support and toxic co-workers). They moved back to Spain to Allariz in Orense, not far from Laura's parents.

In 2017, I forgot to bring their contact details with me, so I could not get in touch. That could have been just as well. After my detour to Rocamadour, I was in two minds whether to resume walking from Mont de Marsan. I decided to resume but I feel sure, if I had their details, I would have taken another detour into Spain to fill that time slot.

This time, I made sure of the details and organised a visit before I left Australia. From time to time, I rang Mat and let him know my whereabouts. In the meantime, Maggie Rose was five; Laura's father had died suddenly, and her mother Suzie was spending time with them. They had also started an English Language School, a highly risky venture.

Getting to Allariz, Spain, involved taking the train to Paris and a flight from CDG airport to Santiago. Waiting for the flight, all around me I heard Spanish. The plane arrived at Santiago about 11:30 p.m., and Mat was waiting. He was the same laid-back Mat, and it seemed as if I had only seen him last week. We drove out of the airport, quite a grand affair for a provincial city, and as we travelled along the freeways, I caught up with the news. The first item was Maggie Rose. She was now five and still a magnificent child. She was fluent in both English and Spanish and was a proficient reader in both languages. She did home schooling; Mat believed she was so advanced that normal school would hold her back. Since Laura's father death, her mother Suzie had been staying with them a few days each week.

The main event in their lives was that their English Language School would be open for business the following day, the first day of the Spanish school year. I felt ashamed that I had kept him up so late before such an important day, but he insisted that was no problem. They were not as anxious as they were the previous year when they had spread their wings with no landing in sight, had ventured into the unknown and started the school. By now, they knew how many students were needed to make the school viable, to break even and even to make a profit. They hoped that last year's students would return and new ones would enrol. Their expectations were built on hope. It was almost as if Mat had come to accept the feeling of not knowing what would happen and had trained himself to enjoy the exhilaration of uncertainty. Now that their wings were unravelled, they were forced to continue their flight, still not quite knowing where they were headed. Their miracle lay in the unfolding of their wings. They had a go at fulfilling a dream and would have been consumed with regret if they decided the venture was too risky. While their wings were spread, their passion, like the wind, would carry them.

After the late night, I was slow in rising. Mat had left early for the school to wait patiently for inquiries and enrolments. I found Laura in the kitchen and was delighted to meet the five-year-old Maggie Rose, a confident chatty little girl, used to mixing with adults. I met Laura's mother Suzie, a refined Spanish lady who had no English. I felt privileged to hear the interchange between Laura and her daughter, sometimes in English and other times in Spanish. They spoke in Spanish when grandma was present. Mat and Laura made certain, Mat told me, that Maggie Rose could speak Spanish to ensure that Suzie would not feel excluded.

While Suzie stayed home to cook and clean, Laura, Maggie Rose and I drove into town to the school. Mat had taken his bicycle just as he used to in Lisbon. The school was light and airy, on the ground floor of a modern building in a new area of town. Everything looked new, the furnishing, books and classroom aids. I'm sure it would have been attractive to even the most reluctant of students. It was an inviting place for learning and fun. Nothing much had happened that morning, which was not unexpected. The real action would begin in the afternoon. Learning English was an after-school activity, which competed with pastimes like sport, ballet classes and music. They expected parents to arrive with enquiries and hopefully enrol their children.

In the afternoon, Laura and Mat were busy at the school while Suzie, Maggie Rose and I walked along the river to a park with a children's playground. Suzie and I communicated through Maggie Rose. We fed ducks, watched clumsy canoeists paddling by, admired an old mill and watched a bridal couple posing for photos. I asked Maggie Rose if she ever confused the two languages. By the emphatic 'no!' I guess she thought it a silly question.

Laura arrived shortly after we returned home. The day had been quiet, but former students had returned. Mat remained at the school to take lessons with adults and did not return home until after 10 p.m. We shared a wine. He was tired but excited that students had returned and other parents had inquired. The sparkle in his weary eyes was the external indication that his heart was brimming with hope.

The next day, I explored the town. Allariz starts at the bottom of a hill where there is a river and park (which Maggie Rose, Suzie and I visited the day before) and climbs up a steep slope to a plateau, which is the main area of the town. The climb requires negotiating your way up a maze of small, narrow and winding cobbled streets lined with medieval buildings, terraces and small squares, giving this old quarter a definite character. The top of the town houses the commercial district – bars, restaurants, shops and the English Language School. This area is busier, and at its centre is a monastery, the bland appearance of which is not improved by a large and dusty car park in front. Next to the monastery is a slender and elegant church that was not open, so I had no opportunity to light a candle for Maris, which would have been the only one in Spain this Camino.

I arrived at the school in time for the afternoon rush. What a buzz! Matt was taking a lesson and was using Beatles' songs to teach his class. Laura was speaking to parents who were inquiring and actually enrolling their children. The children themselves seemed pleased to be there. Some were inspecting the silkworm farm and showing their parents. Indeed, the enrolments were climbing. Each new enrolment was a celebration of a dream becoming a reality. The wings were spread, and the spirit was soaring. I took the time to inspect some of their books, all inviting and brand new. I spoke to some of the students, young Spanish boys and girls struggling with the complexities of English pronunciation. Mat stayed on to take another class, while Laura, Maggie Rose and I returned home.

We had dinner when he returned. Mat and Laura exchanged their news – the students who had returned, new students referred by friends, even enrolments from towns beyond Allariz. Recommendations and word of mouth were the best form of marketing. Mat used Facebook and Social Media, but he focused on the activities of the school such as the progress of the silk farm and the Beatles' songs they were working on. I felt excited with them. They were tackling something, which others might say was impossible, but they were doing it and finding it just could be possible to make a success of an English Language School in a small Spanish town. Mat brought out a smooth old whiskey to celebrate. Their joy was contained. They were not bursting out of their skins yet; they still had a way to go, but they were on track.

Next morning, Suzie left for her home. Since her husband died, she had been staying with Mat and Laura from Sunday night to Wednesday morning. Through Laura, Suzie wished me goodbye. I was touched that, despite the language barrier, we got on well. Mat drove her to Orense where she took the train to her home in A Rúa. When he returned, Mat, Maggie Rose and I went for a walk the opposite way along the river, this time along a rough track with passing evidence of old floods – broken branches and logs. This part of the river was not navigable. We came to a broken bridge half destroyed by the last flood. The crossing was difficult and required scrambling across rocks. Mat was concerned for my safety, but he concluded that if I could walk the Camino at my age, I could negotiate a tricky bridge. Once across, we walked back the way we came. All the way, Mat chatted. He had dreams of one day walking the Camino with Maggie Rose. I mentioned my Danish one-armed friend Michael whom I met in 2011. Since then, every year he has tackled a short section of the Camino, each time with a different grandchild. Mat informed me that I had been trumped age-wise. Just before my visit, a 95 year old American pilgrim walking with her daughter had been found wandering the main road. Allariz is on a Camino route. She was invited to rest for some tea but decided to press on, as they still had about 4 hours of daylight. A lady on horseback asked Maggie Rose directly why she was not at school. Maggie Rose replied that she learned at home. I thought the woman was intrusive, but Mat didn't mind. He believed that normal school would hold her back and bore her. She was fluent in English and Spanish and read well in both. She understood the Galician language, Gallego (similar to Portuguese) but could not speak it (yet!). Maggie Rose asked questions constantly as if on a mission to soak up the world's knowledge. She asked me what 'reject' meant when I used the word. We paused for a coffee at a shop attached to the riding school and had plenty of time to wander around the stables and admire the horses.

In the afternoon, I walked to the school on my own. I found the Camino signage, the familiar shell, and followed them. They led past the monastery that accepts the pilgrims. I didn't see any, so perhaps this is not a popular route. At the school, I found all the family. Mat was teaching; Laura was talking to parents, and Maggie Rose was playing with other children. The air was alive with excitement and learning. New pupils had been enrolling. They had reached 39, ten more to survive and an extra ten to make a profit.

That evening was my last in Spain. I cherished every moment with this lovely, welcoming family because I'll never know if I will ever see them again. In the morning, I said goodbye to Laura and Maggie Rose, and Mat drove me to Santiago airport. On the way, we discussed marketing, how to get those extra enrolments. I arrived at the airport, thankful for the brief opportunity to mix with old Camino mates. The family has embarked on an exciting but scary trip, like walking on the edge of a precipice with a strong wind, needing only an extra unexpected puff to blow them off. I do hope they succeed.

I was happy with my brief encounter with Spain. I had made no preparations for the visit, but each day I remembered more of my Spanish, like picking up on an old skill. With a little more effort, I would have been communicating, not fluently, but effectively. Inside the airport, people with backpacks were waiting, looking as they were homebound after completing their Camino. I was back in the real world of mistrust and suspicion. People avoided eye contact and barged through queues as if oblivious to anything other than their own needs. On the plane to Paris, the lady next to me was a Jack-in-the box, constantly dipping into her bag and never still for more than a few seconds.

*Mat, Noël and Laura 2013*

*Mat, Maggie Rose and Laura 2015*

*Mat, Maggie Rose, Suzie and Laura 2019*

## 21.

*Brother, let me be your servant.* – The Servant Song

Railway unions were on strike on Friday September 13th, but the trains to Périgueux were running. By 2.30 pm I had arrived at the refuge *Association des Amis et Pèlerins de Saint-Jacques Limousin-Périgord* at 83 rue Gambetta. I stayed at this refuge twice as a pilgrim, but this time I would be a hospitalier, ready to put into practise what I had learnt about hospitality from wonderful hosts. Underlying my efforts would be the spiritual meaning I had received at Taizé.

I had accepted hospitality at the other two refuges run by the Association, at La Coquille and at Sorges. Both had supplied an evening meal. At Périgueux in 2017 the hospitaliers, Dominique and Marie Therese, supplied dinner, but in 2019, the practice at Périgueux was to provide a bed and breakfast. It was up to the hospitalier at the time to decide whether to offer an evening meal. Looking at the records, one hospitalier had provided dinner. I asked Annette, the official from the Association who gave me the drum, whether an evening meal was possible. It was up to me as long as I charged an extra 8 euros.

I had one pilgrim on my first night. I apologised that I was not yet organised to provide a meal, but he was special because he was my first pilgrim. Clément did not mind; he was thankful for the refuge and my welcome. Twenty-two and an electrician by trade, he had started in Belgium and was hoping to reach Santiago. He was planning to walk 40 kilometres the following day.

I had time to inspect the resources, beds for eight pilgrims in three bedrooms, two bathrooms, a kitchen and communal area for dining and a bedroom for hospitaliers with two beds. I took over the hospitaliers' room and made up one of the beds with proper cotton sheets, instead of the paper disposable bedwear provided to the pilgrims. A meeting room served as the headquarters of the Association. I was impressed by the extensive library. Every publication in French on the Camino and Compostelle seemed to have been collected, ranging from coffee-table books with many photographs to guide books and pilgrims' memoires.

From the next day on, Saturday December 14th, I offered an evening meal. I had been the recipient of many excellent meals and had a model of what hospitality could mean. A small supermarket was located about 50 metres away, and later I found a larger one with cheaper prices and a wider range of products. Thus began a daily routine of rising early to prepare breakfast, farewelling the departing pilgrims, cleaning the bedrooms and bathrooms (*le ménage*) and then the morning's shopping. I was never sure of how many pilgrims. For the most part, they reserved by telephone, but they also turned up unannounced. That night, I had three – two Aussies and a German. Rolf spoke good English, so we had an English night. Hedley and Lori came from Perth, Western Australia. They were committed walkers and seemed to have hiked everywhere in the world. I could not keep up with the stories of their travels. Rolf was making for Santiago and the only background he offered was that he was the owner of a swimming pool; Hedley and Lori talked so much. The important thing was that the three accepted the offer of a meal, so the four of us sat down to share a dinner of four courses – salad, main dish, cheese and dessert with red wine. That was the French way. If I was going to offer a meal, it should be a decent one.

## 21.

Sunday night I had a full house of eight pilgrims. Five of them, all French, were together and, as this was their last night, decided to celebrate in one of the restaurants. The other three, Jean-Pierre (French), Johannes and Adriana (Dutch) accepted the meal. In fact, they were grateful that it was offered. After a long day's walking, it's a relief to neither cook for oneself nor search for somewhere to eat. There were no eateries in the vicinity of the refuge. Once again, I provided four courses with red wine.

On Monday night, I had five pilgrims and on Tuesday seven, French, German and Dutch. On both evenings everyone accepted the meal offer, and I took delight in seeing them bond into a family. Some had already met on the way, but sharing a meal seemed to bring them together. In contrast, Wednesday saw two pilgrims, Isabelle (French) and Marie-René (Canadian). They were on their last day of walking and ate out. I dined on my own. Wednesday morning saw a meeting of the Association, and I met a number of the members. They seemed intrigued by my presence. One old chap asked if I did the *ménage* as well, as if blokes didn't do that sort of thing. Apart from running three refuges, the Association conducts research into the history of pilgrimage in Limousin-Périgord. Like many voluntary organisations, they have their concerns about falling numbers and finding enough hospitaliers to welcome pilgrims into their refuges.

They seemed interested in me because I was different. None of them knew much English and were happy that I could speak French. Annette was particularly interested and questioned me on my motivation, both for the Camino and for volunteering. I told her about my search for meaning after the death of Maris and my desire to return to others the hospitality I had received. I stressed the importance of providing an evening meal. I mentioned the difference between a 'mechanical' welcome to one which showed sincere warmth. Pilgrims can quickly spot the difference between when they are being genuinely or routinely received.

I asked where I could hire a computer. I told Annette I was a writer and had written two books on the Camino. I was working on another and keen to continue my writing in any spare time. Annette knew of no place, but she loaned me one of the Association's. I was grateful and able to write several thousand words of this manuscript during my time in Périgueux despite the French keyboard slowing me down.

I found the time on Friday to explore the old town and visited the cathedral where I had the opportunity to light a candle. This time, as well as one for Maris, I lit four, one for peace, one for faith, one for love and the fourth for hope. The last was the most important. The light of the first three might go out, but if you hang onto hope and keep that fourth candle burning, it's possible that you can relight the other three.

Friday night saw three pilgrims – Thierry (French), Nicolas (Dutch) and Jorge (German). Nicolas and Jorge arrived by bicycle. An interesting difference between pilgrims: Some you see at registration and that's about all. Others are more dependent and demand your attention constantly. Jorge was in the latter group. He had an air of helplessness, a half-smile and sad eyes as if he were a puppy wanting a pat. He asked many questions and seemed slow to comprehend. He spoke in English, so perhaps he had to translate in his mind from one language to another. He had problems with his bicycle and, up to Périgueux, had been unable to find a mechanic. He asked if he could stay two nights and spend the next day, firstly, finding a mechanic, and secondly, getting his bike fixed. The policy of the Association was one night only unless extenuating circumstances such as sickness or exhaustion intervened. I wanted to help Jorge and thought his problem warranted his staying two nights.

No one wanted dinner. The atmosphere was markedly different. No one seemed interested in talking to the others, and I wondered if temperament or language differences were the main factors that separated them. Some people are outgoing and reach out, others prefer to stay within themselves. Thierry and Nicolas left early, but Jorge stayed. I had to negotiate with him because I would have to close the refuge when I left for shopping. That was the rule of the Association. As it turned out, he was away most of the day. He found a mechanic in the adjacent town of Chancelade, then had to wait while the problem with his gear change was fixed. In the meantime, two new pilgrims arrived for Friday night. Matthias was German, while Nadette was French. She was formal, tense and absorbed in her own issues. She had little to say. Matthias was more relaxed. He mentioned that he had met a Catholic priest who was Australian and also 86 years of age. I would have liked him to stay in the refuge, but I heard no more of him, not even from other pilgrims. Jorge returned late, his bike fixed. No one wanted the evening meal, so once again the atmosphere was cool. No camaraderie developed that night, and once again, my pilgrims failed to bond as a family but left as individuals. As Matthias left in the morning, he made a little speech of thanks. Nadette wished me *Bonne Journée*. Jorge was last. He had so much stuff to organise. As well as a backpack, he had two bags on his bicycle. My practice was not to start cleaning until the last pilgrim left. As part of my hospitality I did not want to appear anxious to get rid of them, but, I confess, I began the chores before Jorge left because I *did* want him to go.

When pilgrims arrived at the front door, the practice was to welcome them and to explain that their boots and backpack were to be left in the garage. They were given a basket to put the items they needed to take up to the refuge. They were also given a set of keys for the front door, the door to the refuge and for the garage. The garage was to be locked at all times for security, as there were other tenants in the building on the second floor. When they left in the morning, they could post the keys in the Association's clearly marked letter box, which was accessed from the garage. Just after she left, Nadette rang to tell me she had posted the keys in the wrong box. I thanked her for letting me know, but I didn't thank her for the problem she'd created. There were two letter boxes for the other tenants. One was a frosty old lady who resented the presence of the refuge and was not on good terms with the Association. She required careful handling. The other tenants were younger and they were noisy, particularly about 1 a.m. Their night was full of shouts and thumps on the floor and sometimes the pilgrims complained. I checked the letter boxes. They were locked, but peering into the slot, I could see the keys in one. I climbed the stairs to the second floor, braced myself for a confrontation and knocked on the first door. A young lady mopping the floor opened the door. I sensed silent hostility and suspicion. *Desolé de vous déranger...(Sorry to bother you...)* I explained I was from the refuge; a pilgrim had posted a set of keys in her letter box. I expected her to say she would retrieve them the next time she opened the box, but she returned inside, spent time finding the key and came downstairs with me. Without a word, she opened the box, which hadn't been emptied for some time. Out fell a stack of leaflets and advertising material along with the keys. I thanked her, and still without a word, she returned upstairs, I guess to her mopping.

    Saturday was market day in Périgueux, so after my chores

## 21.

I went into town. Street after street was lined with stalls and, in addition, an agricultural festival promoting the local Périgord produce dominated the main boulevard. Chooks, rabbits, pigeons, doves of innumerable breeds were on display. Sheep dogs were busy herding both sheep and geese. Miniature horses were the delight of the children as much as the fair rides. Cheese stalls were popular with the adults, and as it was lunch time, acres of food stalls satisfied all tastes. People lined up for a brief appearance on local radio. The festival reminded me of home, the French regional equivalent of an Aussie country show.

I returned to the refuge mid-afternoon to welcome three pilgrims, one German, Peter, and two Frenchmen, Arthur and Jean. All accepted the meal offer, so I was happily cooking for my Camino family. Everyone spoke both English and French, so communication was good, and camaraderie flourished. Peter was 33. He was studying for a higher degree and was working on his thesis. He even produced a laptop from his pack and did some work. Arthur was 23 and a student. Jean was 68. He was walking for a cause and raising money for a small underprivileged village in Bolivia. I was pleased that my efforts at hospitality created a relaxed atmosphere where my three pilgrims of diverse backgrounds felt comfortable to be themselves. I enjoyed cooking and took pleasure in the detail. I had bought flowers at the market and used glasses to display them around the refuge. This was home to my pilgrims, not a bachelor's camp where you made do.

Rain fell during the night and continued in the morning. My family were slow leaving, donning their rain gear and preparing for a wet day. While putting on his boots, Peter made a speech of appreciation. As a German, he was worried how he would be received in France and had embarked on the Camino with some trepidation. However, his welcome had been consistently warm, and Périgueux was no exception. We hugged each other. His words affected me deeply. The Camino helps break down barriers, and here was one example. I thought of the long process of reconciliation that may have taken place between former combatants of World Wars, and here I was, helping with this recovery. I had heard of other young Germans entering France, anxious and wondering how they would be received; this was the first time that I had met this fear at close hand.

Rain washed out the festival, but the food stalls continued to operate, and I ate my lunch under canvas. Back at the refuge, I welcomed four pilgrims. Christian and Michael were German. Patricia was born in the United States but was a French citizen and lived in Paris. She would never return to America; the country had gone mad, particularly under Trump. She loved Paris. Joop was Dutch. Christian and Michael spoke neither French nor English, so communication was difficult but manageable. Joop who spoke both French and English and knew enough German to get any detailed messages across. Patricia and Joop accepted the dinner invitation, but Christian and Michael declined. Instead, they settled for a liquid dinner and knocked off four bottles of red wine, known in Australia as a duck's dinner. I was concerned about the impact of copious alcohol on empty stomachs, but they remained benign, pleasant, laid-back with lots of smiles, the German equivalent of *'No worries, mate! She'll be sweet.'* Joop and Patricia were having problems finding accommodation for the following night and spent some time on their telephones. Patricia found something but not Joop. Through Joop, I inquired of Christian and Michael if they had accommodation, but they maintained their *'She'll be right, mate'* attitudes.

In the morning, Christian and Michael left early, so I did not know if they had heart-starters for breakfast nor their destination. I liked to know where my pilgrims were heading that day, if they had booked ahead or whether they were prepared to take their chances. As I had walked to Mont de Marsan in July, I was able to use my knowledge to advise what lay ahead. In some cases, I rang on behalf of pilgrims, just as others rang for me, particularly for the Germans who weren't confident with their French. I knew their feeling. Patricia decided to quit, as her body was giving her trouble and take the train back to Paris. She gave her accommodation for the night to Joop, another lovely example of one pilgrim helping the other.

I had five pilgrims on Monday, all of whom wanted dinner. Danielle and Alain were French, Gilbert was Dutch, but the two characters were Philipp (German) and Christine (Dutch). Philipp was loud, dogmatic and self-absorbed, ready to express an opinion on any subject. He came first. He said he smoked pot. Christine's reputation preceded her; other pilgrims told me of spending time with a pilgrim who never stopped talking. Christine lived up to her reputation and began talking both in English and in Dutch from the moment she entered the building. She arrived with Gilbert who was as quiet and subdued as she was noisy. I wondered how he could endure this incessant chatter. Danielle and Alain were together but they had their bit to say, so overall, Monday night, with two motor-mouths in competition, was the noisiest night of my Camino. In the midst of this turmoil, I managed to prepare a decent meal of which they were appreciative. Christine amused us by showing us videos she had been making of her Camino. They were impressive, well edited with sound track, all with her smart phone. She was the last to retire to bed and, thankfully, she allowed the rest of us to sleep, but she began early and continued to talk up to her leaving the building. I guessed she bashed poor Gilbert's ear all the way. Despite her eccentricity, she was a likeable person, generous and compassionate, and I wondered if the demons of despair ever confronted her. Despite her talking the leg off an iron pot, she was one of my Camino's lovable characters.

Tuesday night was in sharp contrast; I had one pilgrim. I will call her Edwina. She knocked on the front door, asked if there were a bed available and signalled to two men in a car that they could leave. At first, I thought they were family, but later she told there were two young men she had met in a bar. At registration, she told me she was walking the opposite way to everyone else, towards the north. She usually slept in her tent, but tonight she wanted some comfort. She didn't want the meal. I got the impression she wanted no more questions and just wanted to be left alone. I guessed she was a loner. She had a shower and rest and later emerged to prepare herself a meal. She was ready for a quiet one-to-one chat and spoke good English. On entering Périgueux, she inquired at a bar where was the refuge, and the two young men offered to drive her. I was pleased their motivations were good and they delivered her safely. I chatted about some of the pilgrims and mentioned Christine. Edwina surprised me by asking me not to talk about her to other pilgrims. At that point, she seemed to trust me enough to tell her story. She was walking the Camino to escape a former boyfriend who was stalking her. He found out and was walking the Camino too, inquiring about her along the way. She felt he was getting too close, so she decided to change her route completely to get away from him. She wasn't sure where she was walking; she was just pressing on. Pilgrims talk about each other all the time, the people they had met and where they met. I imagine it could be easy enough to track down someone if you put your mind to it. Behind the innocent gossip and inquiry there can be sinister intent. In the morning, she thanked me for my welcome and concern for her welfare. I hoped she remained safe and I wondered if she had given me a false name and nationality at registration. Keep pressing on, Sister!

I saw Annette every other day, and we became good mates. She had many questions about my story. She asked if she could write an article about me for the Association's biennial newsletter, *Le Petit Jacquaire*. I was intrigued, but I replied *'No worries!'* or the French equivalent. We sat down together, and she made many notes. I stumbled through the interview, translating difficult concepts into French, but Annette was helpful and often supplied the word I was seeking.

All the time I was in France, I felt like an imposter, posing as a French speaker, but everyone assured me that I spoke their language very well and, indeed, were pleased that I was and did not want them to speak English. Many, including Annette, apologised to me for their scant knowledge of the language.

Wednesday night saw four pilgrims, all ladies, all of whom accepted dinner. Martina was Swiss, Anna was Dutch, Angelika and Brigitte were German. Martina spoke French, German and English, and a few other languages as well, a genuine polyglot. Anna spoke some English but no French, while Angelika and Brigitte spoke neither French nor English. All accepted dinner, but the atmosphere was restrained due to language barriers. I did my best to include everyone, and Martina did a lot of translating for the German ladies. Overall, the night was subdued but pleasant. Goodwill prevailed.

Thursday was my last day to welcome pilgrims. I was expecting my replacement hospitaliers, husband and wife team, Sylviane and Jean-Louis. I had already spoken to Sylviane by phone. I was happy to be finishing my shift. Counting that evening's pilgrims, I had welcomed 51 and cooked for 34.

I'd done a good fortnight's work, offering hospitality to all comers. I was hoping to make the transition as smooth as possible. I moved out of the hospitaliers' room into one of the pilgrim rooms and prepared the beds for them. I checked the cupboards and made a sort of inventory of food. I gave everything extra elbow grease in order to hand over a sparkling clean refuge. I had to account for the money I'd collected. The treasurer of the Association was not available, so Annette arrived to do that job. I had found this part of the role the most troublesome. Counting my own money is fine, but others' is a nightmare. Each day, I reconciled what I had collected against what I had spent, and there was always a discrepancy between the figures of what I had left and what I should have had. Fortunately, I had had more money than I needed. The problem was always with the coins. Counting Australian coins is difficult enough, but counting small change in euros is bad news. The coins are small and slip through the fingers. I'm afraid my perfectionist tendencies had me spending hours getting things right, and eventually I felt prepared for the session with Annette. Even she couldn't get it right. *'Quelle horreur!'* she repeated. The small one and two centime coins slipped through her fingers, too. She enjoyed counting money as much as I did. I daresay we were both thankful we were never bank tellers. In the midst of this chaos, she mentioned she had written the article and would send me a copy.

In addition to Sylviane and Jean-Louis, I had three pilgrims. Malik and Jean-Claude were French and Jerry was Australian. I enjoyed listening to his Aussie accent. His story was not good. Despite a tendon problem, he had walked 20 kilometres that day. His foot was giving him a great deal of pain, and he realised he could go no further without seeking medical aid. He planned to visit the hospital. He asked if he could stay an extra day. It was not my decision, I replied, he would have to ask Sylviane. I put the three men in the one room, but Malik mentioned that other pilgrims complained about his snoring, so I let him sleep in the other room. Jerry returned from the hospital. The receptionist, he told me, was not helpful and had difficulty with handling a would-be patient from a non-European Union country. He managed to get past the barrier to see a doctor who told him he needed to rest his foot for five days. He was full of regret that he had not taken good care of himself. He should have stopped walking earlier. I heard echoes of Frederick's French proverb: *He who wishes to travel far spares his mount.* Now he was faced with the possibility of having to quit the Camino. On the positive side, I cooked a good meal, and we managed to enjoy dinner together. Jerry spoke a doggerel form of French, which would have offended the purists. He made himself understood to Malik and Jean-Claude who didn't seem to mind his successful attempts at murdering their language, but I wasn't sure of Sylviane and Jean-Louis, the new hospitaliers, who struck me as conforming, conventional and rule-bound. I felt he was a puzzle to them. He was, in many ways, the brash Australian.

Friday I was due to depart for Paris early afternoon. I decided I wasn't being selfish by allowing the new hospitaliers to do the ménage and give myself an easy morning. I'm happy to clean toilets and fish hair out of the shower drain when I have to, but I was more than content to withdraw my labour and let them take over. My time was all over bar the shouting. I showed them the routine and where things were kept, but much of the time waiting for the train was spent talking to Jerry. The medicine the doctor prescribed had relieved the pain considerably. He was tempted to start walking but decided to follow the advice. I agreed. Although Sylviane had told him he could stay the night, he felt uncomfortable and had already found other accommodation that set no limits on the length of stay. We wished each other well over lunch at the nearby boulangerie.

The railway station was no distance from the refuge. As I was about to step on the train, I noticed Annette in the crowd. 'Are you travelling too?' I asked her. No, she had to say goodbye and wish me safe journey home to *Australie*. I was chuffed. You don't always know the impact you have on others, but it was becoming clear to me that I had made a positive impact on Annette and the Association. Pilgrims are invited to write comments in the Livre d'Or (Golden Book). I suspect that most are formal thanks, a matter of form, the thing one should do, but many reflect a genuine gratitude for the care and hospitality they had received. I felt that the comments pilgrims made about me were in that category. Annette and I hugged each other as if we were family, and she stayed on the platform to wave as the train left.

Annette's article appeared in the December 2019 issue of Le Petit Jacquaire. My rough translation follows:

*Homage to Hospitaliers*

*In the long list of volunteer hospitaliers who put themselves at the service of pilgrims in our refuges and whom we can never thank enough, there are some exceptional personalities. Those who come from afar, those who come again and again over the course of the years, those who deploy treasures of imagination and savoir-faire to prepare meals capable of reinvigorating the exhausted pilgrim, all at least cost. Those who comfort, listen, create the alchemy of an unforgettable meeting, those who* support with a smile the grumpy pilgrim whom nothing satisfies...Those who know how to do these all at the one time.

This year, we have had the pleasure to meet, among others, Noël, to whom we give homage and through him to all the volunteer hospitaliers.

Having come to Périgueux as a pilgrim, Noël wanted this year to be a hospitalier in our gîte for two weeks. This gentleman of 86 years from Australia comes to Europe for three months, has followed numerous Camino routes in France, Spain and Portugal and has formed some lasting links.

This man with a gentle smile and unassuming disposition, psychologist by profession, is also a writer, author of several novels and two books on the Camino. Impatient to publish a third work on the Camino, he looked around for a computer and what was his joy when we allowed him to continue his task. 'You're my friends!' he said.

Following the tragic death of his wife and other women in his family, he questioned greatly the meaning of his life. All his beliefs were questioned and he is continually searching.

In 2005 he visited France, in 2006 he lived at Chambéry and studied French. At church on Sundays seeing pilgrims receiving their blessing gave him the impetus he was looking for. The Camino would give a structure for living.

This year is the sixth time that he has come to Europe. Every morning he rises with a prayer of gratitude, to be here still and to be able to walk across a country. His age raises many self-doubts, but he says to himself, 'If I don't try, I won't know if I can do it.'

This year, he walked 500 kilometres as well as being a hospitalier. He wishes to give to the pilgrims what he has received and believes in the importance of providing a meal. This allows for more interaction. 'The pilgrims arrive as individuals and become a family,' he says. 'Every pilgrim is different. The footprints on the Camino are those of brothers and sisters stretching from the Middle Ages and into the future.'

For Noël, the Camino releases some very positive forces.

In the refuge, he acquitted himself of the job without fuss, did the cleaning and the cooking, inspired by a set of recipes written by a Canadian for use by hospitaliers.

He welcomes with a smile and repeating, 'I don't know if I will ever return again', he inspires us with his passion and dedication.

This man offers us a fine lesson in his humility that he brings to the Association. Thank you, Noël and all the hospitaliers of this year.

Annette

My last two days in Europe were spent in Paris. Saturday, my priority was to buy a few gifts for family and friends, and after I completed my shopping, I walked from Montparnasse where I was staying to the familiar 5th Arrondissement. I was interested to view Notre Dame Cathedral following the fire. It was covered in scaffolding. I checked some of the shops I knew. I bought Christmas cards (Cartes de Noël). My intention was to send them as a gesture of thanks to the places where I stayed with 'big hearts'. I was told it was too early, but I did manage to find some left over from last year. I visited the church Eglise St Jacques de Haut Pas on rue St Jacques and paused under the statue of Saint James. Once again, I had returned to the place where I started. Back in 2010 before my first pilgrimage, I stopped in exactly the same spot and took the same photograph before taking the train to Le Puy-en-Velay. Much has happened in the nine intervening years. I have walked six Caminos through France, Spain and Portugal. I have learned that I can do hard things, overcome obstacles, figure things out, and persevere. I have stepped out of my comfort zone and found opportunities for growth.

On the other hand, one of the major lessons I have learned is that I am not in control. This seems to contradict one of almost unquestionable values of our society – to be in control of one's destiny. How often have I heard 'take control of your life', every self-help book ever written contains that message. On a practical level, that's true, but in the bigger picture, that things go wrong or turn out not as I wished, that my shortcoming and failures get in the way, that I am not in control however much I'd like to be, gives me a certain freedom and awareness that I am being guided by a Divine hand. Reliance on that guidance allows my journey to happen and to walk towards wisdom and truth.

I have learned to accept me as I am. I am thankful both for my gifts and my frailties, for they are the door to change in my life. I embarked on a journey of self-discovery and sought to become a better person. Part of my old self had to die after the death of my beloved Maris; the rest died on the Camino. I like to think that a new self has emerged. I had to accept that I was lost. I didn't know where I was, or who I was. I am still on that path of inquiry and awakening – who am I? Where am I going? What does it all mean? Nevertheless, I feel I'm in good hands as I take on life after the Camino.

On my last night in Paris I burst the budget on a classy French restaurant.

Sunday night I was due to fly home. The weather had turned cold, and the rain cast a grey sombre veil over my view of the Paris roof tops. Not the day for tourism! I was leaving Europe at the right time and looking forward to another summer. I stayed in my little apartment, watching the Rugby World Cup game Australia v. Wales in Japan, until the cleaner arrived. I slowly made my way to Charles de Gaulle airport. It took an hour to find my terminal. Just as well I was early. I still had plenty of time, so I found a seat and watched the scene – people hurrying by, slowed down by enormous cases, others sauntering for exercise before their long flights, soldiers in patrols of six, arms aloft, the younger ones still with pimples, doing their best to assume mean, don't-mess-with-me looks. I was among the first to check-in my baggage, my backpack, the gifts adding a few more kilos. The check-in clerk, a man of middle-age, greeted me amiably. He checked my passport, expressed surprise at my age, rose to shake my hand and said what an inspiration I was to be travelling on my own. With a tear in his eye, he explained his father was 93 and was bed-ridden with dementia. There was no queue, so he came around the front of his desk to push my pack in, then kissed and hugged me. He was very moved, he said. I've been kissed and hugged a few times, but never by a check-in clerk. I'm aware that my story has inspired others, but this time, I was taken unawares. Check-in clerks are usually formal and polite, even friendly, but don't identity with their customers and show emotion. *'It's been a pleasure to meet you'* were his words as he gave me my boarding pass and my pack disappeared down the conveyor belt. I didn't know what to say, so I mumbled I was pleased that I had helped make his day and hoped he would enjoy his shift.

This was a precious sacred moment to end my Camino. As you get older, you're aware that such moments are unexpected. Life is wonderfully unpredictable and so is what happens to you on the Camino. Leave yourself open to these moments. They will enrich your life.

Vivre le Chemin! Vive el Camino! Viva o Caminho! Long live the Camino!

*Statue of Saint James in Eglise St Jacques Paris (Photo taken 24.07.2010)*

*Same spot on 28.09.2019*

# Acknowledgments

The following were my guide books:
*Sur le Chemin de Saint-Jacques de Compostelle. La voie de Vézelay, La via Lemovicensis.* Lepère Editions 2015.

*Miam Miam Miam Dodo Saint Jacques de Compostelle Voie de Vézelay.* Les Editions du Vieux Crayon 2015.

*Chemin de Saint-Jacques de Genève au Puy-en-Velay par le GR 65, Yenne et Chavanay. Via Gebennensis. Chemins de Compostelle en Rhône-Alpes.* 2019.

I am thankful for the following publications for their inspiration:

Beyond Even the Stars. A Compostela Pilgrim in France. Kevin A. Codd. Wipf and Stock. 2018.

The Art of Pilgrimage. The Seeker's Guide to Making Travel Sacred. Phil Cousineau. Conari Press. 1998.

L'Esprit Des Pèlerinages. Gaële de La Brosse et Loïc Mazalrey. Editions Gründ. 2018.

Camino Chronicle. Newsletter of the Australian Friends of the Camino.

Bulletin Camino. Lepère Editions.

Le Petit Jacquaire. Amis et Pèlerins de Saint-Jacques et d'Etudes Compostellanes du Limousin-Périgord.

Thanks, too, to Mat Edmunds for permission to use his photo on the front cover, and to my patient proof reader John Hungerford.

## ALSO BY NOEL BRAUN AND PUBLISHED BY SID HARTA PUBLISHERS

This is the story of Noel who lost Maris, his beloved wife of 42 years, to suicide following years of struggling with depression.

The abrupt ending of a life by suicide can be the most catastrophic of events for those left behind. Survivors experience intense pain and massive guilt. Grief banishes survivors to a place so removed from the normal hurly-burly of everyday life that they feel close to madness. Somehow they have to claw their way back.

Noel accepted there was no way around his anguish and met suffering head on. His pain allowed him to discover the richness within him and to grow in wisdom which he hopes might be of benefit to others.

Maris' death did not shut her out of Noel's life. She remains a very real presence. This is a love story with a difference.

'An involving account of the devastation, guilt and pain commonly experienced by people bereaved by suicide. It is a moving love story and a tale of resilience, offering reassurance and a sense of hope to others similarly bereaved.'
—**Barbara Hocking, OAM Executive Director, SANE Australia**

'Noel Braun gives us the honour of travelling his suicide grief journey after the loss of his beloved wife Maris. He lets us walk with him and understand the devastation that suicide brings and his road of learning to find hope again.'
—**Michelle Linn-Gust, Ph D., President-Elect, American Association of Suicidology**

'Noel takes us into his innermost thoughts, feelings and emotions as he describes, with incredible love and candour, 'losing' his Maris. Noel's story is immensely powerful and the depth and duration of his grief is testament to his enduring love for Maris.'
—**Kate Friis, Counsellor and Psychotherapist**

## ALSO BY NOEL BRAUN AND PUBLISHED BY SID HARTA PUBLISHERS

After a childhood in the Western Australian surf, Vince Kelly, burning with a desire to save mankind, enters the Catholic priesthood. In contrast, his beach mate, Jamie Griffiths, lacking any direction, drifts into a disastrous job and marriage.

Following his unwitting involvement in Jamie's mother's death, Vince suffers an emotional and spiritual crisis, shattering all his former rock solid beliefs. In desperation, he quits both Perth and the priesthood. He crosses the desert to Sydney and settles in Manly, hoping to find new meaning and purpose.

As soon as he sees the quaint Federation house in Whistler Street, he knows it's an ideal refuge for his recovery. He transforms the house into a home, makes new friends and begins to rebuild his life but is plagued with indecision and guilt.

Back in Perth the despairing Jamie cries for help. Already guilt-ridden at abandoning his lifelong mate, Vince leaves Manly, painfully aware that on his return he must make some vital decisions about his own direction.

---

'Braun is a deft writer ... good storytelling ... with a revelation at the end that strengthens the work. A good read.'

—**Wendy O'Hanlon,** *Acres Australia*

www.ingramcontent.com/pod-product-compliance
Lightning Source LLC
Chambersburg PA
CBHW041955080526
44588CB00021B/2752